The Demolition and the Verdict

AF521321

ALSO BY NILANJAN MUKHOPADHYAY

The Demolition: India at the Crossroads (1994)

Narendra Modi: The Man, The Times (2013)

Sikhs: Untold Agony of 1984 (2015)

The RSS: Icons of the Indian Right (2019)

THE DEMOLITION AND THE VERDICT

Ayodhya and the Project to Reconfigure India

Nilanjan Mukhopadhyay

SPEAKING TIGER

SPEAKING TIGER BOOKS LLP
125A, Ground Floor, Shahpur Jat, near Asiad Village,
New Delhi 110049

First published by Speaking Tiger Books 2021

Copyright © Nilanjan Mukhopadhyay 2021

ISBN: 978-93-5447-141-4
eISBN: 978-93-5447-149-0

10 9 8 7 6 5 4 3 2 1

Typeset in Minion Regular by SÜRYA, New Delhi
Printed at Chaman Enterprises, New Delhi

All rights reserved.
No part of this publication may be reproduced, transmitted, or stored in a retrieval system, in any form or by any means, electronic, mechanical, photocopying, recording or otherwise, without the prior permission of the publisher.

This book is sold subject to the condition that it shall not, by way of trade or otherwise, be lent, resold, hired out, or otherwise circulated, without the publisher's prior consent, in any form of binding or cover other than that in which it is published.

Contents

In memory of those who died
in the name of religion

And

For Varsha
An enduring companionship through
all trials and tribulations.

Introduction

To guide a sun beam or create a sun—
To rule ten thousand thousand worlds, or none,
Go, worlds! said God; but learn, ere ye depart,
My favourite temple is an humble heart...

—Phillip James Bailey

The writing of this book was begun around the time when it became evident, during the autumn of 2019, that judicial adjudication of the decades-old temple-mosque dispute in Ayodhya was at long last a certainty. Work on its closure coincided with the declaration that the new Ram temple would be thrown open to devotees in December 2023. The de facto inaugural would strike the opening notes of a triumphalist symphony, which would reach its crescendo when political campaigning for India's scheduled parliamentary election in 2024 nears its conclusion. In more ways than one, devotees lining up to enter the new Ram temple would not just mark a complete circle but also begin a new trajectory, the direction of which remains uncertain at the moment. Much of the path traversed since the early 1980s has been in the name of respective gods. Ironically, people in contemporary India mainly assert their religious identities in a way that is an exact antithesis of moral teachings of any religion. Despite repeating ad nauseam the

Vedic phrase—*Ekam sat, vipraha bahuda vadanti* (Truth is one, wise men describe it variously), most still assert that only their way of reaching the truth is the correct path.

The two-year period, beginning in the third quarter of 2019-20, witnessed humans grappling with the worst existential crisis of the century. Questions of survival in the wake of Covid-19 became uppermost in everyone's minds from early 2020. The subconscious mind probingly asked if anyone amid the current crises could be concerned about a temple-mosque dispute? But contempt and hatred for the 'Other' continued flowing unabated in political and policy narratives. When it became evident that politicians continue to whip up social discord in order to reap political benefits, realisation dawned that there is never a moratorium on propagation of hatred. With politicos pursuing polarising programmes, regardless of the devastating impact of the pandemic on citizens, and whipping up superstition instead of nurturing scientific temper in society, why should critical and reasoned writing on matters that determine the future character of the Indian republic cease?

The aforementioned period also witnessed a number of core objectives of Hindutva getting more or less fulfilled. The list is extensive, immensely gratifying for supporters, profoundly unsettling for adversaries. India's most unwavering swerve towards constitutional majoritarianism began after the BJP secured an enhanced electoral mandate in May 2019. The sense of 'we can do anything' generated by it, first became evident in the government's decision to harshen India's pre-existing anti-terrorism law, the Unlawful Activities (Prevention) Act (UAPA), first enacted in 1967, but subsequently braced up on several occasions by various governments. This coincided with enactment of the Muslim Women (Protection of Rights on Marriage)

Act, 2019, ostensibly to ameliorate the standing of Muslim women within wedlock, but in essence to transmit a clear message to the BJP's core Hindu constituency—that the government was chipping away at 'privileges' of the stereotypical Muslim male.

The government's subsequent decision, nullifying constitutionally-pledged autonomy for Jammu and Kashmir, brought to fruition the BJP's promise for 'complete integration' of the once princely territory into the Indian Union. It sent the signal that in its renewed tenure, the BJP would not limit its mandate to administrative measures and shy away from major alterations to the Constitution. While abrogation of Article 370 was part of the three 'core issues' that were pursued by the sangh parivar for decades, other steps that followed relentlessly could not have been taken had the doorway not been opened by the 'success' of the Ayodhya movement. Whether it was the union government's decision to link citizenship with religious identity by amending the law under CAA, or the actions of several BJP-governed states to curtail religious conversions, illegalise beef consumption, its storage and trade, make inter-faith marriages administratively tedious and socially perilous and disincentivise families with more than two children, each decision was taken with the objective of sending the message that this government had put an end to the practise of 'appeasing' Muslims and shown them their place in the national hierarchy.

The Ayodhya movement is unprecedented in the annals of Indian history. The success of the sangh parivar lies in having ensured that the passion and paranoia aroused in the course of the agitation for the Ram temple, was not limited to merely demolishing the Babri Masjid and constructing a new temple in its place. In addition to it, sentiments stirred in the minds of a large section of Hindus have become integral in their psyche. From a time when the dominant section of Hindus was in principle, of the view that it was obligatory for the majority to safeguard the interests of the minorities, the same people have now begun to think that the obligation is on minorities, to ensure that sentiments of the majority are not hurt. The quote attributed, in a personal conversation, to his mother by a celebrated filmmaker of inter-religious parentage, persistently ricochets deep within the confines of the mind: 'Yeh mulq unka hai' (this country is theirs).

The consensus on India's heterogeneity, multiplicity and complexity has been altered in the course of the Ayodhya agitation. The mosque that existed pre-1992 was successfully depicted as the symbol of a past that had to be undone. With this limited objective now fulfilled, there is greater support for seeing the country and its people from a single national-identity majoritarian perspective. An enhanced agreement now exists for the argument that the majority community, or their representatives, have the primary right to decide what constitutes political and social correctness. It follows from this that minorities, while having the right to 'live' in this country, must adhere to terms set by the dominant community. From a time when social integration was encouraged, there is now a push towards compartmentalisation and existence in respective boxes, coming out during work hours for collective activities, but thereafter retreating to our respective ghettos. We can even say that this 'Gujarat model' has become pan-Indian. The Ram temple may have been 'won', but much remains to be 'done'—this sense drives a significant section of people.

India was not a land of perpetual hostility, a territory constantly labelling people as 'them' and 'us'. Yet, a primary discordance existed in social discourse on how we defined the nation and nationhood, in terms of people and their unitary culture (which is also religion), or as home to a pluralistic society. Differences, divergences, even phases—long and brief—of conflict persisted after Independence. But, the India in which I became socially and politically aware primarily prided itself on its diversity. For a member of the generation of pre- and early teenagers who witnessed the liberation of Bangladesh and events that followed within India, these developments demonstrated the correctness of choice of the founding fathers for steering the nation on a path paved with the principles of secularism, democracy and egalitarianism. After 1971, banter in school was always marked by a sense of one-upmanship insofar as Pakistan was concerned, not for military reasons alone, but for our social character, because religion was not the primary basis of our social identity. Unlike them, we were a nation for all. Likewise, we prided ourselves for being part of the same school assembly despite being pro- or anti-Indira Gandhi, during Emergency and in 1977, as even Pakistan and Bangladesh saw democracy crumbling. In the small north Indian campus town where I grew up, the muezzin's call as well as the temple's gongs were heard without sounding intrusive to anyone.

But dormant social faultlines existed and they were stoked at times to erupt into communal conflagrations. One such incident that I got to witness as a neophyte journalist were the riots in Meerut in September-October 1982. Now forgotten by more macabre violence and state participation in 1987 in the city and in several episodes in different cities and towns in India, the series of these riots actually turned out to be a trial run for what followed. With time, the 1980s came to be regarded as the decade when religion and religious conflict became an integral part of politics and elections. Unfortunately, much of what lay at the root of these incidents of communal violence, mainly reported by the media from an episodic perspective, stayed unexamined because of professional inadequacies.

The Ayodhya issue struck a chord with a significant section among Hindus due to the success of the RSS-VHP in stoking their anxieties after the mass conversions in Meenakshipuram, Tamil Nadu in early 1981. From the mid 1980s, campaigns for a Ram temple at Ayodhya and protests against these, often triggered violent clashes between Hindus and Muslims. Initially, almost every secular political party and most members of civil society parroted about India's 'inherent secularism'. They dissed arguments that the RSS-VHP-BJP would eventually occupy the centre stage and frame the parameters of political discourse.

Despite limited experience in reporting communal conflicts, the Ayodhya issue became an early preoccupation for me. I was fortunate to work with editors in the late 1980s and early 1990s who too sensed the emerging centrality of the Ram Janmabhoomi agitation. They agreed that with the temple demand finding resonance among Hindu masses, the sangh parivar was gradually owning up to Hindutva, as a word in political discourse and as an ideology. The opportunities to report on these developments from the ringside, also fructified in my first book, *The Demolition: India At The Crossroads* in early 1994.

As a writer, it was somewhat comforting to return to a familiar subject matter more than a quarter of a century after that book. But it soon became apparent that Ayodhya was not just a singular issue which raised a political demand and then faded away after the goal was achieved. Instead, it acted as a catalyst for changing India intrinsically. Much has been written by reputed academics as well as by journalists, including me, on what has altered in the country in the past few years, especially after 2014. While this appears more compelling now, premonition of this was visible early in the course of the Ayodhya movement. It was clear to me in 1993 while writing the first book, that the 'face of Indian polity has undergone a dramatic change in the last decade, and a new political and social order appears to be around the corner'. To understand how this metamorphosis is upon us, well and truly, it is important to revisit the entire socio-political canvas of the issue.

The agitation for a Ram temple at Ayodhya gradually segregated a distinct Hindu political constituency, although it took more than two decades for the BJP to electorally harness this. The time gap between emergence of this vote bank and for BJP to begin reaping it in elections, almost matches the time the Muslim League took before it became seen as a 'natural' representative of Muslims in British India. The League began isolating a Muslim political constituency from the 1920s and by the mid-1930s such an electorate was in existence. Yet, it was only in the 1945-46 elections to the Central Legislative Assembly and Provincial Assemblies, that the League emerged as the primary representative of the community. Like the League's performance in the last elections of British India, the BJP in 2014 benefited from the second wave of religious homogenisation. This process continued and benefits keep accruing to the BJP and its affiliates within the pyramidal political clan over which the RSS presides as an ideological fountainhead.

India changed irrevocably from the early 1990s after this unchannelized throng of voters was mobilized behind the BJP. Most importantly, large segments of societal memory from the pre-demolition era got erased. More than fifty percent of Indians are below thirty and in their living memory, the Babri Masjid structure does not exist—what remains is the temple that is now coming up and the city of Ayodhya being transformed into a must visit, once-in-a-lifetime destination for Hindus. Salman Rushdie created the demographic category of midnight's children. Likewise, 'high-noon's children' exist in India. These are people whose memories took shape only after the sun passed the meridian over Ayodhya's skies on that cold 6th December Sunday in 1992. That's when India entered the post-demolition phase of history.

Issues of belief and devotion are non-negotiable now and mythology is routinely presented as history from the highest of the country, President and prime minister included. In an era when a Ram temple and 'reconstruction' of several other 'disputed' shrines are *fait accompli*, most people remain unaware of a time when the RSS-VHP wished to 'prove' their case. The argument that 'matters of faith' are not open to scientific scrutiny was incorporated into the political discourse after archaeological surveys questioned the believed antiquity of modern-day Ayodhya. The identity of the 'Other' has been widened from being limited to 'descendants of Babur'. It now comprises anyone who poses a hurdle in the path of a strong and defiant majoritarian community and their political representatives. This new 'enemy of the people' includes even members of the judiciary who do not comply with their wishes. Others routinely clubbed in this 'gang' include the entire opposition, large sections of civil society, feminist groups, academia, the old-guard in the media and of course Muslims and other religious minorities. Abusive words are part of daily vocabulary and hurled at people with progressive, liberal or left-of-centre viewpoints; the most famous pejorative for journalists, 'presstitutes', was also invented by a former army general who remains a member of the union council of ministers.

A significant section of today's 'young India'—no linkage with Mahatma Gandhi's weekly of that name or the demographic group he reached out to—grew up seeing vocal section of Indians, including Hindus, mournful for the demolition of the mosque on December 6, 1992, and committed to its reconstruction. Unable to fathom their political grief, this group of Indians categorised these lamenters as inimical to the Hindu cause. They unabashedly ask why the will of the majority should not prevail in India—after all, it does in Pakistan? The choice of what we decided to be in 1947 is immaterial. A far greater number of people in the country now equate being Hindu with being Indian. Diffidence in donning the 'Hindu' identity is a sentiment of the past. Past generations of Hindus who grew with a sense of victimhood yet hesitated to give it expression, are now vocal about dislike or hatred towards the 'Other'. The perpetually unapologetic and outraged Hindu who needs to substantiate his rage, has emerged in the course of this agitation and is lined in a single file behind the BJP. Only a small section of Hindus are willing to reach out and convince Muslims in concluding that their forefathers did not choose the 'wrong' nation during Partition. It is forgotten that they not just refused to become citizens of Pakistan, but also forsook the system of separate electorates. They had enjoyed this privilege since the enactment of Morley-Minto Reforms (Indian Councils Act, 1909) although this deprived them of adequate representation in the legislature.

In the agitation for the Ram temple at Ayodhya, extra-legal demolition of the Babri Masjid was an unwritten objective. Thousands of kar sevaks repeatedly assembled in Ayodhya at the clarion call of RSS-VHP-BJP (the last joining the platform formally later than the other two affiliates). Parallels were later drawn between their collective act and the mythical tale of Hanuman's burning of Lanka. It is a different matter that Lord Ram in the epic, was portrayed as being displeased with his obedient follower's act. But unlike the disapproval of the epic hero, Babri Masjid's demolition evoked a sense of achievement and tales of valour survive. The sense grew that the symbol of Hindu subjugation in medieval India was obliterated. Although this reduced in intensity and extent in support for future agitations and campaigns, it enabled large sections of Hindus to see the shrine's tearing down as evidence of the community's power to unwrong history. Undeniably, the unrestrained destruction of the sixteenth century mosque made Muslims aware of their identity and what it meant being a Muslim in India. There is certainty that the Supreme Court verdict and the construction of the Ram temple will further alter Indian polity, inter-community relations and self-awareness of Muslims.

The BJP floundered electorally in the aftermath of the demolition. It was thereafter forced to moderate its stance on uncompromising principles. Yet, adversaries of the BJP did not muster courage to provide consistent and coherent ideological alternative to the party. Consequently, the sentiment of majoritarianism thrived and became further widespread. If we plot an imaginary index of Hindutva and place the years on the 'X' axis over a period of forty years since 1980, and the value of ideology on the 'Y' axis, few would deny that the graph has risen consistently, never declining, at best showing retarded growth in some years.

Although the Ram Janmabhoomi Movement was India's biggest post-independence mass agitation, temple construction was not its primary objective. Spearhead of the temple agitation, Lal Krishna Advani, asserted on several occasions that the Ayodhya issue was not limited to this. As he says in his autobiography, *My Country, My Life*, for him, 'it became a symbol of struggle between genuine secularism and pseudo-secularism' and provided the basis 'for a sharply polarised debate between two opposite conceptions about the source of India's nationhood and national identity: the unifying concept of cultural nationalism and the dividing concept of anti-Hindu nationalism.' Advani was not the only one who felt 'vindicated' by the Supreme Court verdict.

In this book, I have tried to place the Ayodhya issue in its entirety, encompassing the rise and growth of the Ram legend to his use as political icon in Chapter One. The next chapter presents the scientifically established history of contemporary Ayodhya from antiquity to the modern day. Chapter Three recreates the events in 1949 that led to the installation of the idol of child Ram in what was until fairly recently a functional mosque. Chapter Four revisits the process of how the RSS and its affiliates reinvented their political representation and tactics, a period when from being a marginal force in Indian political and electoral space, it began to move closer to the centre stage.

The Giant Leap, is the fifth chapter and describes how the demand for the Ram temple was conceptualised, the way in which the RSS-VHP-BJP went about it, the key personalities involved and the major turning points in this process. Chapter Six presents an account of the events and the build up to 6 December 1992 when the Babri Masjid was demolished. In Chapter Seven, I have surveyed the history of the legal conflict over the shrine and analysed the watershed verdicts, including the concluding judgement of the Supreme Court. The concluding chapter, 'The Silent March Ahead', assesses events following the demolition, the moderate phase of the BJP, the rise of Narendra Modi and how he has marshalled India to the trajectory it is now pursuing.

Nilanjan Mukhopadhyay

October 2021

1

Ram

From Mythical Hero to God to Political Icon

'If you look back at the great classics and the epics and myths, they were for everyone. Different people got different things from them, but everyone was invited to participate.'

—Chitra Banerjee Divakaruni

In the last week of May 2019, days after the BJP was re-elected to power, when Prime Minister Narendra Modi was weighing his new ministerial team, chief of the RSS, Mohan Bhagwat, proclaimed, 'Lord Ram lives in everyone, and *Ram ka kaam* [Ram's work] is everyone's responsibility.' Undoubtedly, the phrase 'Ram's work' was an allusion to the proposed temple at Ayodhya and a polite reminder to Modi and his team of the 'unfinished agenda'. It is anybody's guess whether the prime minister would have become a national leader but for the infamy, as well as the glory, that came his way in the wake of the 2002 riots following the Godhra carnage. The horrific incident, just after the Sabarmati Express rolled out from the railway station of this nondescript Gujarat town, would not have occurred had boisterous VHP activists not been returning from Ayodhya after participating in yet another programme to keep the embers of the Ram temple agitation smouldering. In assembly by-elections held days before the carnage, the BJP, under Modi's stewardship, did not perform well, an indication that the party's prospects at the impending state polls were not very good. The turn of events, however, enabled Modi to give voice to the angry majoritarian Hindu and he benefited politically.

But, Bhagwat's prompt to the re-elected government was questionable. If, as Bhagwat affirmed, Ram 'lives in everyone', why insist that the temple be built at exactly the same spot in Ayodhya? This incongruity gets further accentuated if one juxtaposes this sequence of events with the most popular Malayalam rendering of the Ramayana, the *Adhyatma Ramayanam* by Thunchaththu Ezhuthachan. It narrates an episode of Ram visiting Valmiki's ashram and asking where he should stay. The sage replies that since Ram dwelled in the hearts of every individual, it was immaterial which material space he chose to occupy. Certainly, Hindutva votaries who also claim to be devotees of Ram are not satisfied with God residing in their minds and hearts. Occupation of a public space is a political victory. But for whom—Ram or his politicized admirers?[1]

Related to this is the question of Ram's plurality. Bhagwat articulated the views of his political clan—that there is but one dimension of Ram. There is an interesting tale from the Ramayana that stands in contrast to the Ram that Bhagwat alluded to. Once, as the story goes, after Ravan has been vanquished, Sita has been banished and Ram is on the throne, his ring falls on the ground and disappears into a hole. Ram tells Hanuman, who has the power to change his size, to go into the hole and get his ring back. The monkey god's travails begin when he slips into the netherworld and is caught by aides of the king of spirits or the *bhooton ka raja*.

Hanuman is put on a platter for the king as part of his dinner. Worried, Hanuman chants Ram's name ceaselessly. When he hears the mantra and spots Hanuman, the king of spirits asks him who he is. Hanuman explains and requests the king to enable him to fulfil his mission of finding Ram's ring. The king of spirits pushes forward a large dish in which there are countless rings. 'Take your pick, they are all Ram's rings,' the king of spirits says. Befuddled, Hanuman looks at the king of spirits who explains that there have been as many Rams as there are rings and whenever one incarnation or avatar of Ram is about to be over, his ring falls and is collected in the platter. In a flash, Hanuman understands that the time on earth of the Ram he knows is over and returns empty-handed.

As far as Bhagwat and others in his fraternity are concerned, the Ramayana's protagonist has outlived his utility in their political narrative and his next avatar will be in the form of an installed deity in a temple that will be symbolic of the Sangh Parivar's political hegemony.

The RSS committed itself to an agitation for a temple in the Uttar Pradesh temple town as late as 1984 even though the dispute was more than a century old. However, the organization had since its inception built its socio-political profile around the revered legendary prince's public following and the epic centred around him. The original tale which became most popular was a linear poetic narrative of Ram, a prince, Sita, his wife, and Lakshman, his half-brother. The story recounted their adventures and escapades when banished to the forest by a cunning stepmother. Valour, duty and love were the primary moral messages of the story. The original kernel of the saga, however, was retold with each narrator incorporating elements from different regional cultures, languages and religious traditions. Well before early twentieth century, especially within sections of Hindu upper-caste society, from which the founders and initial leadership of the RSS emerged, the Ramayana had evolved into a religious text and Ram had already been deified and put on the pedestal as God, Vishnu incarnate.

When Keshav Baliram Hedgewar and his associates chose the day of Dussehra in September 1925 as the founding day of the Rashtriya Swayamsevak Sangh (RSS), the attempt was to establish a symbiotic link with the epic's extant version and its philosophy. In Hindu mythology and historical legends, multiple narratives converge on this day. The festival is also referred to as Vijaya Dashami, and is celebrated in different ways in various parts of India. In north, west and parts of south India, the festival marks the day when Ram slayed Ravan, symbolizing the victory of good over evil. In contrast, in eastern India, while remaining true to this symbolism, the day denotes the end of Durga Puja, more than a day after Goddess Durga killed the demon Mahishasur on the cusp of the eighth and ninth day of the ten-day-long ritual.

Within mythological narratives surrounding Durga, a parallel 'family' tale is interwoven. According to this, the goddess is on an annual visit to her paternal home with her children, Lakshmi, Saraswati, Ganesh and Kartik. The visit comes to an end on this day and she begins her return journey to her marital home in the Himalayas, symbolically depicted by immersion of the idols in the nearest river or waterbody. In parts of west India, especially Maharashtra, this day is also celebrated as *simollanghan* (crossing of the border) which, legends say, marks Shivaji's armies crossing his kingdom's frontiers to fight the enemy, thereby heralding the beginning of the war season. The birth of the RSS was intertwined with this Hindu religio-militaristic tradition and the choice of the founding day indicated that not only were ancient Hindu values part of the RSS's foundational philosophy, but the Ram myth would also continue being an integral part of the political vocabulary of the RSS.

Multiple mythological strands associated with the founding of the RSS have enabled the organization to position itself as a religio-political organization although its stated brief remains mobilizing and strengthening Hindu society. From the time it codified the organization's tenets, the RSS contended that its symbolism was based not on religion but on culture. In its contention, dharma was not religion per se and was part of the people's *sanskriti* or culture. From the onset, RSS leaders fashioned themselves and the organization as Ram's own. It is no wonder that with a 'magnificent' temple to mark his birthplace remaining an unfinished agenda, it was time for the BJP to pay back thc favour to the god for riding on his back and reaffirming the party's status as India's dominant political force. Bhagwat's assertion was made in this backdrop.

*

The BJP or its affiliates were not the first political party or organization to publicly celebrate Dussehra. There is a long history of political appropriation of religious festivals in different parts of India. As such, the Indian model of secularism, as it developed post-Independence, was placatory and prioritized societal equilibrium. It was not primarily driven by the impulse to separate religion from state. After Independence, Jawaharlal Nehru created several public events—for instance, state tableaus during the

Republic Day parade—which emphasized the diversity of Indian cultural tradition, often depicted through religious motifs. As a result, he failed to stay away completely from publicly participating in religious festivals. Pictures of him with Indira Gandhi, published in the Dussehra souvenir, together with Kullu dancers, integral to Kullu Dussehra, testify to this. The festival was provided government aid in 1960 at the initiative of a local Congress legislator who convinced seniors in his party and government that the Dussehra festival in the famous hill town was 'the most important cultural heritage of the Valley'.[2] Similar patronage of religious festivals, for instance Durga Puja committees in West Bengal, by political parties, has given strength to the Hindu nationalistic viewpoint that religion overlaps culture in India.

Nehru and Indira or others from non-BJP stables who followed, may have participated, and continue doing so, in religious festivals and talked glowingly about the characteristics of mythological characters. However, they never forced their interpretation of the character, mythology or epic on citizens. Each individual was left free to find their own spiritual meaning in the epical tales they had grown up with and in their own time. These leaders imbibed from local cultures and tradition whenever they turned out to join festivities and did not try to impose a unitarian version of the Ramayana or a one-dimensional or static imagination of Ram.

This, however, has never been the case with leaders of the Sangh Parivar. From the beginning of the Ayodhya temple agitation, they insisted on a particular interpretation of the Ram legend, presenting it as the only correct reading of the hero-turned-god. The Sangh Parivar's projection of the epic emphasized the political dimensions of the Ram story, his greatness and victories. Moments in the legend when Ram sought 'inner repose', when he underwent tremendous anguish because of acting as sovereigns must, and did not act according to his 'natural karuna' or compassion, 'sidelining it for some kingly duty', were never highlighted.[3] Refusal by anyone to accept the Hindu nationalist rendition of the Ram legend and its vital characteristics without demur invited nothing short of being branded anti-national.

Among the first such instances was one by Advani in 1990, the year his supporters orchestrated a failed campaign to get him voted as BBC's Man of the Year, in a bid to signal the BJP's emergence on the international arena. This move was also aimed at enlisting the support of the Indian diaspora for the Ram temple. Advani claimed that Ram was not just a god, but an embodiment of India's national character. He delivered numerous rousing speeches in the course of his political-discourse-altering Somnath to Ayodhya Rath Yatra, the first of several motorized chariot processions he embarked on over the years across the length and breadth of India. In these he said that the BJP extended support for a Ram temple because the campaign's successful culmination would lead to a reassertion of the Indian identity, which in his mind was 'primarily Hindu'.[4]

Advani represented the suave face of the BJP, and his relatively mild yet seductive political vocabulary enabled the party to convey its viewpoint to the intelligentsia. The crassness required to take the set of arguments to the hoi polloi was left for other leaders in the fraternity. From 1990 onward, much before the accusation of being lesser patriots was hurled at political adversaries, scathing graffiti also became commonplace. One such stated: *Ram drohi, rashtra drohi* (One who betrays Ram betrays the nation), illustrating that Hindutva advocates did not consider citizens not backing the demand for a Ram temple as being worthy of a future in an India governed by them.

'Sri Rama is the unique symbol, the unequalled symbol of our oneness, of our integration, as well as our aspiration to live the higher values.' With these words, Advani began his foreword to the BJP's 'White Paper on Ayodhya' released in April 1993. This tone was at odds with his word selection four months ago after the Babri Masjid was demolished, when Advani had termed 6 December 1992 as the 'saddest day' in his life. Yet, in the foreword, he also argued that the BJP's opponents had allowed separatist tendencies to 'mar public discourse in India to the point that the word "Hindu" became something to be ashamed about, to the point that nationalism became a dirty word…'

From the late 1980s onward, when Advani personally took charge of the Ayodhya agitation, his campaigns were two-pronged and were amplified by others in the Sangh Parivar. The template he created has been followed ever since, even after the Supreme Court verdict and as the process of constructing the temple began. The first aspect of Advani's presentation was a unidimensional image and interpretation of Ram. The second element of this campaign was to link public imagination of the mythical hero-turned-god with the nation, and anyone disagreeing with the Sangh Parivar's understanding was affixed the slur of anti-national or traitor. At no point was any reference made to touch on anything but Ram's political triumphs. Aspects that Valmiki or later Tulsidas focussed on considerably, when the character was gripped with 'inner torment, at war with his better, more compassionate self', were brushed aside.[5] A flaw in Ram's character, or an inherent contradiction may be acceptable in a central character of an epic but certainly not in someone who drives the process of civilizational assertion.

Advani's arguments were paraphrased, paradoxically in his absence, by Modi on 5 August 2020 after he laid the foundation stone of the new temple. In his speech, the prime minister declared that Ram was in the 'ideals of India' and that he 'resides in India's philosophy'. Although made twenty-seven years apart, the core of the two arguments was the same: that Ram symbolized the essence of India and a temple to him at Ayodhya would be a tribute not just to him but India too. Atal Bihari Vajpayee too as prime minister in December 2000 had asserted in a speech in the Lok Sabha that the agitation symbolized national aspiration.

It would be incorrect to dispute the importance Indians—this includes people of faiths other than Hinduism—accord to the Ramayana and Ram, although they emphasize different aspects of the mythical tale. The worry is that a monochrome depiction of Ram would strip him of his humanness and apotheosize the character worshipped by people who do not understand the reasons why the personality occupies, in Advani's words after the Supreme Court verdict, 'an esteemed place in India's cultural and civilizational heritage'.[6]

Significantly, prior to the VHP taking up the agitation, the notion of Ayodhya being the birthplace of Ram was well known to Hindus but the temple town was not a hugely revered pilgrimage centre drawing thousands from remote corners of India through the year. This is self-evident in Modi's assertion at an official meeting, held on 26 June 2021, to draw up a development plan for Ayodhya. He declared that his government would provide the city with 'futuristic infrastructure' so that the 'coming generations should feel the desire to visit Ayodhya at least once in their lifetime'. The claim that the disputed site held a 'special and sacred place in the hearts of crores of our countrymen in

India and abroad'[7] prior to 1986 can only be taken with a pinch of salt.

*

The epic has undoubtedly played a significant role in shaping perceptions of Indians for the past two millennia. But people's readings of Ram's story and the epic are varied. Arguing that every Indian should have a similar perspective on the tale and the character strips plurality from multiple narratives that the original epic spawned over centuries. In the initial years when the Ram Janmabhoomi agitation gathered momentum in the 1980s, India's state-run broadcaster, Doordarshan, ran the televised serial, *Ramayan*. It not just brought everything to a standstill during the telecast but also ended up projecting a 'correct' and unidimensional character of the protagonist and various episodes in Ram's life. Imposing a linear perception on everyday responses and basic outlook of citizens negates the essence and beauty of the tale and pushes away significant sections of Indians from the classic story.

Mythology, like history, is not made up of unidimensional characters. Moreover, 'which' Ramayana is our national epic and 'which' Ram is the epitome of Indian nationhood? The question arises because even Advani accepted the multiplicity and diversity of the Ramayana tradition and the Ram story. In the foreword to the party document cited earlier, he scored a self-goal of sorts: 'There is hardly any language in our country into which the Ramayana has not been translated. There is scarcely a folk tradition which does not celebrate the life and legend of Sri Rama.'[8] He may have also added that the spread and continued popularity of the Ramayana were not just restricted to India. Although

Advani erred in using the word 'translation', the versions emphasized different aspects of the epic. Yet, with his submission, Advani partly admitted that the Ramayana, over centuries, transcended geographical as well as religious boundaries. Ironically, as we shall see, his ideological brotherhood lives in denial mode and campaigns contrary to this reality.

In January 2018, India hosted a commemorative summit in New Delhi to celebrate twenty-five years of association between India and the ASEAN (Association of South-East Asian Nations). Its leaders were also chief guests at the Republic Day functions. As part of the event, the Indian Council for Cultural Relations (ICCR) put together a five-day-long Ramayana Festival to underline the common cultural heritage of India and South-East Asian nations. Cultural troupes from these nations presented different performances from the epic. Significantly, the renderings were diverse. Modi expressed delight at the event, stating that this demonstrated 'India's deep civilizational and historical relations with the ASEAN region'. The foreign minister at the time, Sushma Swaraj, also noted that the Ramayana, alongside Buddhism, connected India and the ASEAN. A telling evidence of this connect is the continuous performance of the Ramayana Ballet since 1976 at Yogyakarta, the only Indonesian city still ruled by a monarchy. Till the point of writing, almost sixteen thousand performances had been staged without fail at an open-air stage, shifting indoors only if and when it rained.

But as the ASEAN cultural fair or the nightly ballet at the Indonesian city reaffirmed, no retelling of one story, whatever be the language, region or country, is identical. The diversity and vibrancy of the Ramayana tradition and the character of Ram stand in contrast to the singular, or fixed, imagination thrust by the BJP and its affiliates. This underscores that Ram and his story have been used primarily as a political tool and not as a cultural symbol which unites people across different cultures, regions, nations and faiths.

*

On one hand the BJP and the RSS proclaimed the multidimensional characteristic of the Ramayana and Ram legends to underscore the epic's cultural richness. On the other, it presented a one-dimensional narrative, necessary for political mobilization and to fell its adversaries. This dichotomy became sharply evident within months of the Babri Masjid's demolition. Sahmat, the cultural organization established in memory of the Communist Party of India (Marxist) (CPIM) activist and street-theatre pioneer, Safdar Hashmi, organized an exhibition in seventeen cities across India in August 1993. The display, titled *Hum Sab Ayodhya* (We Are All Ayodhya or invincible), depicted the characteristics of the religious city, what it stood for and, most importantly, showcased the tale of Ram through multiple narratives. As against popular perception of Ayodhya having come to represent the epicentre of Hindu–Muslim conflict in India, the objective was to convey the message that the temple town was representative of the whole of India and its people.

The exhibition comprised eighty-three display units which used extensive texts. These were cross-referenced with archaeological, historical, artistic and photographic citations and representations. The panels encompassed history and the people of Ayodhya from ancient times to the present. The display boards used contrasting tales from the Ramayana, including one from *Ram Katha* (the original story which ceased to exist after it was rewritten as the Ramayana). In this particular text which became a matter of conflict, there were references to Buddhist and Jain versions of Ram's story. Citation of a Buddhist *Dasaratha Jataka* tale, which antedated Valmiki's Ramayana, was the subject of much controversy for it portrayed Ram and Sita as siblings.

The immediate drum-beating from the RSS and the BJP was that Sahmat had committed sacrilege by depicting the two chief characters of the epic as brother and sister, and had hurt Hindu sentiments by allusions to an incestuous relationship. Offended political groups of the Sangh Parivar accused the exhibition—which had been advanced a sum of Rupees 25 lakh by the Union human resource development (HRD) minister, Arjun Singh, under his discretionary powers—of a communist conspiracy to denigrate Hindus and defame Hindu epic traditions. Way back in the 1960s, Madhav Sadashiv Golwalkar, second sarsanghchalak of the RSS, who has had the longest tenure as the head of the organization, started clubbing communists as anti-Hindu, alongside Muslims and Christians. In his book, *Bunch of Thoughts*, now troublesome for the RSS–BJP combine, there is a chapter titled 'Internal Threats', with subsections on Muslims, Christians and communists. He also popularized the slogan 'Not socialism but Hinduism'. In contemporary political discourse, no effort is spared to denigrate the imaginary 'left liberal cabal', unreal because liberals and communists have little in common.

The Sahmat exhibition was held without controversy across India except in Faizabad/Ayodhya and later in Delhi. In the temple town, activists owing allegiance to the VHP stormed the exhibition and tore down display panels. Additionally, criminal cases were registered against Sahmat under several sections of the Indian Penal Code (IPC) paradoxically under central rule. Its functionaries were accused of promoting enmity between religious groups, deliberately wounding religious feelings and being part of a criminal conspiracy. Significantly, the VHP and its allies chose to kick up a storm over the show only in Ayodhya and not in any other city, although the same panel was mounted in each venue. The exhibition, the public response to it and the HRD ministry's financial support became the subject of inflamed arguments in Parliament for almost an entire week during the ongoing monsoon session.

*

In Delhi, the nature of the controversy was different. The show was held at the Nehru Memorial Museum and Library (NMML) at the Teen Murti House. On 21 August 1993, Lok Sabha Speaker Shivraj Patil—significantly, he was from the Congress party—ordered the removal of the 'offending' panel. The same day, Sahmat decided to take down the exhibition in Delhi. Before they could begin the exercise, the city police, under orders from the lieutenant governor (LG), swooped down on the exhibition and confiscated the text panel using powers granted to it under Section 95 of the Criminal Procedure Code (CrPC). This section empowers the police to seize various types of publications which are punishable under sections of the IPC. Cases under the IPC had already been filed in Ayodhya and the same sections were used once again in the capital. Thus, the government of the time, strangely enough that of the 'secular' Congress party, implicitly accepted the Hindutva argument that Hindu religious and cultural traditions were unidimensional. The action against the Sahmat exhibition also signalled that public propagation of Buddhist and Jain renderings of the Ramayana would henceforth be disallowed and that the RSS–VHP–BJP combine could decide on the form of the public rendering and depiction of the Ramayana.

The outcry at both places was due to panels which referred to the Buddhist *Dasaratha Jataka* tales, certainly one of the oldest versions of the Ram story. The objection arose because the cited text was suggestive of Ram and Sita, shown as siblings, being involved in an immoral relationship. No critic chose to consider the original narrative as an instance of the writer/compiler suggesting that the two, despite being brother and sister, entered into a conjugal relationship to establish a pure royal line in conformity with the traditions of the time. Even if one faults this argument, there is no denying that the text was not a fictional imagination of Sahmat members, written with the intention of creating mischief and denigrating Hindu gods. There is little doubt that this rendering of the Ram and Sita story is also part of the Indian tradition but the Valmiki Ramayana did not follow this storyline and instead altered it. This could have been because social norms altered and marital relations between siblings were no longer considered acceptable by the time the Valmiki Ramayana was composed.

Sadly, rational responses were in short supply in August 1993. Sahmat was singled out for criticism even by parties and groups antithetical to the RSS and the BJP. It was accused of not being pragmatic on matters of faith, which became the political norm as years went by. The organization and its key members were furthermore accused of being blind to realpolitik. Vast sections of secularists argued that Sahmat should have realized that following widespread communal strife in the wake of the demolition of the Babri Masjid, flagging a quasi-extinct ancient tale, at variance with the currently accepted representation of epical characters, would certainly provoke anger. The putting down of Sahmat even by people who shared its world view was an instance of political and ideological opponents of the Sangh Parivar accepting that Hindu nationalists could be contested only on their terrain, and that their understanding of the Ramayana and Ram had to be universally accepted. Undoubtedly, much before the BJP's emergence as the principal pole of Indian politics, avowed opponents too were bowing to pressure and choosing silence over contestation.[9]

Emboldened, belligerent sections of Hindu nationalists turned their attention to a programme in which some important people were involved. The Uttar Pradesh government sponsored the annual Ramayan Mela at Ayodhya in January 1994. The organizing committee of the traditional annual fair was headed by Mahant Nritya Gopal Das, vice-president of the VHP-backed Ram Janmabhoomi Nyas and one of the bigwigs of the Ram temple agitation. He is currently the chief of the Shri Ram Janmabhoomi Teeth Kshetra Trust, established by the government at the Supreme Court's behest to oversee construction and manage the new Ram temple. Obviously, his past patronage of a touchy publication was overlooked because of his clout among Hindu seers. A souvenir was released during the event. Its publication and circulation resulted in a furore because one of the articles had also drawn from the Jataka tales and the Jain *Ram Kavya*. This piece too referred to the celestial couple as brother and sister. Additionally, flowing from the Jain Ramayana, Ram was shown as an evolved Jain male character who has not just conquered his passions, but is also in his last birth. As a result of this, he is reluctant to kill Ravan and the task is eventually passed to Lakshman. It led to public protests and created upheaval within the organizing committee. This was despite the article remaining faithful to the epic's Jain tradition which is totally devoid of Hindu values and considered Ravan a noble person. Significantly, Hindu nationalists consider Jainism to be an Indic religion and Article 25 (2) of the Constitution of India also states that 'reference to Hindus shall be construed as including a reference to persons professing the Sikh, Jaina or Buddhist religion'.

*

Despite opponents of the BJP practically throwing in the towel, the party spent the major part of the post-demolition years in the 1990s and the first decade of the new millennium moderating its cultural-nationalist stance. It positioned itself as a middle-of-the-road political outfit after concluding that it would remain a political pariah unless it shed its extreme right-wing social outlook. After the National Democratic Alliance (NDA) lost the general elections in 2004, Vajpayee bemoaned inaction after the 2002 Gujarat riots and suggested it was one of the causative factors. Paradoxically, however, although the BJP remained out of power for a decade thereafter, there was no cessation in the growing approval of the idea of Hindutva or support for its stand on Ram, the Ramayana and the Ram temple. Despite the Congress's comfortable majority during the first tenure of the United Progressive Alliance (UPA) government—this improved after the 2009 parliamentary elections—various outfits of the Sangh Parivar kept up its campaign on the Ram story. These organizations kept looking for opportunities and one such came up in 2008. On 25 February, activists of the Akhil Bharatiya Vidyarthi Parishad (ABVP) vandalized Delhi University's Department of History and assaulted its head of department and eminent scholar of medieval Indian history, Saiyid Zaheer Husain Jafri. Their objection was to an essay on the Ramayana by the historian, poet and litterateur A.K. Ramanujan, a Padma Shri awardee. The paper was part of the reading list for the concurrent discipline course on culture in ancient India in the University of Delhi for second-year honours students not doing history. The essay was titled 'Three Hundred Ramayanas: Five examples and Three Thoughts on Translation'.[10] The ABVP activists were backed by another Sangh Parivar affiliate, the Shiksha Bachao Andolan Samiti (SBAS). Importantly, the campaign had the blessings of former HRD minister, Murli Manohar Joshi. The SBAS positions itself as an organization of nationalist historians with the objective of purportedly rescuing India from Marxist and Wahabi historians, unsurprisingly put on the same plane. It had already acquired infamy for campaigning against books of the National Council of Educational Research and Training (NCERT) the previous year. The body of RSS-connected historians was anchored by Dinanath Batra, a known 'history and thought police'.[11]

The ire against Ramanujan stemmed from him raising an ingenious question: 'How many Ramayanas? Three hundred? Three thousand? At the end of some Ramayanas, a question is sometimes asked: How many Ramayanas have there been?' This starting premise was against the Hindu nationalistic framework that there is just one Ramayana and one Ram, and the interpretation cannot vary from the representation presented by Advani in his foreword to the BJP's 'White Paper on Ayodhya'. More than a month prior to the attack on him, Jafri was forwarded two memoranda by the university's vice chancellor. These spelt out objections to Ramanujan's essay. But after consideration, the history department decided to retain the essay in the study list. The department asserted that the essay was included in the reading list because it would make students aware of India's literary richness and diversity. The department's note stated that the course and the reading list had 'gone through all the due administrative procedures and the readings have been all approved by the relevant bodies. We see no reason to drop it from our reading list.'[12] The ABVP and its partners in the campaign claimed that Prime Minister Manmohan Singh's daughter, Upinder Singh, was the compiler of the volume which contained Ramanujan's essay although the allegation had no grain of truth.

The return of the UPA government to power in the 2009 Lok Sabha elections did not dishearten the affiliates of the RSS and they kept up pressure on the history department to drop Ramanujan's essay. The primary objections, besides mention of multiple versions of the epic the poet-writer recounted and commented on in the paper, were due to certain descriptions of important characters which Hindu nationalists found objectionable. They took these phrases out of context and highlighted several 'objectionable' references. For instance, they contended that the essay termed Hanuman as a 'ladies' man', 'trusty henchman' and even 'tiny monkey'. However, those demanding action against the controversial text did not take note of the fact that Ramanujan did not make these statements of his own accord but merely listed out various ways in which the characters had been depicted. For instance, he wrote that in 'Southeast Asian texts … Hanuman is not the celibate devotee with a monkey face but a ladies' man who figures in many love episodes'. Hanuman was further called Ram's 'trusty henchman' elsewhere. Likewise, while recalling various versions of the Ramayana, Ramanujan mentioned that 'The Santals, a tribe known for their extensive oral traditions, even conceive of Sita as unfaithful ... she is seduced both by Ravana and by Laksmana'. Ramanujan also quoted the Tamil story of *Satakantharava* (which) 'gives Sita a heroic character; when the ten-headed Ravana is killed, another appears with a hundred heads: Rama cannot handle this new menace, so it is Sita who goes to war and slays the new demon'. These versions, Ramanujan meaningfully argued in his essay, would be to the 'shock and horror of any Hindu bred on Valmiki or Kampan'. Given the consistency with which the Sangh Parivar affiliates pursued their campaign against his essay, Ramanujan's assessment was bang on target.

The SBAS even moved the courts, first a lower one and later the Delhi High Court seeking directions to Delhi University to remove the essay. But the judges stated that this was an internal matter of the university. Batra, however, persisted and filed a civil case in the Supreme Court in 2010 and this time met with partial success. The apex court directed the university authorities to establish an experts' committee to examine the essay and submit their viewpoint to the Academic Council. The committee comprised four historians who remained unidentified. Although three of them did not find the essay objectionable, the fourth, despite accepting Ramanujan's scholarship, declared that these variations (from the most popular narratives) 'are bound to affect the sensibilities of impressionable minds. If the teacher explains the background of these versions, the students may be convinced, but I doubt if college teachers are well equipped [sic] to handle the situation.' This was strange reasoning because the committee was attributing the poor quality to teachers from colleges affiliated to a premier university. Certainly, the story around Ram was being sanitized under public pressure. The historian who was in minority also revealed a communal mind when contending that the problem would 'become more difficult in the case of a non-Hindu teacher'. This historian was in effect arguing that courses on religious traditions or practices must be taught only by people of that religion. Following from this, non-Muslims would have no business to teach a course on either history of Islam in India or even on political Islam. In November 2019, this dystopian possibility became a reality when protests rocked Banaras Hindu University (BHU) against a Muslim assistant professor, Firoze Khan, who was selected on the faculty of the Sanskrit department. Sadly, this agitation succeeded and the teacher was forced to resign.

Back in 2011, a member of the BJP-aligned teachers' organization, National Democratic Teachers' Front (NDTF), declared that while they did not intend to 'challenge the academic credentials of Dr A.K. Ramanujan', he certainly was 'not a historian, and his essay deliberately highlights those narratives of the Ramayana which paint Rama, Sita, Hanuman, Laxmana, etc., in dubious hues. This essay is partly pornographic.'[13] This argument was odd. To write his essay, Ramanujan did not require the skills of a historian. A literary critic was better placed and he was suitably qualified in this discipline. Eventually, the years' long campaign met with success and in October 2011, the vice chancellor, with the backing of the Academic Council, dropped the essay from the reading list. It was unfortunate that the university did not have the courage to stand up to 'thugs who seek to violently limit the intellectual freedom of a university'.[14] Students opting for this course would thereafter learn that Valmiki's Ramayana or Tulsidas's *Ramcharitmanas* was the only book retelling the story of Ram. Or at worst, think that the television serial was the only 'true' story of Ram and the essence of Ram's character was just what Advani had written in his foreword to the BJP's White Paper. The RSS–BJP conglomerate succeeded in ensuring that people began to perceive the story of Ram and the epic as they wished them to see it, not in the multiple ways in which Ram's character could be interpreted with his goodness as well as flaws.

In the popular version of the Ram story, the smaller narrative around Ahalya, the eternal woman who responded to her inner urges and was seduced by Indra, king of gods, was very significant because Ahalya is freed of her curse by Ram. Ramanujan narrated how this sequence was contrastingly treated in Valmiki's Ramayana and in Kamban's *Ramavataram* in Tamil although the divergence on the core event of this tale is very nuanced. In Valmiki's version, Indra seduces a willing Ahalya while in the latter's rendering, she is aware of her 'straying' but cannot let go of the proverbial 'forbidden fruit'. Analysis of this sub-tale of the larger Ramayana story is mostly absent in Hindu nationalistic narratives because Ram is not central here. Yet Ramanujan's recounting of an incident, which shows Hindu celestial beings too were at times subject to human foibles and failings, became problematic because it was a hurdle to sanitizing the public image of the characters. The opposition to Ramanujan's essay can be understood keeping in mind the Hindutva need for Ram and Ramayana to be flawless. The article was all the more troublesome for the RSS–BJP–ABVP combine because Ramanujan wrote that Ram's 'character is not that of a god but of a god-man who has to live within the limits of a human form with all its vicissitudes'. Over decades, whether it was a party publication penned by Advani, a prime ministerial speech delivered by Modi, or a government function anchored by the foreign minister, multiple narratives of the Ramayana were cited to establish the epic's influence across geographical territories. But depiction of what was contained in these diverse renditions was not allowed.

In the most commonly accepted version of Valmiki's Ramayana, the first and last books, 'Balkand and Uttarakand have been regarded by scholars as the handiwork of latter-day interpolators as there are not only discrepancies in style but also contradictions in the core of the epic poem'.[15] Some scholars contested this viewpoint and preferred to see Ram as divine at all periods of the Ramayana's development. In addition to contending that no one can question 'whether the poem was ever written without its religious outlook', they viewed 'major figures as temporal representations of the Hindu triad: Ravana and Vibhishana of Brahma, Rama of Visnu and Indrajit of Siva'.[16] There was considerable academic debate preceding the campaign to proscribe Ramanujan's essay from the academic curriculum and this was conducted within a democratic space. By constricting open-ended discussions, the protagonists of the Ram temple movement were negating diversities of Hindu narratives and reducing vast quantities of spiritual texts into dogmas.

*

The principal reason for Hindu nationalists to oppose viewpoints highlighting the Ramayana's multiplicity of renderings stemmed from the political necessity of presenting Ram's story as history. Hindu nationalistic claim on the disputed shrine in the initial years of the agitation was built around the assertion of 'proving' the site as Ram's birthplace and the existence of a Ram temple beneath the Babri Masjid. The tack was changed subsequently and the claim was presented as a 'matter of faith' which did not require 'proof'.

In recent years, conversations around Ayodhya have made it appear as if the events depicted in the most popular narratives actually occurred. However, the reality is that instead of the story being based on history, the epic has its own history. As Romila Thapar argued, the narrative 'does not belong to any moment in history for it has its own history which lies embedded in the many versions which were woven around the theme at different times and places'.[17]

In the Ramayana's history there have been moments where different readings, critical essays and even fiction based on the epic have generated humungous controversy. In contemporary India, it is inconceivable that Periyar E.V. Ramasamy Naicker's (EVR) critical interpretations of the Ramayana in Tamil—*Iramayanakkurippukal* (Notes on the Ramayana) and *Iramayanappatirankal* (Characters from the Ramayana)—would be allowed to be circulated and discussed. In fact, the Hindi translation of his first book, *Sachchi Ramayana*, was banned temporarily by the Allahabad High Court in December 1999 for offering an image of Ram different from the popular representation.

Periyar's reading of the epic mirrored his politics—its anti-Brahminical thrust primarily. His texts, written in 1930, although translated in the late 1950s, lambasted almost every revered character of the epic and were generous with admiration for Ravan. The analysis is also driven by the 'desire to see in it a struggle between North and South India'.[18]

For Periyar, the dominant readings of the Ramayana were

driven by the objective of ensuring north Indian Brahminical domination over Dravidian southern India. Ramasamy did not just target the epic but also the 'respect with which Tamilians have traditionally viewed the Ramayana, arguing that the story is both an account of and a continuing vehicle for northern cultural domination'.[19] The critique advocates that north Indian propaganda has misled Tamilians into believing that Ram is an exemplary personality, the ideal man in each of his relationships, whereas, EVR reasoned, the truth was the opposite. For EVR, the Ramayana was full of flawed characters: 'Dasaratha enslaved by passion, Sita overly fond of jewelled ornaments, Laksmana desirous of Sita, Kausalya as excessively ambitious for the success of her son, and Laksmana too hot-headed to control his flaring temper.'

In the eyes of Richman, Periyar's 'denial of the epic's sacrality echoes his own youthful disillusionment with Hinduism, while his condemnation of Rama as an agent of North Indian oppression parallels his attack on Brahmins as dominating both the Congress Party and local positions of power'. With Ram's installation by Hindu nationalists in the political space, even in north India, Dalit thinkers and activists have at times seen reason in Periyar's arguments although they have been somewhat uncomfortable with his strong advocacy of Dravidianism and his framing of the epic as an Aryan versus Dravidian conflict. Significantly, the anthology of essays which Richman edited was first published in 1991 in the United States and included Ramanujan's paper. Fortunately, both the collection of articles and Ramanujan's controversial article remain available in India, online as well as in bookstores. Yet one never knows when hot-headed Hindu activists will 'discover' this 'sacrilege' and launch another stir against 'defilement' of Ram and the Ramayana.

It is ironical that the first book banned in independent India was not the handiwork of a government driven by the idea of Hindu nationalism. Instead, it was done by a regime headed by the icon of secularism, Jawaharlal Nehru. In 1955, *Rama Retold*, a fictional spoof on the Ramayana was banned. It was written by Aubrey Menen, born of an English mother and Indian father, who grew up in India as well as in England but made Italy his home. It would be far-fetched to contend that Menen reflected the Dravidian position on the Ramayana, so 'subversive' of the popular readings of the epic. Yet it was beyond the pale of doubt that he was 'only continuing the tradition of demystifying [perhaps a trifle drastically] the epic'.[20]

Although Menen is almost totally forgotten as a writer in India, an interview of his appeared in *India Today* in January 2015.[21] In this, he said he wrote *Rama Retold* because he wished to 'secularize a religious story in Jawaharlal Nehru's secular state ... [He] was afraid of being criticized. *Jesus Christ Superstar* packed the Cambridge Theatre in London for five years, largely with sincere Christians. People like Nehru, who believe nothing, are often the most sensitive when it comes to religion. Childhood guilt, I imagine.' The Nehru government, 'despite all claims to have a free democratic republic where we are entitled to free expression, the native system, like its British overlords, exercised extreme caution when it came to religious matters'.[22] *Rama Retold* was criticized sharply by C. Rajagopalachari, custodian of numerous constitutional posts and founder of the right-wing Swatantra Party. Later, he also translated an abridged translation of the Ramayana into English. He termed Menen's book as 'nonsense but of the unreadable kind, i.e., pure nonsense'.[23] M.V. Kamath, the journalist known for his not-so-unsympathetic opinion regarding the

Indian right wing, too, found the book abominable because 'in no culture is virtue and decency laughing matter'.[24]

Menen spared no character in the epic. But besides his description of Dasarath as a womanizer, Lakshman as a brawny loyalist with little mind of his own and Sita as someone whom one has just to 'put up with', it was *Rama Retold*'s irreverence which irritated those who had begun idolizing Ram. In addition, Sita was blasphemously shown as having gone to Lanka with Ravan of her own free will to suggest a crush. Menen also introduced the character of Valmiki who was at times depicted as the protagonist and running an ashram of gluttons where Ram stays during his *vanavas* or banishment.

Menen may have hurt Hindu sensibilities, but the response of the state, and especially Nehru's, foretold how groups claiming their 'sensibilities' were hurt, especially in matters of religion, would impinge on the freedom of expression in India. Yet, despite compromising his much-vaunted secularist posture in the face of criticism from conservatives within his own party and outside, Nehru did not permit political use of the Ram legend.

The final footnote in the *Rama Retold* story was inserted in its narrative on 13 February 1989. On that day, Menen died in Thiruvananthapuram after suffering from throat cancer for some time. In faraway Srinagar, that very day, one person died and more than a hundred people were injured during a protest against the publication a day earlier, in the United States, of Salman Rushdie's *The Satanic Verses*. The angry crowd mirrored actions of Muslim conservatives in Pakistan who had raged against it the day before. The violence in Srinagar was despite the Indian government proscribing the book in October 1988 after several Indian political leaders, including former diplomat

Syed Shahabuddin, petitioned it. Tragically, this decision would be taken by Rajiv Gandhi, Nehru's grandson. Neither those who demanded the ban on the book nor the ones who accepted this demand had read the book. The next day, Ayatollah Khomeini spoke on Radio Tehran. He delivered one of the most scathing speeches on a work of literature. In the course of his monologue, he called for Rushdie's execution, accusing him of apostasy and blasphemy.

Twelve days prior to Menen's death, on 1 February 1989, the VHP organized a *sant sammelan* (conclave of Hindu religious leaders) in Allahabad during the ongoing Kumbh Mela where it was decided to conduct a ceremony in Ayodhya to lay the foundation of the new temple on 9 November 1989, the occasion of the annual festival of *utthanaikadashi* or *devothan ekadashi* (a religious festival when the gods are supposed to have risen). After this ceremony was contentiously completed, the VHP leaders declared that the foundation of Hindu Rashtra had been laid. Menen's passing could not have been at a more ironical period in Indian history!

Menen's novel may have lacked literary depth, but it paved the way for numerous scholars, writers, essayists and even animators to retell Ram's story. Many earned the ire of the Sangh Parivar and its raucous brigade of thought police. In 2008, American animation film-maker Nina Paley decided to make a film, *Sita Sings the Blues*, which drew parallels between the breakdown of her own marriage and Sita's *agnipariksha* or test by fire. She decided to set her images to blues music sung by the famous American jazz artist Annette Hanshaw. Significantly, she told a newspaper reporter: 'I didn't set out to tell The Ramayana, only my Ramayana. I was moved by the story. It seemed to speak so much to my life at the time [when she made the film]. And it was cathartic to re-tell it.'[25] Although first exposed to the Ramayana through the Amar Chitra Katha comic series, parallels between her life and Sita's came in the aftermath of receiving an email from her husband dissolving their marriage: 'The question that I asked and that people still ask is, "Why?" Why did Rama reject Sita? Why did my husband reject me? We don't know why…'

Hindu zealots, however, did not like Paley's effort, especially the film's tagline: 'The Greatest Breakup Story Ever Told'. The film was a take-off on feminist renderings of the Ramayana, references to which were drawn by Nabaneeta Dev Sen, writer and academic, who wrote about 'many versions of the Ramayana written by women, including the Telugu Ramayana written by Molla and the Bengali Ramayana written by Chandravati in the 16th century'. The two were the first women to write the Ramayana in their regional languages. Of the two, the latter looks 'at the Ramayana through a woman's eyes and critiques Rama from a woman's perspective'.[26]

Sita Sings the Blues was released online and remains free for viewing on www.sitasingstheblues.com. But the film immediately enraged Hindu nationalists, and one group called the Hindu Janajagruti Samiti (HJS) led protests in cyberspace demanding that the film be banned and criminal proceedings initiated against those who made, funded and assisted in its distribution. Although efforts of the HJS came to naught and little was heard about the campaign after the initial pitch, the group succeeded in furthering the objective of playing victim and claiming that Hindu traditions, epics and revered gods were being maligned in public eye.

Brave creators, however, continued to tread the path of danger and possible proscription. In 2011, film director and editor Shikha Sen made *Anek Ramayan*, a film which recounted how in 2007 a group of parents at a Delhi school decided to get together to stage a play on the Ramayana for their children. The script soon became a matter of severe contestation as different parents had grown up on various versions of the Ramayana. Some wished the character of Ram to be that of the ideal, perfect man. While for some others, it would be better if he was depicted as a multifaceted personality and not necessarily perfect in every sphere. Ultimately, after much debate they agreed that the representation would be as in different texts. The film underlined that there were 'more than a thousand written Ramayans, written all over the country, at different times and different regions, in different languages. Given the social and period variances, there are variations in the different interpretations of certain incidents.' The director acknowledged that some of the details, which she as a Bengali might have grown up with, were different from those of others who had been reared on the Odia, Malayalam or Tamil versions. 'And all of these would be vastly different from the Tulsidas [version] that most here [in Delhi] have grown up on. And there are many which many of us take as granted, which are not even there in Tulsi!' The multiple versions of the Ramayana were mentioned even by Modi in his speech on 5 August 2020 when he laid the foundation stone of the Ram temple. But while he listed these out to argue that 'Rama is the faith of India', their existence is testimony to multitudes of perception among people regarding the character and epic.

The director was aware that the film was in several ways 'saying the same thing that Ramanujan's essay brought out … that the epic is a vibrant story teeming with wonderful differences right through our written history. The existence of different versions says that we are a diverse country and this diversity should be celebrated rather than denied.'[27] Fortunately, this film too escaped the Hindutva radar and remains available on the Internet.

*

The history of the Ramayana which Romila Thapar mentioned becomes evident when analysing the evolution of the epic through various stages. In the first stage, the epic was primarily martial in character and the protagonist was a noble hero, a fact that becomes clear when Ram says that even his future is determined by fate. In this phase, the pantheon of gods is Vedic in character and not Puranic. Throughout the first and the second stages, Ram and Lakshman are compared to Indra, Brahma and other gods like Vayu, Agni and Marut representing the forces of nature. The nature of the narrative altered greatly in the third stage as the 'Balkand' and the 'Uttarakand' got incorporated into the epic's extant version. The stress here onward was on Ram's divinity and the composition began its transformation from a simple narrative to a complex religious text. By that time, descriptions of Indra's moral degradation had begun appearing in several religious and mythological scripts of the time. Ram could no longer be compared to Indra. At about the same time, Vishnu and Shiva started emerging as the main gods of the Hindu pantheon, and by the time the epic went into its fourth stage of development, the two gods had completely displaced Indra and Brahma from the altar although the latter still remains part of the Holy Trinity.[28]

Over centuries, social structure also moved from the Vedic to the Puranic; the caste system emerged by the fourth stage of the epic's development. The four varnas or castes were also clearly spelt out. Attitude towards women underwent a change and emphasis was more on subservience to the husband and chastity. A woman was also often considered—by the third stage—a seductress, and by the end of the fourth stage, there was further decline in the status of women. The wife stopped having an identity of her own, and instead was of just ornamental value to the husband. Widowhood began being considered inauspicious, and there were occasional references to the practice of sati. In terms of social custom, women by that time were expected to eat after the menfolk of the family. The change in attitude towards women in society corresponded to the time when interpolations were made in the Ramayana about Ram doubting Sita's chastity after the death of Ravan, and even later when the gossip mill in Ayodhya forced Ram to banish Sita to Valmiki's hermitage.

Significantly, Ram's entry into the pantheon of Hindu gods happened only after the medieval Bhakti poet, Goswami Tulsidas (sixteenth/seventeenth century), composed his version of the Ramayana, the *Ramcharitmanas.* He evidently wrote this poem in the closing decades of the sixteenth century when he lived in Ayodhya. Importantly, in Tulsidas's work, 'Ayodhya [identified as Avadhpuri in his work] appears neither as a place with a temple of Rama nor as an important place of pilgrimage for the Hindus'.[29] Additionally, although Tulsidas emphasized the 'virtues of remembering Rama and repeating his name, nowhere in *Ramcharitmanas* does he speak of the worship of idol of Rama; had a temple existed in Ayodhya it could not have escaped his attention.'

Earlier, and by the time the Ramayana was in its third stage of development, various bardic interpolators were actively expanding the epic. There were also several other writers who were using the extant version as a base for their independent creations. They had also begun translating Valmiki's original into other languages. The legendary story of Ram began spreading far and wide in India, and in other parts of Asia through traders and other workers. The urge to come up with new readings of the epic was naturally irresistible for several writers. Among the first such exercises is the 'Ramopakhyana' of the Mahabharata, an abridged version of the Ramayana. The oldest known examples of the classical literary tradition using the kernel of the Ramayana's story are the two plays, *Pratimanataka* and *Abhishekanataka*, both currently attributed to Bhasa and written sometime in the third century AD. The two plays differ from one another and the latter starts with the episode of Ram killing Vali by sleight and the subsequent reproach by the dying Vanar king.

Among the early classical literary works, the most well-known one based on the Ram story is Kalidas's long poem *Raghuvamsa*. The genealogy that Kalidas follows is in contrast to the one in the Ramayana, but is closer to the one presented in the *Vishnu Purana*. There are several other renderings through the centuries which indicate the growing popularity of the Ram story. Not all of them contain the entire Ram story but emphasize a few episodes of the entire epic.

One of the first adaptations in an Indian language other than Sanskrit and Prakrit was *Ramavataram*, a Tamil version written by Kamban. It was most likely written between the ninth and the tenth centuries. Kamban's work heralded the adoption of the Ram story in a big way by various writers from south India. While Abhinava Pampa, also called Nagachandra, wrote the *Pampa Ramayana* in Kannada in the eleventh century, it was followed by the Malayalam versions titled *Ramacharitram* and *Ramakathapattu*. There were other versions also in various south Indian languages, including the *Adhyatma Ramayanam* by Ezhuthachan, possibly the best-known Malayalam version. Significantly, adaptations of the Ramayana in south India were done before such attempts were made in other north Indian languages.

By the late fourteenth century several adaptations were being done in other languages in India. The first major adaptation of the Ramayana, in an Indian language other than Sanskrit, Prakrit, or any of the south Indian languages, was the Bengali version composed by the poet Krittivas in the fifteenth century. This version gave rise to a spate of Bengali adaptations, including one by the poetess Chandravati in the sixteenth century and others by Dvija Madhukantha, Kavichandra and Nityananda Acharya. In the version penned by Krittivas, there are indications of Buddhist influences, possibly because there were still several remnants of Buddhism in Bengal at that time. During the same period, adaptations were also done in many more languages—Odia, Assamese, Gujarati, Marathi and, of course, Hindi. But none of these adaptations led to the kind of popularization of the Ram story as the *Ramcharitmanas* did. The poem became immensely popular even during the lifetime of Tulsidas. Prior to this, Ram's legend remained restricted to the court and to the theologists. But in a single stroke, Tulsidas managed to make the Ram story popular among people and gave it a mass character. Tulsidas was not the only bhakti poet who, while translating, created a new version of the story of Ram. It was done in Marathi also by the medieval poet Eknath. But he died in 1599, leaving the *Bhavarth Ramayana* incomplete.

By the time the bhakti movement became a nationwide

phenomenon, the story of Ram had started spreading not only to every nook and corner of India but also in several other countries of Asia. Ram's story travelled to China, Japan, Tibet, Indonesia, Burma (now Myanmar), Vietnam, Cambodia, Malaysia, Laos, Thailand and the Philippines. It was taken to these countries mostly by travellers and pilgrims who had visited India, and by the end of the seventeenth century, there were many versions of the story in these countries. The trend of adapting the primary plot continued with some of these versions presenting Ram as a person who was Buddha in his previous life. These texts were based on Buddhist philosophy as its theological core. In some countries the story of Ram became so popular that the kings started adopting the title of Ram. It is important to note that in all these versions, Ram's popularity was related to his martial abilities and sense of morality. Kings who adopted the title of Ram did so for these reasons, and not for any association of divinity with Ram's character.

By the nineteenth century the story of Ram was hugely popular and his kingdom and mode of governance were considered the model to aspire to. Hindu nationalists were not the first to use Ram as political motif: Gandhi talked of Ram Rajya during the freedom struggle and it was natural that sooner or later someone would use the legend for sectarian purposes. Once Ram was introduced to the political space, it was a matter of time before the process of multiple appropriations of the Ramayana and Ram's story would begin. When the Ramayana began travelling across territorial boundaries and cultures, it was appropriated in myriad ways. But with political leaders installing Ram on the political platform, there was need for a singular Ram. Gandhi was clear that his Ram was the character depicted by Tulsidas for he considered it 'as the greatest book in all devotional literature'.

Much of the consolidation of the singular image of Ram which helped the Hindu nationalistic political agenda happened during the late 1980s and coincided with the period when Doordarshan telecast Ramanand Sagar's serial. It ran for seventy-eight weeks from January 1987 to August 1989 (with a break for some months) and brought everything to standstill every Sunday when the serial was telecast. This was roughly the period when the movement metamorphosed from being a disquieting yet insignificant agitation, waged by a handful of angry-sounding Hindu zealots whose political vocabulary was grossly incorrect as per the extant value system, to a mainstream political issue which would mutate the basis of India.

The telecast of the serial strengthened congregational Hinduism, a trend which was first started a century ago by Bal Gangadhar Tilak with public Ganesh festivals and also as manifested through publicly organized or community Durga Puja in Bengal. Prior to this, religious worship was a personal matter at home or in temples. The serial fed into middle-class imaginations and aspirations and marginalized other versions of the Ramayana besides also giving a greater sense of the Hindu collective. It has been argued that the serial triggered 'subtle changes in this pluralistic and decentralised religion [Hinduism], long divided into sects, each worshipping different deities, lacking a holy book, a unique and singular god, or a single capital of the faith … [the serial] contributed enormously to the VHP's movement to "liberate" the birthplace of Ram. Hitherto one of the many gods worshipped by Hindus, Ram was increasingly being seen, courtesy of the serial on television, as the most important and glamorous of them all.'[30] This formulation was further substantiated by Arvind Rajagopal in his book, *Politics After Television*. He quoted the president of Vishva

Hindu Parishad under whose stewardship the Ram temple agitation became dominant, Ashok Singhal, as accepting that the serial 'was a great gift to our movement. We owed our recruits to the serial's inspiration.'[31] He also recounted Mahant Avaidyanath, spiritual predecessor and guru of Uttar Pradesh chief minister Yogi Adityanath and president of the Shri Ram Janmabhoomi Mukti Yagna Samiti that was established in 1984, as saying that Sagar had spread *prachar prasad* or auspicious publicity for Ram and the movement. He also noted that by commissioning the serial, and the subsequent one on the Mahabharata, the Congress government had 'violated a decades-old taboo on religious partisanship, and Hindu nationalists made the most of the opportunity'.[32]

In terms of its creative characteristics, Sagar's take on the Ramayana was considered a popular and mixed account of Valmiki's and Tulsidas's versions and 'would become the "reigning literature" if the RSS clan comes to power in India'.[33] In *India After Gandhi*, Ramachandra Guha cited anthropologist Philip Lutgendorf as writing that 'never before had such a large percentage of South Asia's population been united in a single activity'.[34] This common activity contributed, in time, to the rise of much disunity, communal strife and intercommunity alienation in India.

Ramanand Sagar's serial also contributed in no small measure to the alienation of Indian Muslims from their understanding of Ram as a moral ideal. Ironical as it may sound in contemporary India, the Ramayana thrived in the Urdu language from 1860 when it had not yet become tagged as the language of Muslims. After Munshi Jagannath Lal Khushtar's translation (beginning with *Bismillah ir Rehman ir Rahim*) that was published in that year, there were almost 300 versions of the Ramayana in Urdu, many in verse and called *Manzum Ramayana*.[35] Even as Urdu got the Islamic tag, the high point of Ram's depiction in Urdu literature was possibly reached in the first decade of the twentieth century when Allama Iqbal composed his poem on Ram. He may have been closely identified with the idea of Pakistan by the end of his life, but the poet termed Ram as *zindagi ki rooh* (the soul of life) and *roohaniyat ki shaan* (the pride of spirituality) before bestowing on the epic hero the title of Imam-e-Hind. This couplet read:

> *Hai Raam ke wajood pe Hindustaan ko naaz*
> *Ahl-e-Nazar samajhte hain us ko Imam-e-Hind*
> (India is proud of the existence of Ram
> Spiritual people consider him prelate of India)

If Hindu nationalists wish India's religious minorities, especially Muslims, to accept the universality of Ram as a *mahapurush* or a revered person of the land, they have to allow Muslims to read 'greatness' in the character within their spiritual tradition. Ironically, Muslims have been told that the Ram story is not theirs. In October 2016, Nawazuddin Siddiqui, the film star, while vacationing in his hometown in Muzaffarnagar district, wished to be part of the ongoing Ramlila and approached the committee organizing the show. He was to enact the role of Marich, Ravan's uncle, and even rehearsed with the team. The plan was however aborted as local Hindu zealots opposed this, saying that being a Muslim, Siddiqui had no right to be part of the Ramlila. The police did not back either the actor or the committee, instead advising them to go back to the original plan and stage the show with a Hindu actor.

As a new Indian republic appears a distinct possibility, for once Valmiki's words appear to be wrong. He had concluded the epic by writing: 'Here ends the story and its sequel, the prime Ramayana graced by Brahma and composed by Valmiki.' There is little doubt that there is further to come in the political narrative triggered by the fruition of the agitation for a temple to Ram at Ayodhya.

2

Ayodhya

From Antiquity to the Present

'What is history but a fable agreed upon?'

—Napoleon Bonaparte

The fifth of August 2020 was a watershed day not just in the political agitation for the Ram temple; it was also a day when much of reconstructed history and popular belief were given a stamp of authority by the prime minister of India. In his speech at Ayodhya after the Bhoomi Pujan ritual, where he was the *jajmaan* (person performing the rite), Modi remarked that the day marked the end of centuries of the Ram temple's saga of destruction and resurrection. But his assertion was at odds with that reading of history which was relied upon by the Supreme Court while hearing the sensitive case.

Modi's affirmation put the official seal to the partly incorrect and somewhat distorted history peddled since 1984 in the course of the religio-cultural movement for a Ram temple. Over three-and-a-half decades, efforts have been made to historicize contemporary Ayodhya's association with Ram and establish the epic hero's historicity. In this process, much of Hindu mythology was also depicted as history. As a consequence, the town became the stage where mythical stories were spun into modern metaphors and in turn converted into political tools utilized to garner support for the agitation.[1] The conversion of mythology into history dovetailed into the process of weaponization of history. The incorporation of 'this' history into their political schema provided individuals with plausible self-articulated explanation or logic and was necessitated by the need to provide a rational veneer to an agitation entirely grounded in faith and belief. The spearheads of the movement were aware that the moment religious conviction became the driving force of the agitation, it would provide the opportunity to manipulate, politicize and mobilize people emotionally. Although driven by subjective feelings, people—especially the intelligentsia—required the pretence of a reasoned position, and thus the need for fabricated history.

This effort was in sync with repeated attempts to alter history curricula in schools and colleges. After 2014, this effort was given greater thrust by appointing as chairperson of the Indian Council of Historical Research (ICHR) someone who once headed the Akhil Bharatiya Itihas Sankalan Yojana (ABISY), the history wing of the Sangh Parviar. Within months, the ICHR declared that historical research would thereafter give greater weightage to folklore, custom and oral traditions. Yellapragada Sudershan Rao, the new chairman who quit in sixteen months of his appointment because of a quibble with the government over the amount of his honorarium,[2] was of the view that 'the Ramayana and the Mahabharata are true accounts of the periods in which they were written ... Western schools of thought look at material evidence of history. We can't produce material evidence for everything. India is a continuing civilisation. To look for evidence would mean digging right though the hearts of villages and displacing people … In continuing civilisations such as ours, the writing of history cannot depend only on archaeological evidence. We have to depend on folklore too.'[3]

This was not the first time that Narendra Modi or someone else in the Sangh Parivar was playing fast and loose with fact, trying to pass off mythology/legend as history. Modi had claimed incredulously in 2014 that plastic surgery and test tube babies were common practices in ancient India: 'We worship Lord Ganesha. There must have been some plastic surgeon at that time who got an elephant's head on the body of a human being and began the practice of plastic surgery … We all read about Karna in the Mahabharata. If we think a little more, we realise that the Mahabharata says Karna was not born from his mother's womb. This means that genetic science was present at that time. That is why Karna could be born outside his mother's womb.'[4] In October 2019, the Union home minister, Amit Shah, at a lecture in the Banaras Hindu University called for rewriting history from an 'Indian point of view', underscoring how important altering perspective on history was for the Hindu right wing.[5]

In the course of the Ram Janmabhoomi agitation, much effort was made to transform the temple town's history and synchronize it with the popularly believed Hindu account. It is noteworthy that emphasis in this narrative was on Ayodhya as a geographical location to buttress the claim of this town as the birthplace of Ram. This reversed a crucial notion in Tulsidas's *Ramcharitmanas*: '*Avadh tahan jahan Ram nivasu*' (Wherever Ram dwells there is Avadh or Ayodhya). The centrality of the poet's contention is that

Ayodhya can be located even in hearts of devotees. Yet, emphasizing on 'this' Ayodhya being the actual birthplace of Ram was essential for the agitation to gain strength because it was necessary to situate the proposed temple at the precise spot where the Babri Masjid once existed.

Significantly, the idea of a fixed location for the mythological Ayodhya was based on secondary sources from the nineteenth century onwards, one of which—A.S. Beveridge's translation of *The Baburnama*—was termed by the Supreme Court as not very authentic because 'she had neither read the original nor is there anything to indicate that she was in a position to translate it'.[6] Protagonists on behalf of the temple were aware that the sources cited to 'prove' or argue that the 'claimed' or popular history of Ayodhya was the same as its 'actual' history were insufficient. Therefore, an argument was put forth from the late 1980s, similar to the contention forwarded by several nationalists including Mahatma Gandhi, that on matters of faith, 'literal truth' was often unnecessary.[7] Gandhi was never keen to demonstrate his religious or spiritual belief as being founded on rational evidence. He was of the view that individuals were entitled to religious conviction however unscientific it might appear to others. Likewise, from the late 1980s, the issue of contemporary Ayodhya being the birthplace and the mosque being located on the precise spot where Ram was born was presented as 'a matter of faith' not open to scrutiny of any sort, academic or legal. Just as the popular narrative of Ayodhya was increasingly projected as the temple town's real history, Ram too stopped being depicted as just God, but also began being projected as a historical character in whose life, various events, most importantly his birth, occur at the sites pinpointed by proponents of the movement.

'Hindu histories' on Ayodhya showcased among the masses are chiefly based on booklets and monographs of questionable scholarship which began being published and widely distributed between 1986 and 1991. To lend credence to this publicity material, academic credentials of purported writers were highlighted. These booklets were not limited to merely depicting contemporary Ayodhya as the historical seat of events in Ram's life but also detailed a chronology of events and 'battles' waged by Hindus over several ages to 'liberate' the Ram Janmabhoomi.

With a few variations in details or dates, these pamphlets laid down the following timeline: Ram was born 900,000 years ago or in the *Treta Yuga*. A battle took place in 150 BC during the Greek and Kushana periods. The Ram temple was built in 100 BC by Vikramaditya. Two battles took place during Salar Masud Ghazi's time, four during Babur's to liberate the Ram Janmabhoomi, ten during Humayun's period, twenty battles during Akbar's reign, thirty during Aurangzeb's tenure, ten battles during the rule of Awadh emperors including Wajid Ali Shah, and two during the British period (1912 and 1934). Divine intervention led to the 'miraculous appearance' of Ram Lalla's idol in 1949. Finally, the gate was unlocked in 1986. The period between March 1984 when the VHP launched the agitation and 5 August 2020 when Modi conducted the Bhoomi Pujan ceremony for the temple marks the final battle Hindus 'waged' for the temple, it is claimed. The construction of the temple will mark the conclusion of the final phase of the crusade, the narrative contends.

According to this chronology, Ayodhya is presented as the theatre of nearly ninety battles to 'liberate' the Janmabhoomi, a struggle in which Hindus always 'clashed' with the mightiest. Modi alluded to these battles in his speech after performing the groundbreaking ceremony of the temple at Ayodhya in August 2020 when he claimed the day marked the 'culmination of that centuries-old penance, sacrifices and resolve'.[8] With the past 'history' of struggles, it was only fair to ask the entire community to close ranks and make another bid at regaining possession of the *janmasthan*. The *mandir waheen banayenge* (shall build the temple at the precise spot) clarion call made a case for the argument that the basis of agitation was historically sound, besides being a long-standing demand for more than a millennium. These pamphlets enabled temple proponents to push 'history' to a completely new readership—those who pick populist stories in which folklore and belief are presented as truth. The booklets were sold at pilgrimage centres and other common places of assembly. These 'histories' were also packaged in various other forms—as diaries, calendars, posters, videocassettes and audio cassettes containing devotional songs set to popular Hindi film tunes. These histories were often 'prefaced or headed frequently with "Om", a mantra, or a long prayer to Shri Ram'.[9] As a result, the dividing line between religious text and history was blurred.

*

There are five visibly delineated epochs in the recreated story of Ayodhya. The first epoch began 900,000 years ago when Ram is believed to have been born. This period continued till 1528 when Babur is understood to have visited Ayodhya. While there, he is presumed to have ordered construction of a mosque after demolishing a Ram temple atop the hillock referred to as Ramkot. Most events believed to have occurred during this epoch are based on suppositions.

The second epoch began from when the Babri Masjid

was believed to have been built and continued till the late 1850s, when the first violent skirmish between Hindus and Muslims took place over possession of the shrine. The last decade of this period marked the beginning of publicly recorded conflict between the two communities and increasing assertion by Hindus of the site being the exact birthplace of Ram.

The third epoch began thereafter and continued till December 1949 when the idol of Ram Lalla was forcibly installed beneath the central dome of the Babri Masjid, marking the de facto dispossession of Muslims from the mosque and its desecration. In this phase, conflict between the two communities was recurring and the dispute entered the legal arena for the first time.

The fourth period in Ayodhya's history lasted from 1949 till the demolition in December 1992. In this phase, there were two well-demarcated sub-periods—the first from 1949 to 1986 when few in India knew about the dispute as it remained localized. The second sub-period started with the unlocking of the disputed shrine and it being opened for Hindu devotees in February 1986. It concluded with the shrine's demolition in December 1992. During these years, the monument and matters connected with it became the overarching theme in national polity.

The final epoch of the Ayodhya story began with the demolition and continues to unfold. It was in this phase that the Hindu political constituency, created in the 1980s with the onset of the agitation, was eventually harnessed by the BJP with Modi as its leader.

Accounts pertaining to the first era are dependent solely on faith and belief. While various Hindu accounts mention the birth of Ram in today's Ayodhya 900,000 or more years ago, archaeological evidence completely contradicts this contention. Popular or traditional history asserts that Ayodhya was the capital of the kingdom of Kosala, although with the rise of Buddhism in the fifth or sixth century BC, the capital was moved to Saket. Many historians, however, argue that the two towns or cities were one and the same. Whatever its name, the city declined during the Buddhist period. Scholars owing allegiance to the Hindu or 'nationalistic' school of historiography claim that Ayodhya's 'rehabilitation' was initiated by Vikramaditya in mid-fifth century AD, when Buddhism was on the decline. In the course of the Ram Janmabhoomi agitation, it has also been claimed—but again not sustained by archaeological evidence—that the Ram temple which was destroyed by Babur had been built by Vikramaditya. This is the period when the Gupta kings were at the helm. However, there are divergences over the identity of Vikramaditya, as it was the title for more than one Gupta king.

Romila Thapar argued that Chandragupta II (tenure lasting from AD 375 to 415) assumed the 'title of Vikramaditya/sun of prowess',[10] although many scholars from the other school contend that Skanda Gupta, who was the last king of this dynasty and died in AD 467, was also the last king to be bestowed with the title of Vikramaditya. In recent years, Gupta kings have emerged as a vital icon in Hindu nationalistic historical discourse. Skanda Gupta is idolized for annihilating Huns in AD 455 and preventing India from meeting the fate of other civilizations which were completely overrun by the invaders. The Gupta kings are depicted as being among the early rulers who played an important role 'in the unification of India in ancient times'.[11] The history seminar at which this claim was put forward made news in October 2019 because Amit Shah was the guest of honour. It was centred around Skanda Gupta, and

Shah too spoke favourably about the king. He also released a book whose author asserted that Skanda Gupta's study was essential in present-day India 'for the "resonances" his life holds for "contemporary times"'.[12] Shah further complained that Indian history was studied from a foreign or leftist perspective, that 'in spite of having saved the nation from invaders, and having freed the region around Kashmir, history has not registered the contributions of Skanda Gupta or given him his due'.[13]

*

Archaeology and evidence-based history draw from one another and it is no different in the case of Ayodhya. There is no gainsaying that the early history of the temple town is bereft of 'action' witnessed since the middle of the nineteenth century. The *Imperial Gazetteer* (1908) stated that 'early history of the district is purely legendary'.[14] Almost a century later, there had been no change in this assessment and a modern historian, in an important book on the Babri Masjid's history in 1991, noted that 'historical study of Ayodhya in the ancient period is difficult because of the scanty and doubtful evidence available. There are long gaps which cannot be substantiated by archaeological, epigraphic or literary data.'[15] As mentioned earlier, there is enormous disagreement among scholars regarding the location of mythological Ayodhya. While some argue that the contemporary town is not the place referred to in Valmiki's epic, others swear to the contrary. Ancient scriptures and texts use a multiplicity of names to identify the town. In Buddhist texts it is Saketa, while in Jain scriptures the town is called Vishaka, Viniya or Vinit. Other sources refer to the town as Kosala, Maha Kosala, Ikshvakubhoomi, Rampuri and even Ramjanmabhoomi.

Whatever may have been the name of the town in history and legendary narrative, it evoked great interest among archaeologists and official historiographers from the beginning of the nineteenth century. The British organized the first archaeological survey in 1862–63. This survey, conducted by Alexander E. Cunningham, founder and first director general of the Archaeological Survey of India (ASI), concluded that Saketa and Vishaka were identical to Ayodhya. He went along with the viewpoint, widely prevalent by then, that the town was associated with Ram although no remains of ancient Hindu temples were discovered. Not surprisingly, he agreed with popular belief and did not draw his conclusions from evidences of Buddhist structures he found. But he did not identify any spot as the birthplace of Ram over which a mosque existed. Instead, he referred to the Mandir Janam Asthan or 'Birth-place temple' which stood 'in the very heart of the city' and a quarter of a mile away from the bathing ghat, which hc said was known as Lakshman Ghat, where Ram's epical brother bathed. This temple was located less than a hundred metres north of the Babri Masjid and was demolished in August 2020 to make way for the new temple being constructed at the site where the mosque existed till December 1992.

Before the next survey in 1870, P. Carnegy, posted as officiating commissioner and settlement officer, Faizabad, wrote 'Historical Sketch of Faizabad with Old Capitals Ajodhia and Fyzabad'. It had been more than a decade since the first recorded clash between Hindus and Muslims over the shrine. Carnegy based his conclusions on what was 'locally affirmed' and wrote down that at the time of the 'Mahomedan conquest', there were 'three important Hindu shrines, with but few devotees attached, at Ajudhya, which was then little other than a wilderness'. Of the three, one was the Janmasthan temple and he said that Babur had built the mosque.

Archaeology in mid- and late nineteenth century was primitive and many deductions were based on oral traditions. For instance, Cunningham noted that there were 'several very holy Brahmanical temples about Ajudhya, but they are all of modern date, and without any architectural pretensions whatever'. This is certainly based on physical observation of the place. Subsequently, however, the report stated: 'There can be no doubt that most of them [the temples he saw] occupy the sites of more ancient temples that were destroyed by the Musulmans.' This remark was undoubtedly based on hearsay or belief, not on archaeological findings. Clearly, antiquity of contemporary Ayodhya was not established during colonial rule although myths and legends surrounding Ram, the Ramayana and the Ram Janmabhoomi were repeatedly perpetuated. More on this later.

*

Much time elapsed before methodical archaeological excavations were taken up, first in 1969–70 and then a few years later. Although Ayodhya and the region surrounding it witnessed socio-political tumult in 1949–50 after the idols were forcibly installed inside the Babri Masjid, the matter did not linger on as a source of conflict. Consequently, both archaeological expeditions were conducted in strict adherence to standard protocol and procedure. The first of the two archaeological teams was led by scholars of the Banaras Hindu University's Department of Ancient Indian History, Culture and Archaeology. The second was partially sponsored by the ASI and conducted under the project entitled 'Archaeology of Ramayan Sites'.

The BHU project was restricted to excavations at three spots in Ayodhya, and driven by the academic objective of tracing the site's cultural sequence. None of these small cuttings were close to the Babri Masjid. In contrast, the ASI-backed project excavated two spots of which the first was a trench on the western side of the Ram Janmabhoomi mound. The other was in an open area west of Hanumangarhi, near the highway which pierced through Faizabad and Ayodhya. Later, a total of fourteen sites were excavated. These included sites in the temple town, as well as other locations mentioned in the epic like Sringaverpur, Bharadvaj Ashram and Chitrakoot. Based on the findings, the report concluded that human settlement in Ayodhya could be dated from the beginning of the seventh century BC. The excavations also indicated absence of significant settlement between the third and the eleventh centuries AD.

This report was disconcerting, not only for the scholars arguing in favour of the mythological Ayodhya being the contemporary town, but also for the supporters of the Hindutva idea, as it went against their historiography of habitation and the Ram temple. The report, however, was restricted to academic journals. But the publication of the survey's findings in mainstream media in the late 1980s put the Sangh Parivar in a quandary. Even if one believed in the existence of Ram in history, the claim of 'this Ayodhya' being 'Ram's city' could no longer be proven as VHP leaders had claimed till then. Eventually the political triad steering the movement put forth the argument that the existence of Ram and Ayodhya being his birthplace and kingdom was a matter of faith that could not be subjected to legal or scholarly scrutiny.

This discomfort was most apparent in the writings of B.B. Lal, who led the ASI-sponsored archaeological expedition and later emerged as one of the principal archaeological resource persons for the VHP and the RSS. Yet in 1985–86, before his association with the temple movement, Lal wrote: 'This site may go back to the beginning of the seventh century BC at the earliest. This indeed is very uncomfortable evidence, for no one had expected the beginnings of Ayodhya to be as late as that, particularly when one considers that the Painted Gray Ware associated with Mahabharat sites like Hastinapur, etc., antedated Ayodhya.'[16] Furthermore, Lal's argument 'took away' or 'relocated' the mythical city from the contemporary one. He contended that examination of a wide variety of Vedic verses showed that these did not contain allusions to a city called Ayodhya as many other scholars had claimed. Instead, 'the word "ayodhya" was found to have been used in the sense of "invincible", and the reference in these verses was to the human body which, as abode of god, is invincible'.[17] More damaging to the Hindutva cause, because of the claim that the so-called magnificent temple had been built by (one of) the Vikramadityas, was Lal's assertion in yet another journal: 'It is rather remarkable that the Gupta period is not significantly indicated at the site—a fact also noted in the first season's dig in 1975.'[18] This is the period that the VHP had initially claimed the Ram temple was constructed. The same journal also noted that the 'antiquity of Ayodhya, thus, on the basis of these excavations, is ascribable to the early seventh century BC'.

From Lal's findings it is clear that while Ayodhya came to be an important urban centre in the third century BC—there was evidence of fortification—it declined in the late ancient and early medieval periods and ceased to be so after the third century AD. The ASI survey in 2003 conducted after an order of the Allahabad High Court noted evidence of a 'stone structure' during the Kushan period—first to third centuries AD—but added that its nature 'is not very clear'. As far as the Gupta period between the fourth to sixth centuries is concerned, the ASI excavations were limited to 'presence of terracotta figurines and a copper coin'. Historical evidence of the subsequent period exists in the form of the writings of the Chinese traveller Xuang Zang, who left China in AD 629 and returned in AD 645. He visited Ayodhya (called O-yu-To in his accounts) when it was a part of the kingdom of Kannauj under the reign of King Harsha. He wrote about the prosperity of Ayodhya, although this is at odds with the archaeological findings, and stated it was a famous Buddhist place. The ASI report for the post-Gupta or Rajput period between the seventh and the tenth centuries mentions a 'circular subsidiary shrine'. Given that the Chinese pilgrim reported Buddhism as thriving, it is possible that this shrine was actually a stupa, hence the reference to a 'circular' shrine. Buddhists in India often claimed ownership of the disputed property, even as late as May 2020,[19] but this was neither examined nor did it become a politically contentious issue because of their limited political clout. The entire political movement for a temple at Ayodhya would have had a different character if Buddhists were a numerically significant political constituency.

The post-Gupta period in fact provides diverse narratives. After its 2003 excavation, the ASI drew attention to the 'existence of a circular shrine together with a *makara pranala* indicative of Hindu worship dating back to the eighth to tenth century'. This suggests that this temple structure was either built after demolishing the previous Buddhist temple or that the structure had these architectural features even while being a place of Buddhist worship. Whatever be the case, it certainly was not the structure, constructed in the twelfth century, that the Supreme Court referred to as being the last structure before the Babri Masjid was ordered to be built.

*

During raids by the Turks in the region in the eleventh century, Kannauj was invaded by Sultan Mahmud of Ghazni in 1018–19. This kicked off a long period of attacks and retreats. For nearly two centuries, the territory controlled by the rulers of Kannauj remained unsettled because after every Turk invasion and their retreat, local Hindu rulers regained control of the kingdom, only to be humbled by the next wave of invaders. After the first attack on Kannauj, the next targets included Ayodhya. Records show that the first Turk attack on Ayodhya was led by Saiyad Salar Masud Ghazi, whose tomb is in Bahraich. An account says: 'After the rains, Masud led his army against Ajudhan. Although in those days, that place and its vicinity was thickly populated, it was subdued without a struggle. Masud was delighted with the climate of Ajudhan and, as it was a good hunting ground, he remained there till the end of the following rains when he set off for Delhi.'[20]

There was another attack on Ayodhya, this time led by the governor of Lahore, Ahmad Niyaltigin. Prior to Ahmad's appointment as the chief administrator of Lahore, he was treasurer of Mahmud of Ghazni. After Mahmud's death in 1030, his son, Masud, appointed his father's fund manager once he decided to focus on India. Significantly, on his appointment, Ahmad issued the following edict for all his (Muslim) officers: 'They were not to undertake, without special permission, expeditions beyond the limits of the Punjab, but were to accompany Ahmad on any expedition which he might undertake; they were not to drink, play polo, or engage in social intercourse with the Hindu officers at Lahore; and they were to refrain from wounding the susceptibilities of these officers and their troops by inopportune displays of religious bigotry.'[21] The Ghazni representative soon led a successful expedition to Benares in 1034 and 'either he himself or one of his chiefs went to Ayodhya'.[22]

Two significant deductions can be made from Ahmad's directive. First, that the Ghazni empire had co-opted local Hindus who were appointed to high positions. Second, that the regime was not given to, or encouraging of, religious intolerance among its officials. This appears to be at odds with the history of temple destruction attributed to invading kings and their armies. Given the non-discriminatory policies of Masud and later Muslim rulers, at least insofar as the religious profile of their bureaucracy, military and local allies, it would be erroneous to view their actions from the modern prism of religious conflict. Instead, a wiser window through which these actions can be viewed would be the impulse to leave behind a lasting legacy. In the medieval era, legacy could be best built by constructing forts, palaces, garden pavilions and of course temples or mosques. Quite often, mosques which replaced temples were more grandiose in architecture and construction.

After the Turks withdrew from the area, Hindu chieftains regrouped, and the Rashtrakuta dynasty is said to have ruled Ayodhya remotely from Kannauj. The Ghaznavids raided Kannauj again between 1086 and 1090 and, after their withdrawal, there was a change of guard with the Rajput clan of Gahadavalas headed by Chandradeya assuming power. There is no mention of Ayodhya being ruled independently by a powerful ruler, or by a strong local chieftain, in this period. It appears that Ayodhya too came under the control of the Rajputs. After the initial claims of the Ram temple having been built by Vikramaditya were modified, the VHP put forward the assertion that the temple destroyed by Babur was in fact constructed during this period. The ASI report of 22 August 2003 however put twelfth century as the period of the last temple-like structure built before the disputed mosque.

Turkish interest in the area remained even after the Gahadavalas assumed control. Yet it was not till the 1190s that Kannauj and Ayodhya were raided again, this time by Muhammad Ghori. H.R. Neville's *District Gazetteer of the United Provinces of Agra and Oudh: District Fyzabad*, 1909, claimed that several Hindu places of worship were destroyed during this attack on Ayodhya. Instead of considering this assertion, undeniably picked up from local oral sources, as the Gospel truth, there is need to examine if evidence indeed existed to prove this. If Neville's claim was true, would it be correct to presume that the demolished shrine was the one that the ASI found evidence of and was the last one constructed on the mound before the mosque? Does this mean that Ghori was the one who demolished the temple and Babur merely built the mosque over its ruins?

The 9 November 2019 Supreme Court verdict states that the pillar bases of the temple-like structure excavated by the ASI were of twelfth-century antiquity. The ASI, the court further notes, did not specify the characteristics of the temple, whether it deified Ram, any other Hindu God or maybe even the Buddha. When Babur ordered the construction of the mosque over the ruins, the judges conclude, there was no evidence to suggest that remnants of the pre-existing structure were used for the purpose of constructing the mosque. It states that the 'pillars that were used in the construction of the mosque were black Kasauti stone pillars. ASI has found no evidence to show that these Kasauti pillars are relatable to the underlying pillar bases found during the course of excavation in the structure below the mosque.'

No Hindu ruler controlled Ayodhya after Ghori's departure. For a brief period after 1228, the town was under the suzerainty of Shams-ud-din Iltutmish who was appointed governor of Oudh, and Ayodhya was part of its territory. The Supreme Court observes that the ASI report noted, 'There is a time gap of about four centuries between the date of the underlying structure and the construction of the mosque. No evidence is available to explain what transpired in the course of the intervening period of nearly four centuries.'

The court's observations certainly brings down the curtains on the first epoch in Ayodhya's history with the two primary claims of the temple proponents remaining unproven. First, that Ram was born in today's Ayodhya and at the spot claimed as his birthplace or Janmabhoomi where the Babri Masjid once stood. Second, that Babur demolished a dazzling temple, deifying Ram and befitting his status, to build a mosque either as an act of religious bigotry or otherwise. With these two beliefs negated with due scholarship and excavations, the Sangh Parivar was forced to change tack on how it presented the 'case' for the Ram temple. Yet this failed to convince not just loyalists of the RSS, BJP and VHP, but also a large community of Hindus who have come to believe myths as authentic histories, whereas 'desacralised, demythicised histories based on historical records are false'.[23]

*

The principal reason for disagreement on the popularly accepted notion of the Babri Masjid being constructed in 1528 on orders of the Mughal dynasty's founder is that *The Baburnama* has no entries from 2 April to 8 September 1528. In one of the last entries before this void in the diary, Babur recorded that on 28 March, he and his forces were stationed north of Avadh at a junction of two rivers. One of the two rivers was the Ghaghra, known as the Sarayu when it flows past Ayodhya. The proponents of the view that the 'Babri Masjid was built by Babur' are of the opinion that he thereafter visited Ayodhya and asked Mir Baqi to construct the mosque. With formal records of Babur's life in these five months missing, the history of this period is largely based on popular stories and incorrect interpretations by British writers. The Supreme Court did not examine this matter and the three Allahabad High Court judges in their verdict of 30 September 2010 were unable to evolve a consensus view.

Whether Babur personally visited Ayodhya or not may remain an unresolved question, but he certainly controlled territories in the Avadh region. However, after Sher Shah defeated Humayun, the region came under the rule of Afghan nobles and the situation remained unchanged until Akbar secured power over Avadh, Jaunpur and Benares in 1559. A significant development took place in Ayodhya after this. This subsequent episode disproves the Hindu nationalistic claim of the Babri Masjid–Ram Janmabhoomi issue being a source of Hindu–Muslim conflict at that time. It was in this period that Goswami Tulsidas lived and worked in Ayodhya, writing his magnum opus, *Ramcharitmanas*, his version of Ram's story in Avadhi. He began his monumental work in 1574 in Ayodhya and completed it three years later in 1577. *Ramcharitmanas* became immensely popular even during Tulsidas's lifetime and remains one of the most popular versions of the story. This version is virtually the 'standard' Ramayana in several parts of India. Given the gradual rise of the Ram story from the tenth and eleventh centuries, the time was ripe for the emergence of a writer to popularize the story and take it to the masses, and Tulsidas stepped in to fulfil this role.

By the beginning of the sixteenth century, several additions had been made to the original kernel of Valmiki's composition, but public following was never huge. The story had grown through the centuries, several minute details were incorporated and public perception of Ram too had undergone transformation. Although Ram's deification had been more or less completed, he was still not part of day-to-day conversation among people. Tulsidas's composition was instrumental in making Ram a people's god and hero. The traditional staging of Ramlila, a popular form of theatre on Ram's life, is primarily based on Tulsidas's work and is staged even today in most parts of India, especially north India. In fact, the actual onset of the 'Ram cult' in India began with the popularization of Ramlila.

Significantly, there was a gap of less than half a century between the time that Babur was believed to have built a mosque and the period when Tulsidas wrote *Ramcharitmanas*. Several people, including Justice S.U. Khan, noted that 'if a temple standing on the premises in dispute had been demolished and a mosque had been constructed thereupon less than 50 years before Tulsidas wrote Ram Charit Manas [the spelling he used] at Ayodhya, there was no reason for not mentioning the fact by him in his famous book. Even if it is assumed that the mosque was subsequently constructed by Aurangzeb, still Tulsidas should have mentioned in Ram Charit Manas that a specific small piece of land measuring 1500 square yards or a temple standing on such a site was birth-place of Lord Ram.'[24]

Additionally, William Finch, the first European traveller to visit Ayodhya between 1608 and 1611, described bathing ghats in the town and a fort in ruins but made no mention of a mosque built by Babur after demolishing a temple. Although Finch recorded that by that time, Ram was considered an incarnate of Vishnu and someone who had taken human form, he made no mention of the belief that the town was considered to be his birthplace. Abul Fazl's seventeenth-century chronicle in Persian, *Ain-e-Akbari*, also contains a description of Ayodhya and referred to the town as 'one of the holiest places of antiquity'.[25] Yet he too did not 'mention the existence of a temple dedicated to a person with spiritual and temporal power and its replacement by a mosque. Nor does he record any religious strife in the area.'[26]

*

The Supreme Court recalled the ASI report of 2003 suggesting little trace of human activity in Ayodhya after the twelfth century. The same appears to be true for the sixteenth and early seventeenth centuries. But the cult of Ram began growing steadily in the decades after Tulsidas's composition and during Akbar's tenure when the bhakti and Sufi traditions thrived. During Aurangzeb's reign, noted for being punitive towards Hinduism at certain places, Ayodhya too bore some of the brunt. Although some temples were demolished in this period here, there are no references to any of them being connected with the birthplace or the Janmabhoomi. But after his death, when the Mughal Empire began to disintegrate, Ayodhya was wracked by 'conditions of anarchy and civil war'.[27] Not all history of Ayodhya was about greatness and glory, either in reality or in the world of make-believe.

With the decline of the Mughals, political power passed to a new ruling dynasty in Awadh. Faizabad became its capital and remained so till Asif-ud-Daulah shifted the capital from here and established Lucknow in 1775. Social life in Ayodhya till this time was 'harmoniously adjusted despite the striking difference in religion and race between the ruling classes and the common people'.[28] Intercommunity relationship was marked by a composite culture and 'all festivals were celebrated irrespective of religious denomination. In several cases, both Hindus and Muslims revered the same *peer* or *sant*.'[29] The principal religion-based conflict that kept recurring was the 'fierce battles' between Vaishnava Bairagis and Saiva Sanyasins 'over the question of the possession of religious places'. But British chronicles had begun planting seeds of discord between Hindus and Muslims by fostering the story of the mosque being built on a demolished Ram temple. This was greatly assisted by the fact that the kingdom of Awadh was in its final stage of decline by the middle of the nineteenth century. Hindu–Muslim conflict had begun making its ugly face visible too in this period. Although Ayodhya remained part of the sovereign state of Awadh, it was under the administrative and revenue control of the British Resident based in Lucknow after the treaty of 1819. The parallel historical and legendary beliefs regarding Ayodhya gained credence thereafter.

Forty years after Faizabad ceased being capital of Awadh, the British moved into the twin towns in 1816. This was seven years after a communal riot occurred in Benares, the adjoining district. It was from this time that British administrators, writers and historians began viewing

Indian history and social relations in its entirety through the framework postulated by James Mill in his Indophobic book, *The History of British India*, also published in 1816. Mill's viewpoint of Hindus and Muslims being preoccupied with religion and at loggerheads with one another all the time became the steady framework for all British chronicles of India and this did not spare Ayodhya too. In his 1838 report, more than two decades after Mill's volume was published, Montgomery Martin, a British officer deputed by the East India Company to survey eastern India, highlighted Aurangzeb's alleged role in the destruction of several Hindu temples. He claimed that this triggered deterioration of relations between Hindus and Muslims, a depiction at odds with what administrators found. Actually, they 'were surprised to find that despite Muslim rule in Avadh, Hindus had been living peacefully and Hinduism had not been undermined in this area'.[30]

Colonial chroniclers had not yet begun endorsing what later became the complete theory regarding Ayodhya and the shrines. Martin, while evaluating claims of stories that there were once as many as 360 temples in Ayodhya, wrote: 'If these temples ever existed, not the smallest trace of them remains to enable us to judge the period when they were built; and the destruction is very generally attributed by the Hindus to the furious zeal of Aurungzebe [sic].'[31] It is evident that even as late as 1838, Babur was yet to be accused of having demolished any temple. Yet, within two decades, the narrative began altering. In 1870, P. Carnegy endorsed what Mill postulated, adding that the Mughals destroyed temples because Muslims were driven by the will to impose 'their religion on all those whom they had conquered'.

*

From the first half of the nineteenth century, British chroniclers and administrators started portraying the history of Hindu–Muslim relationship in Ayodhya as a story of continuous conflict, depicting Hindus as 'humiliated victims' and Muslims as 'jubilant victors'. But it was not due to this that relations between the two communities deteriorated in this period. In fact, the schism between the two communities was not an overnight development but the result of a slow burn among Hindus, first across north India and later to other parts of the country. This process was also triggered by the decline of the Mughals after Aurangzeb's passing in 1707 which increased the dependence of Muslim official authority on Hindu aristocracy. This process hastened in Faizabad after it ceased to be the capital of Awadh. Around the same time, more so from the early nineteenth century, Muslims in Ayodhya, as in many other parts of north India, were not as significantly represented in the ruling classes. Muslims also included large numbers of converts from the lowest strata of Hindu society who gravitated towards Islam after perceiving Muslim society as relatively more socially egalitarian. The altered power equation as a consequence, coupled with the new social balance as a result of conversions of low-caste Hindus to Islam, triggered conflict between Hindus and Muslims which 'both sides attempt to decide in their own favour by any means, including the use of force'.[32]

Violent clashes between the two communities in the 1850s marked the end of the second epoch of contemporary Ayodhya's history. Interestingly, however, the first intercommunity clash in 1853 was not over control of Babri Masjid or the alleged demolition of a Ram temple by Babur. Furthermore, these clashes not only widened the gulf between Hindus and Muslims, but also underscored sharp divergences between Shias and Sunnis in Awadh and its neighbourhood. The prominent twentieth-century Hindi writer Amritlal Nagar visited Ayodhya in 1957 to research for a novel on the 1857 rebellion. Among other objectives, he also wished to unravel the odd sequence of events in Ayodhya. After all, the major communal conflict in 1853 was followed four years later by unrivalled Hindu–Muslim unity during the uprising against the British in 1857. How could this paradox have arisen? he wondered.

While researching, Nagar stumbled on a news report dated 20 June 1902 in the *Pioneer* newspaper mentioning the inflammatory role of a Bairagi sadhu in triggering the clash by spreading unsubstantiated rumours. Evidently, he was expelled from the monastic order as a consequence of a conflict with the chief of the Hanumangarhi temple and in rage converted to Islam. Thereafter he went to Lucknow where he spread the canard that Hanumangarhi sadhus were giving finishing touches to their plan to lay siege to the Awadh capital.

Historically, the fortress-like Hanumangarhi at the base of the Ramkot hillock was the most important Hindu temple in Ayodhya. A hundred years after the events, Nagar was struck by the oddness that while there was no proper 'home' for Ram and his family in the town, 'his humble servant, Hanuman, should be housed within an armed fortress'.[33] Hanumangarhi was constructed on seven bighas of land donated to a Hindu Bairagi saint by Nawab Abul Mansur Safdarjung, the second nawab of Awadh before his death in 1754.[34] Inside the compound, a Qanati Masjid (temporary mosque) was located and this was demolished by custodians of the temple. The act incensed Muslims, not just of Ayodhya but of the neighbourhood as well. The local administration refused to intervene, as a consequence of which some Muslim groups gave a call for jihad to restore this mosque. Those who called for a religious struggle to reclaim the mosque also feared attacks on other Islamic sites in the temple town. The conflict drew in officers of the East India Company but they, along with officers of the nawabi administration, were accused by local Sunni Muslims and those from Rohilkhand of being hand in glove with the Bairagis.

Clashes ensued over restoration of the Qanati Masjid and numerous Muslims were killed by Bairagis. There are no authentic reports on losses among the Hindu saints. This led to further mobilization of Muslims, this time under the leadership of one Maulvi Amir Ali, a *pirzada* of Amethi and descendant of the family of a famous scholar from Mughal emperor Akbar's period. The maulvi was joined by people from Amethi and Lucknow and also from Rohilkhand in large numbers. Wajid Ali Shah, the nawab of Awadh, tried to smoke the peace pipe and appointed an inquiry committee. Meanwhile, Shia and Sunni theologians disagreed with one another over the call to continue the jihad, exacerbating the dispute between the two sects. Eventually, the maulvi lost patience and began marching towards Ayodhya with armed followers. But he died alongside many loyalists when forces of the East India Company lined up with Rajput chieftains to attack the brigade. Different historical accounts attribute Amir Ali's killing to various forces. For instance, the *Imperial Gazetteer of India* (Vol. 5, p. 292) states he was 'defeated and killed by the king's troops'. Whoever may have led the charge against the maulvi, an estimated 500–700 Sunni Muslims were killed at the place of the clash in present-day Barabanki district. Muslim landlords of the region turned up the next day to honourably bury Amir Ali. Wajid Ali Shah also had to face the fury of Muslim poets and writers who compared him 'with the hated Ummayad ruler Yazid b. Muawiya (AD 683), the most hated figure in Shia psychic'.[35]

Earlier, when news of Maulvi Amir Ali starting his march to Ayodhya reached Muslims in the temple town, they too stormed Hanumangarhi. But the Bairagis repelled the Muslims who took refuge in the Babri Masjid, following which the Bairagis launched a counterassault. In the clashes, in 1855, many Muslims were killed. They were buried in front of the mosque and the place came to be called Ganje Shahidan (martyr's place). This graveyard was dug up first by the VHP in 1989, when it performed the ritual of shilanyas ostensibly to lay the foundation stone of the proposed new temple, and later by the BJP state government in early 1992, when the disputed land was acquired to be handed over to the VHP for constructing the temple. The graveyard had been targeted earlier too during the riots that broke out in the aftermath of the Partition in 1947. Evidently, the Bairagis in 1855 also gained possession of the Babri Masjid for some time. The Ram Chabutra was built during the time when the priest warriors had control over the mosque and this platform became a basis for Hindu claim over the shrine.

While the situation in Ayodhya remained volatile, another Muslim leader, the rebel Ahmadullah Shah, arrived in Lucknow. After campaigning for some time, he headed towards Ayodhya but cast anchor at Faizabad where he preached jihad, while his band of followers visited the tomb of Amir Ali daily. Sensing that he was influencing the Muslims, the British imprisoned him. But Shah managed to escape from prison during the 1857 uprising when the rebels stormed the jail to free inmates. Ahmadullah Shah was declared as people's leader and implored to lead the fight against the British. It was indeed paradoxical that a person who embarked on a march to Ayodhya to avenge the killing of Amir Ali became a leader of Muslims as well as Hindus in the struggle against the British. This shows that colonial efforts to construct a historical divide between the two communities and a long history of clashes over the Babri Masjid had failed to put one against the other, at least on this occasion.

But the British did not relent. During the period after the clash outside Babri Masjid, British administrators erected a railing inside the compound to divide the property into an inner area and an outer portion around the Ram Chabutra and Sita Rasoi which also came up subsequently. The Supreme Court in its verdict noted: 'The railing provided the genesis of the bifurcation of the inner courtyard (in which the structure of the mosque was situated) and the outer courtyard comprising the remaining area.'[36] With Muslims hereafter allowed entry to offer namaz only through the north gate while Hindus entered from the east gate, the colonialist succeeded in creating a physical wedge between the two. The apex court recalled an 1860 application by a local Muslim pleading for the removal of the railing and Ram Chabutra because the 'Azaan of the Moazzin was met with the blowing of conch shells by the Hindus'.[37] Because this submission was not heeded, the dispute had only one route to follow: that of escalation, and paved with law, politics and statecraft.

3

The Desecration

'O double Sacrilege on things Divine,
To rob the Relic, and deface the Shrine!'

—John Dryden

The Hindu Mahasabha was linked to the two most treacherous incidents to fracture India decisively before it was proclaimed a sovereign democratic republic on 26 January 1950. The first tragedy struck the newly independent nation on 30 January 1948, when Mahatma Gandhi was assassinated. The Mahasabha's inspirational former president, V.D. Savarkar, and scores of his party leaders were arrested and tried for being part of the conspiracy. Charges against him and several others remained unproven and they were acquitted. Savarkar, among the last Mahasabhaites to remain in detention because he was tried alongside Nathuram Godse, Narayan Apte and others, was eventually acquitted in February 1949. The remaining seventeen years of Savarkar's life—he died in February 1966—were spent under the shadow of doubt. Speculations continued that he knew more about Godse's plan to assassinate Gandhi than what was established in court.

Despite this, and even after a judicial commission, the Jeevan Lal Kapur Commission, wrote in 1969 that 'facts (established by the Commission) taken together were destructive of any theory other than the conspiracy to murder by Savarkar and his group', the process of rehabilitating Savarkar's public memory continued. From the time Indira Gandhi ordered the release of an official commemorative postal stamp on the Mahasabha leader's birth anniversary in 1970, India has witnessed the elevation of Savarkar into an iconic freedom fighter. The reverence shown by secularists to his memory while chastising his ideology is representative of the discrepancy between the stated and the implied or intended.

The second act, that of criminal transgression, in which the Mahasabha was involved at the dawn of the Indian republic, did not end in a single episode of tragedy like the Gandhi assassination case. Instead, the impact of that illegal act created a deep schism in the Congress party and pushed Jawaharlal Nehru on the warpath against a few of his colleagues in the state of Uttar Pradesh. Thereafter, the impact of the incident continued to torment India, particularly since 1984. This sinister act, which bore fruit in the dead of the night, was meticulously planned over several years with vital roles essayed by a wide variety of people, including those in government employment, active in politics and involved in the management of religious institutions. Yet, none batted an eyelid while violating legal and moral boundaries of the land and culture they professed to uphold as well as the sanctity of a shrine revered by one community. More importantly, the entire episode, when looked at with the benefit of hindsight and with the availability of information from multiple sources, reads like a taut political thriller.

Two men in their forties, born within one year of each other in the early years of the twentieth century, met for the first time in 1946 at a Hindu Mahasabha conference and discovered that although they lived in Ayodhya, their paths had oddly enough never crossed. Over the next two years, they continued meeting at political gatherings. The personal association between them deepened when they were lodged in the same prison for three months after Gandhi's assassination. Over time, their lives got incontrovertibly intertwined as they collaborated in one of the earliest instances of political and religious subterfuge in independent India. But in 1946, Gopal Singh Visharad and Abhiram Das did not know how they would become principal characters in a plan that would alter the nation's political flow. Ironically, besides steadfastness to the Mahasabha's worldview, they had little in common—one was a lawyer and the other a priest.

Almost at the same time, barely a hundred kilometres away from where Visharad and Das resided, it was passion for tennis that brought three men together, although the youngest and oldest were two decades apart in age. The youngest, then thirty-two, was born into abundance. Maharaja Patweshwari Prasad Singh was the ruler of Balrampur state, north-west of Ayodhya, and on this day in August 1946, he reached out to the newly appointed district magistrate of adjoining Gonda district. K.K.K. Nair, the second man, was a thirty-nine-year-old civil servant and an unlikely sparring partner for the maharaja—Nair was an Alleppey-born Malayali in contrast to the Thakur ruler. Yet, their cultural divergence survived time and distance, even after Nair was transferred from Gonda in 1949. It was not just the attraction for tennis which kept the two together—they were bound on another matter which altered India's destiny.

The third in this unlikeliest of trios was the eldest and oddest. Mahant Digvijaynath was fifty-two and despite a fondness for tennis, managing a sprawling religious ashram and furthering Hindu nationalistic politics were his primary commitments in life. Born Nanhu Singh in Rajasthan's Udaipur, he lorded over a religious mutt that inspired much awe, the Gorakhnath monastery in Gorakhpur which drew its spiritual lineage from an eleventh-century Hindu saint. Born in 1894, Digvijaynath was not just the presiding mahant or chief priest of the mutt, but also one of the most powerful Hindu Mahasabha leaders of the United Provinces. Strangely enough, despite being adopted by the Gorakhnath Sampradaya (community) when just four and growing up to become a stalwart of Hindu nationalism, he studied at a Christian college, St Andrew's College, Gorakhpur.

The association between the three underscored the ease with which a feudal lord could draw an important bureaucrat alongside an authoritative political and religious leader into his inner circle and collaborate on a project that would violate the boundaries they were obligated to safeguard either by law, moral convention or religious edict.

By early 1947, large parts of India were enveloped in communal flames leading up to the Partition. It was against this backdrop that the maharaja organized a grand yagna in his kingdom to which he also invited another leading Hindu saint, Swami Karpatri, who had founded and headed the Dharma Sangha and nursed nascent political ambitions. In time, Swami Karpatri established the political party, Ram Rajya Parishad.

According to a 1991 report in the Mahasabha's central mouthpiece, the weekly *Hindu Sabha Varta*, Digvijaynath presided over this meeting between the maharaja and

Swami Karpatri. The mahant conveyed Savarkar's views that 'Hindu religious places which had been under occupation of foreigners must now be liberated'.[1] The next day, Nair joined the deliberation and the 'mahant laid before (Nair) the strategy to get back Sri Ramjanmabhoomi in Ayodhya, apart from Kashi Vishwanath Temple in Varanasi and Sri Krishna Janmabhoomi in Mathura'.[2] But, for all his seriousness and urgency to 'liberate' the three important shrines, Digvijaynath did not pursue his plan for more than a year. He had more pressing matters to attend to.

*

Towards the end of January 1948, it was evident that there was a huge risk to Mahatma Gandhi's life. He had earned the ire of Hindu nationalists by embarking on what turned out to be the last fast of his life on 13 January. His demand, which was accepted to get him to break his fast, that the Indian government must promptly release Rs 55 crore to Pakistan as part of the agreed Partition settlement, was for Hindu nationalists the proverbial last straw—final proof of Gandhi's consistent 'appeasement' of Muslims. On 20 January 1948, Madanlal Pahwa made an unsuccessful bid to assassinate Gandhi in Delhi. Detained thereafter, he uttered the three most ominous words of the times to his interrogators: '*Woh phir aayega*' (He will come again).

It was against this backdrop that the Kapur Commission noted that Digvijaynath along with his Mahasabha colleagues, 'at a meeting held on 27th (January) at the Connaught Place under the auspices of the Delhi Provincial Hindu Sabha, said that Mahatma Gandhi's attitude had strengthened the hands of Pakistan. They criticised the communal policy of the Government of India and the measures taken by Mahatma to coerce Indian cabinet … Mahant Digvijay Nath exhorted the gathering to turn out [sic] Mahatma Gandhi and other anti-Hindu elements to Pakistan … Shouts of "Long Live Madanlal" were raised. Besides this, there were other slogans.'[3]

As it turned out, Gandhi's assassination provided a breather to the Babri Masjid because most Hindu Mahasabha leaders of any consequence were arrested by the government to unravel the conspiracy as well as contain the sense of outrage among people who were attacking Mahasabha and RSS leaders and their properties. Unlike the RSS, the Mahasabha was not banned by the Central government, partly because Syama Prasad Mookerjee, a minister in the Nehru government, was still a member of the Hindu Mahasabha executive. He cleverly secured a reprieve for his party. At an extraordinary meeting of the Mahasabha, summoned a day after Savarkar's arrest, on 5 February 1948, Mookerjee asked for the party to either cease 'its activities and limit itself to social, cultural and religious problem' or abandon 'its communalist composition (…) and open its doors to every citizen, regardless of religion'.[4]

Mookerjee's proposal was discussed at the Mahasabha's Working Committee on 15 February and it was decided to go with the first option in order to avoid censure from the government. Mookerjee thereafter began lobbying to secure reprieve for senior leaders of the party. He wrote to Sardar Patel on 4 May 1948 and said that he hoped none from the Mahasabha would be prosecuted because of their 'political convictions'. Mookerjee also requested that the top brass of the Mahasabha, including Digvijaynath, be allowed 'to attend meetings (of the Mahasabha Working Committee and the All India Committee) unless they are implicated in the murder trial'.[5] Patel's reply in two days pointed out that the leaders mentioned, including the mahant, had indeed 'made very nasty speeches on 27 January for which they are being put on trial. Their release at his particular juncture ... would be fraught with considerable risk.'[6]

*

The Hindu Mahasabha and the RSS may have been on the defensive in the aftermath of Gandhi's assassination, but Hindu nationalism as an idea and other national leaders who tacitly endorsed the ideology were certainly not pushed on the back foot. Evidence of this was the heated debate in the Constituent Assembly when the Hindu Code Bill was presented in the House in April 1948, barely two months after Gandhi fell to a maniacal Hindu's bullet. The opposition to the proposed law demonstrated that the Father of the Nation may have died, but the idea that took his life was thriving. That this malaise was not limited to the Mahasabha and the RSS, but had taken firm roots in the Congress further became blatantly evident during the campaign for the 28 June 1948 by-election for the Faizabad–Ayodhya seat in the United Provinces Legislative Assembly.

The election proved to be a battleground for two arch rivals—UP chief minister Govind Ballabh Pant and Acharya Narendra Dev, stalwart of the Congress Socialist Party (CSP), which though beginning as an adjunct of the Indian National Congress had decided to branch out in early 1948 and its members relinquished membership of the Congress. The two leaders were not merely mutual antagonists, but represented distinct worldviews holding divergent notions of the Indian nation and nationhood. This was expressed not merely on matters related to religion and politics, but on language too. Leaders like Pant shared the Mahasabhaite view of Urdu as a 'Muslim language' and Hindi as the 'national' language with Devanagari as the script. Pant was in step with Purushottam Das Tandon who in a couple of years would be locked in a massive confrontation with Nehru on ideological matters. Tandon viewed language as an expression of culture and his position was very close to the Hindu nationalistic framework where culture is posited within the folds of religion.

In his address to the Hindi Sahitya Sammelan on 3 December 1947, Tandon asserted that one must 'forsake all attraction (*moh*) to useless ideas and groups and stand under the banner of one nation, one language, one script one culture' if we wanted to have a 'national' (rashtriya) vision of the country.[7] In the same vein, Pant declared in front of mahants of Ayodhya during the campaign for the by-elections: 'We are proud to be the sons of Bharat which has given light to the world in the ancient past. Now it is our duty to regain that position and restore our ancient culture.'[8] These assertions of Tandon and Pant, and the ready embrace of this opinion by a significant section within the Congress party and the people, underscored a rising acceptance of the unitarist view of India as against its diversity.

'Oneness', which Tandon emphasized, and Pant's commitment to restore India to an imagined 'pristine past' which has been destroyed by 'foreign' invaders, were the recurring themes of the Hindu right wing. All over the world, regimes have imagined a glorious past with the intention of foisting it on a mundane present, for which blame is apportioned on those 'responsible' for 'terminating' the era of magnificence. Articulation of such viewpoints by Congress stalwarts substantiated the characterization of the party as an umbrella organization offering space as well as legitimacy to the entire spectrum of political opinion. When Tandon and Pant made the above comments, our nation builders had merely agreed in principle to commit, at least on paper, to a Constitution that promised a non-discriminatory state. These statements were testimony to the fact that in practical politics, boundaries of such a state had begun to be already tested much before the country formally proclaimed itself a republic.

In an India literally torn asunder by religion-based nationalism, communal strife and the nascent emergence of politics of 'othering', this was neither a vocabulary of comfort for the minorities who chose to stay back in the country of their birth, nor did it reflect the inclusive spirit envisioned by Gandhi and other secular nationalists. In the Faizabad–Ayodhya by-election, Narendra Dev was the symbol of this inclusive worldview that Tandon and Pant wished to marginalize. To achieve this objective, the UP chief minister used questionable tactics.

The election 'marked the end of the grand old party as a representative of the national movement and the beginning of the Congress as an electioneering machine, fuelled no longer by the idealism of the freedom struggle but by pragmatism in politics'.[9] To this end, Pant was driven by the sole objective of defeating Narendra Dev. Narendra Dev had been the sitting legislator but had resigned along with some other party colleagues to set a moral example (in an era when the idea of defection was non-existent) after thirteen CSP members of the House had walked out of the Congress to establish CSP as a separate political party. The by-election was necessitated because CSP members were driven by idealism and political naivety and never imagined that Pant would perceive the electoral contest as a personal challenge.

The first indication that the UP chief minister wished to humiliate his bête noire came when the official candidate was replaced with Baba Raghav Das, a Deoria-based Hindu ascetic, known for his advocacy of political Hinduism. Das was also a friend of Hanuman Prasad Poddar, the promoter of the Gorakhpur-based Gita Press, pioneers in publication of books and periodicals propagating religious and Hindu nationalistic ideas from the 1940s. Poddar was also a close associate of Digvijaynath and the two evidently collaborated on the latter's 'project Ayodhya/Ram Janmabhoomi'. For the by-election, the battlelines were drawn by Pant—a conservative Hindu politician was pitted against a leader who did not hide his atheism and materialistic outlook. Not content with replacing the candidate, Pant, in an era when high-voltage campaigning by a top-ranking leader for a by-election was not the norm, made several visits to Ayodhya and mounted a slanderous campaign, accusing Narendra Dev of not believing in Lord Ram. Pant emphasized that Narendra Dev 'did not wear the *chot*, the tuft of hair worn by devout Hindus'.[10] Pant also made a virulently communal charge that Muslims and zamindars were 'trying to undermine the Congress'.[11] Eventually Pant had his way, and Narendra Dev was defeated by almost 1,300 votes.

As we have seen, the dispute over the Babri Masjid was simmering in Ayodhya for several years prior to this. Seeing the chief minister of the province siding with Hindu communalists, the proponents of the Ram Janmabhoomi movement got emboldened and decided to step up their activity. But in the absence of any leadership, this sentiment was not channelized till the time Mahasabha leaders, most prominently Digvijaynath, were absolved of the charges levelled against them. The short jail term paradoxically benefited the Mahasabha and the Ayodhya plan, providing the opportunity for Visharad and Abhiram Das to get to know one another while in jail and discuss the idea to occupy the Babri Masjid. The mahant was eventually set free in November 1948 and he planned his next move. It was time to set in motion what he had confided to the other three in Balrampur almost twenty months ago. With the Mahasabha no longer constrained by the advice of Mookerjee, it was also an opportune time for the organization to showcase the cause of Ram Janmabhoomi at the national level. Such backroom support and astute planning were all that was required to secure the Ram Janmabhoomi's liberation. By the middle of 1948, local Hindu priests, partly encouraged by Pant's proxy victory, had already begun making preparations to seize control of the Babri Masjid.

Muslims were prevented from offering prayers at the mosque and would frequently be stoned by Hindu residents when proceeding to the Babri Masjid. The police stationed at the site took scant notice of these attacks. The Babri Masjid was under the management of Uttar Pradesh Central Sunni Board of Waqfs and reports of the impending threat to the Masjid reached its headquarters. The Board deputed one of its inspectors, Mohammed Ibrahim, to visit Ayodhya and assess the situation in the town. His report, dated 10 December 1949, stated: 'Hindus do not read the Ramayan during the day. During the night, if any Muslim was to stay in the mosque, Hindus and others would trouble them. Any Muslim going towards the mosque is accosted and called names. I went to the mosque and realised that many of the rumours are true. There is danger to the mosque from the Hindus. It appears that an application be lodged with the Deputy Commissioner Faizabad, requesting those coming for namaz should not be troubled and since the masjid is Waqf property, it should be protected.'[12]

*

In hindsight, three occurrences between June and August 1949 make it obvious that there was a well-thought-out design behind the de facto Hindu occupation of Babri Masjid with the incident on the night of 22-23 December 1949. This involved considerable planning and necessitated involvement of politicians and people from the bureaucracy and judiciary. First, on 1 June, K.K.K. Nair was transferred from Gonda to Faizabad–Ayodhya to begin a nine-month-long tenure in the course of which he facilitated the alteration of the town's narrative. The promptness with which Nair drew other officers and magistrates into his fold and the rapidity of his actions suggest he was posted to the district with the specific brief of speedily enabling the takeover of the mosque. Initially, however, the intention was to construct a temple over the seventeen-foot-wide, twenty-one-foot-long and six-foot-high Ram Chabutra. But soon, the plan was altered and de facto conversion of the mosque into a functional temple became the objective.

The second of these developments began with Nair identifying a steadfast loyalist in Guru Datta Singh, the Faizabad city magistrate who also doubled up as Nair's assistant. The two asked a few Hindu residents to seek permission from the government to construct a temple on the Ram Chabutra. This application was forwarded by Nair to the government in Lucknow and he was asked in July 1949 to examine if the land was municipal or nazul land.[13]

In his reply in October, Nair wrote that there was 'nothing on the way and permission can be given as

Hindu population is very keen to have a nice temple at the place where Bhagwan Ram Chandra Ji was born'. Nair's recommendation was faulty and withheld the information that the Faizabad sub-judge had dismissed a similar plea in 1885 on the ground that 'if permission is given to Hindus for constructing a temple then one day or the other, a criminal case will be started and thousands of people will be killed'. Moreover, as a rational and fair administrator he should have highlighted the existence of Lord Ram as a 'belief' of Hindus instead of accepting it as factual history. Nair's note mirrored his pro-Hindu bias and exposed the purpose for which he was deputed to Faizabad.

Finally, that the whole thing was a carefully choregraphed conspiracy was clear from a resolution adopted by the United Provinces Hindu Mahasabha on the eve of the second anniversary of India's Independence Day in 1949. This endorsed a prior demand of the all-India body of the Mahasabha for 'restoration of the temples of Shri Vishwanathji at Kashi, Shri Ram Janam Bhumi at Ayodhya and Shri Krishna Mandir at Mathura which were converted into mosques in the Mughal times and the remains of which are still there'. The Mahasabha cited the case of restoration of the Somnath temple and demanded that government should pursue the 'same policy in respect of these temples' too.[14] It's worth recalling that Sardar Patel had unilaterally announced reconstruction of the Somnath temple and in January 1949 a trust was established to oversee the project. At Mahatma Gandhi's insistence, the government had been kept out.

Nair was forced to explore other means as the state government turned down his recommendation to permit construction of a temple on the Ram Chabutra because it received reports of imminent breach of peace due to the overbearing attitude of local sadhus and Bairagis towards Muslims. Paradoxically, the Hindu Mahasabha too contributed to government anxieties. Immediately after adopting the resolution on the three shrines in August 1949, the Mahasabha formed the All India Ramayan Mahasabha in Ayodhya. It announced a nine-day-long *akhand path* (continuous recitation) of Tulsidas's *Ramcharitmanas* at Hanumangarhi from 20 October.[15] By this time, Visharad had been appointed president of the Hindu Mahasabha in Ayodhya and, along with Abhiram Das, was drawn into Digvijaynath's plan to take over the Babri Masjid.

What really made the temple town a tinderbox, forcing administrators in Lucknow to be more watchful, was the support of the Congress legislator and vanquisher of 'secular' Narendra Dev, Baba Raghav Das, for the programme. He joined Digvijaynath and Swami Karpatri on the stage on the concluding day. His presence was a major achievement for the Mahasabha as this demonstrated that its plans were backed by almost the entire political spectrum except the socialists. Alarm bells rang within government echelons when it was announced during the concluding function that from 24 November, another nine-day-long akhand path would be organized. Apprehensions were heightened because the venue for this was no longer Hanumangarhi, but the Ram Chabutra. The day chosen for the start of the second phase of the programme, now at Babri Masjid's doorstep, was what is celebrated as the annual *tithi* or the lunar day of Ram Vivah, the marriage of the Lord to Sita.

The proposal for this programme was moved significantly by Baba Raghav Das and not the two Mahasabha bigwigs. The objective of the event was to 'persuade' Ram Lalla (the idol of child Ram enthroned on the Ram Chabutra) to 'shift' to the 'original janmabhoomi'. This decision sent two messages. First that Ayodhya's sadhus and Bairagis, backed by the Mahasabha and the Congress legislator, were getting more belligerent and moving closer to the Babri Masjid. In hindsight, this appears merely a preparation for the eventual takeover of the mosque on the night of 22-23 December. Second, this decision marked the 'invasion' of the Ram Chabutra, hitherto controlled by the Nirmohi Akhara, by sadhus of Hanumangarhi who were members of the 'rival' Nirvani Akhara. This indicated the beginning of rivalry for the control of the eventual 'grand' Ram temple, which was witnessed throughout the decades-long legal dispute. What would be the impact of this intrusion into the space of a rival clan was a moot question, especially when the Nair-led local administration appeared to be backing the Hanumangarhi sadhus.

A rare ground report from Ayodhya was frightening and made abundantly clear the hazards of being a Muslim in the town in the aftermath of India attaining Independence. *Harijan*, the magazine started by Mahatma Gandhi, reported the plight of Muslims in Ayodhya in November 1949. It stated: 'In the middle of this graveyard [where those who died in the 1855 clash were buried] was a foundation known among the Muslims as Kunati Masjid. A platform was being raised on its site. Muslims were full of fear. Under Section 145 of the CrPC, they made a petition to the City Magistrate, but no action was taken.'[16] The report also mentioned that Akshay Brahmachari, often called the last Gandhian standing in Ayodhya, who also happened to be the secretary of the Faizabad District Congress Committee, was beaten by a mob on 15 November after he mentioned these incidents to Nair. The *Harijan* report added: 'This [recitation of *Ramcharitmanas*] was followed by some days of feasting and distribution of food in front of the

Babri Masjid. Propaganda was carried on for this purpose through loudspeakers installed in the tongas and motorcars proclaiming that the birthplace of Ram was being regained ... People went in hundreds. Speeches were delivered telling people that the Babri Masjid was to be converted to a Ram Mandir. Government officials were attending the recitations. Some more old tombs and holy places were demolished and idols of Hindu gods were installed in their place ... The people thought that all this was being done with the sanction of the government.'[17]

One does not know if the waqf inspector, Mohammed Ibrahim, was driven by premonition when asked to revisit the Babri Masjid in less than a fortnight. On 22 December 1949, he reported that Hindu priests were more aggressive. He wrote that the Ramayana recitation was continuing at the Ram Chabutra and the surrounding graveyard was being excavated. The report said that policemen were present at the site while it was being dug up. But they took no action. Eventually, four people were arrested but all of them were bailed out. The tomb of a Sufi saint in the vicinity was also dug up and a saffron-coloured flag was hoisted over it by a Bairagi. On Friday afternoons, the mosque would be opened for two or three hours, cleaned and, after namaz, locked up again. The report stated that when the Muslims left 'a lot of noise is created and from the surrounding houses, shoes and stones are hurled. The Muslims, out of fear, do not utter a word. I have spent the night in Ayodhya and the bairagis are sure to forcibly take possession of the masjid.' Little did he know that this would happen within a few hours in the stealth of night.

*

The intervening night of 22-23 December 1949 marked Ayodhya's hours of ignominy, a disgrace etched in time so incontrovertibly that seventy years later India's highest court too accepted the illegality of the act committed in those few hours. It was also the night of glory for Abhiram Das and as recognition of the immense significance of his act, the people of Ayodhya referred to him as Ramjanmabhoomi Uddharak (the saviour of Ramjanmabhoomi), or Uddharak Baba, till his death in December 1981. The government-established trust to oversee the construction of the Ram temple intends to build a 'museum' on Ram besides an open-air theatre, library and research centre within the complex. Would such a site, besides romanticizing tales of the Ramayana, Ram and the Ram Janmabhoomi and the 'struggle' for its 'liberation', also devote a section for the galaxy of Ayodhya's 'heroes'? If such a section is earmarked in the possible 'museum', would its curators stick to the myth of Ram making a divine appearance in the form of the idol of the child god, or would they give Abhiram Das due recognition?

Questions that the Kapur Commission raised twenty-one years after Gandhi's murder and the facts it unearthed pointed to the Hindu Mahasabha's deeper role in the conspiracy behind the assassination. Yet, these were never probed by investigating agencies. Likewise, while the police arrested Abhiram Das and his close associates who were personally associated with the desecration of the Babri Masjid,[18] the role of the Hindu Mahasabha and several of its leaders, including Savarkar, Digvijaynath and Narayan Bhaskar Khare, was never investigated although sufficient reasons existed for their roles being probed. Because the Mahasabha had adopted a resolution asking for restoration of the three shrines in UP to Hindus, investigators should have explored if the goal was partially accomplished with the involvement of its leadership—local or national.

The conspiracy to install the idol was planned at two levels. On the political plane, the idea came from 'above' and was steered by Digvijaynath. On the other hand, the detailed scheme was hatched by officers led by Nair and assisted by Guru Datta Singh, 'Thakur' Bir Singh, the civil judge of Faizabad, and Babu Priyadatta Ram, chairman of the Faizabad-cum-Ayodhya Municipal Board.[19]

Digvijaynath's personal role in the takeover from 1946 onward was well established but he too was spared. It was only due to public pressure that the easiest target, K.K.K. Nair, was relieved of his job on 14 March 1950 but no criminal action was initiated against him. It did not hamper either his continuing efforts in accumulating large tracts of lands or pursuing a political career with zest. His wife, Shakuntala Nair, was elected to the first Lok Sabha in 1952 from Gonda as a Hindu Mahasabha candidate. She was thereafter re-elected to the House twice in 1967 and 1971, on both occasions as a Bharatiya Jana Sangh (BJS) candidate from Kaisarganj, adjoining Gonda.

K.K.K. Nair too became a member of Parliament in 1967 from Bahraich, also as a BJS nominee after two failed attempts in 1957 and 1962. Significantly, in 1962, Nair's co-conspirator in Ayodhya, Digvijaynath, too was in the fray, but both lost. The mahant was eventually elected from Gorakhpur in 1967, although as an independent candidate because by then, the Mahasabha was electorally a spent force. He however remained committed to its ideology. In the fourth Lok Sabha there were three members who had played a key role in desecrating the Babri Masjid—the Nair couple and the Hindu Mahasabha leader. The seamless shift of the Nairs from the Hindu Mahasabha to the Jana Sangh was indicative of the common purpose of the two parties. It must be noted that in 1951, despite the events of 1949–50, the Mahasabha or Jana Sangh failed to field candidates from the two seats in Faizabad district. From the adjoining constituency of Basti-cum-Gorakhpur, Digvijaynath too lost the poll. This suggests that the gains on the Ram Janmabhoomi project notwithstanding, electoral returns were not accruing to Hindu nationalists who between them won just seven seats in a House of 489.

This could be partially due to the tactics adopted by Pant and Tandon who embraced the sentiment in favour of the Ram temple as their own, while keeping the Mahasabha at arm's length. It was also possibly the first sign of pragmatic communalism—or 'soft' Hindutva as many refer to this ploy—the Congress and other parties embraced in time to come whenever needed. Even locally in Faizabad, Priyadatta Ram, the chairman of the municipal board was an important Congress leader who at times sparred with Hindu nationalist leaders as well as paired with them on occasion. For all his professed secularism and commitment to separate religion and politics, Nehru was a mere bystander on several matters within his party.

There was further evidence of Nehru's inability to prevent the Faizabad unit of his party being corroded by Hindu nationalistic sentiments between 1957 and 1962. Nair's 'collaborator', Guru Datta Singh, the civil judge who was no longer in service, had developed political ambitions by 1957. He contested for the Lok Sabha from one of the two seats in Faizabad as a Jana Sangh nominee. However, he lost. Congress nominees bagged both seats. The Congress strongman in Faizabad, Madan Mohan Varma, was a state legislator and aligned with the C.B. Gupta group in the faction-ridden UP Congress. Opposing him within the Congress was paradoxically another Rambhakt and proponent of the Ram temple cause, Priyadatta Ram, who was aligned at the state level with the Sampoornananda group. By being politically bipolar, Priyadatta Ram underscored a rising trend in post-Independence politics of secular politicians, avowedly opposed to communal politics, often ending up utilizing it to consolidate political power.

Despite the vertical divide in the Congress unit in Faizabad, Jana Sangh candidates, including Guru Datta Singh, lost because Madan Mohan Varma and Priyadatta Ram broke bread after they sensed a surge in popular support for the Jana Sangh. They agreed that the former would support the latter during the next municipal board elections, due in two years, in return for Priyadatta Ram's support in 1957 for Varma for the state assembly election.

His loss in the parliamentary polls notwithstanding, Guru Datta Singh's quest for an elective office knew no bounds and he was willing to settle for anyone enabling him to pursue this goal. When the polls for the chairman of Faizabad Municipal Board were called in 1959, he decided to throw his hat in the ring and got Madan Mohan Varma to renege on his commitment to Priyadatta Ram. As a result, Guru Datta Singh became chairman of the municipal board and, although records do not confirm this, possibly also the ex-officio 'receiver' of the locked Babri Masjid. He, however, was soon accused of financial fraud and sacked.

As the 1962 general elections approached, Guru Datta Singh made yet another attempt to become a lawmaker, and secured the Jana Sangh nomination for the state assembly seat from Faizabad. This time, however, he got the support of Priyadatta Ram and his faction who were more intent in ensuring the defeat of Madan Mohan Varma although he was a Congress candidate. Securing revenge for his humiliating loss in the municipal polls in 1959 was more important for Priyadatta Ram than ensuring the defeat of a resurgent Jana Sangh candidate. This demonstrated how personal affiliation and political ambitions determined the strategic choices of political leaders. But this unscrupulous duo's effort came to naught and Guru Datta lost to Varma by almost seventeen thousand votes.[20]

This discomforting reality was all the more grave because in the few years that Guru Datta Singh had been in politics, he had shown himself a person with a 'messianic dedication to Hindu spirited values and his single-minded dedication to actualize them in the political arena'. The former civil judge's 'fundamental incapacity to translate vision into reality' had also been noticed within a short period of his entering public life. The American social scientist Harold A. Gould raised a fundamental question on seeing the dependence of the Jana Sangh on unscrupulous leaders like Guru Datta Singh at the local level and their inefficiencies. He asked if this 'incapacity (would) be less likely to manifest itself if the Jana Sangh should become powerful enough some day to rule all India?' Many would believe or find evidence to show that Gould was a soothsayer.[21]

The details regarding the installation of the idol inside the mosque is in effect a subplot, albeit important, of the larger story of Ayodhya and the Ram temple. This inglorious tale of what transpired in the intervening night of 22-23 December 1949 and the role of Hindu Mahasabha leaders would have remained obscure but for the meticulously researched book by journalists Krishna Jha and Dhirendra Jha. Besides providing a blow-by-blow account of the events, it also named people instrumental in planning the planting of the idol in the medieval mosque, the extent of complicity of the local administration, chiefly Nair, Guru Datta Singh and the police, immediate response of people who got to know about this stealthy operation, and how people and other key personalities responded once this became public knowledge.

Before darkness on the fateful night lifted, one of the chief custodians of the mosque, by virtue of being the district magistrate, Nair, already knew about the successful execution of the plan. While Abhiram Das had played the designated role, his planned partner in the 'crime', Mahant Ramchandra Paramhans Das of Digambar Akhara, developed cold feet at the eleventh hour and did a no-show. But Abhiram Das continued on his own and accomplished his task before the stroke of midnight, when the friendly guard on duty was to make way for the constable on duty in the next shift. Constable Abul Barkat would certainly not play blind if the mosque was defiled on his guard and Nair had given specific instructions to complete the 'job' before his shift started. Das accomplished his task along with two siblings he enlisted to get past the crisis precipitated by Paramhans Das's absence. His old prison-mate Visharad spent the night undertaking a vital job: getting posters and handbills printed at a 'friendly' press to spread the word of Ram Lalla making an 'appearance'.

*

Hindus of the twin towns of Faizabad–Ayodhya woke up to the 'good' news while Muslims picked up information they dreaded. The Babri Masjid muezzin since long, Muhammad Ismael, who was present in the mosque that night when Das and his siblings entered and subdued him, had fled and run through the night for more than two hours before finally halting at the Muslim-majority village of Paharganj Ghosiana on the outskirts of Faizabad. An out-of-breath Ismael woke up residents and merely managed to convey the message that Muslims had been dispossessed of the Babri Masjid. He never left this village thereafter and assumed the role of the village muezzin till his passing in the 1980s.

The next morning, the mosque and its surroundings resembled a veritable fair ground, thanks to the akhand kirtan which Shakuntala Nair hereon took charge of, a role for which the Mahasabha duly rewarded her with a nomination to contest the parliamentary election. Government action was crucial in the initial days but K.K.K. Nair was intent on disallowing a reversal of the takeover and the Babri Masjid's restoration to its rightful owners. From the beginning, efforts were made to obfuscate, as well as distort, the legal process and present the country with a fait accompli.

The events in Ayodhya and Lucknow occurred on anticipated lines and the *Harijan* commented: 'The burden of a lingering litigation has been laid on them [the Muslims].' The magazine also mentioned another incident that illustrated that the Muslims were not dispossessed of just the Babri Masjid but that this was taking place elsewhere too in the twin town. A restaurant, named Star Hotel, located on the main square of Faizabad, was owned by a Muslim resident of the town. He was an old nationalist Muslim and was boycotted by the Muslim League for his views. During Partition, when the League actively encouraged Muslims to migrate to Pakistan, this man opposed the League. However, one day the district magistrate was misinformed that the restaurant was being used to store arms. A raid was conducted and although nothing was found, four people on the premises were arrested. The restaurant's proprietor was asked to vacate the premises immediately and he complied with the order in the presence of the district magistrate. The building was handed over to a Hindu trader who renamed the restaurant Gomati Hotel. The DM and other local officials were present at the inaugural function of the new hotel. Later, however, the old owner moved court and was eventually successful in securing the restoration of the restaurant to him. The Babri Masjid, sadly, did not have a similar judicious and happy ending!

*

On 22 December 1949, Ayodhya was not the only place where the Hindu Mahasabha cadre was exultant. Several hundred miles away, in the heart of India, a train halted at Nagpur railway station while on its way to Calcutta from Bombay. The platform was chock-a-block with people eager to have a glimpse of Savarkar who was on the train, travelling to attend the annual conference of the Hindu Mahasabha, the first after Gandhi's assassination and the release of Savarkar. The sprightly man stepped out to address his admirers. He did not say anything new and merely reaffirmed his party's commitment to Akhand Bharat and Hindu nationalistic thought. But what mattered was his confidence: 'Our goal is nearer than ever ... Mahasabha, after two years of travails and suffering, has emerged stronger with its principles fully vindicated by the events during the period.'[22] Barely a month before India was to adopt its Constitution, such chutzpah was surprising. Did the Mahasabha leader's self-belief stem from acquittal of all Mahasabha leaders in the conspiracy to assassinate Gandhi? Or was this due to the knowledge that occupation of the Babri Masjid was expected any day? Although no charges were ever levelled against Savarkar in the conspiracy to install the idols in the mosque, he always guided the Mahasabha on crucial issues. It can be assumed with a fair degree of certainty that Savarkar would have endorsed, if not authored, the Mahasabha resolution of 14 August 1949 for 'restoration' of the three UP shrines.

By the time Savarkar arrived in Calcutta and the Mahasabha conference began the next day, the venue was agog with news about developments in Ayodhya. Khare, no longer prime minister of Alwar state or member of Constituent Assembly (he was dropped in February 1948), assumed the Mahasabha's presidency. In his acceptance speech, he stated that 'the ideology of secular state must be given up and the ideology of the cultural state must be adopted. Hindus being the 85 per cent of the population, their culture would be the culture of the state or Rashtra ... It is my firm belief that to solve the problem of this nation there should be a change of constitution. Muslims should be regarded as second class citizens. They should be allowed freedom of movement everywhere. They should be permitted to enter trade or commerce, practise their culture, their money, property should be protected. But they should stay away from politics. They should not be permitted any part in the political life of the country.'[23]

Khare's call for dumping the Indian Constitution before its adoption remains the first known call for a new anthology of national statutes and reflected the ideological gains made in the two years since Gandhi's assassination. Khare merely verbalized this realization, and this sense of power would have been bolstered with the successful execution of the plan in Ayodhya. In another year, the Mahasabha was further heartened by subsequent developments in Ayodhya, and its leaders were now willing to own up the act as their own. A resolution at the special session in December 1950 in Poona stated: 'During this year, (the) Hindu Mahasabha undertook the work of regaining the Ram Janma Bhoomi temple at Ayodhya. Shri Mahant Digvijay Nath, Shri V.G.

Despande and Shri Tej Narain went there and the Ram Janma Bhoomi shrine is now in the possession of the Hindu Mahasabha.'[24] By the end of 1950, the Babri Masjid was indeed in the control of Hindus although not exactly under the Mahasabha's charge. However, there was no denying that those managing the daily affairs of the 'captured' shrine were sympathizers of the Mahasabha.

*

It merely required a righteous civil servant to ensure that the principle of rightful restitution was followed and the Babri Masjid restored to its original owners subsequent to its desecration. It would also not have been a tall task for an officer with the extent of power district magistrates have in India to prevent the build-up to the events on the intervening night of 22-23 December. Even if he had faltered, the political leadership merely needed to be firm and issue instructions to the executive that regardless of inherent dangers, rule of law should prevail in Ayodhya and that the idol and other artefacts should be removed and the mosque restored to its original state. This, however, was not done and in a span of less than a year, the three arms of the state—the executive, the legislature and the judiciary—collaborated to convert the Babri Masjid into a de facto temple. Thereafter, the only questions that remained to be settled were when, how and by whom would a new Ram temple be built after reducing the Babri Masjid to rubble. It eventually took seven decades before these questions were completely answered. Although it was evident from the morning of 23 December that Muslims were waging a losing battle insofar as this mosque in Ayodhya was concerned, the Supreme Court verdict on 9 November 2019 marked the end of hope. Subsequent events have only added to the torment.

Although most accounts hold Nair responsible for allowing mob sentiment to dictate the takeover of the Babri Masjid, the political leadership was in no way less responsible. In defence of Nair, it may be said that howsoever reprehensible his role may have been prior to the installation of the Ram Lalla idol and its immediate aftermath, once he sent a much-delayed radio message to Pant, the chief secretary and the state home secretary at 10.30 a.m. on 23 December, he followed the brief that Lucknow gave. Nair was among the 'first to reach the spot'[25] after Abhiram Das went inside the mosque along with his siblings. Clearly, Nair was among the handful in Ayodhya who did not sleep that night in anticipation of the developments. However, when he reached the Babri Masjid before dawn, he did not act because 'he wanted the news to reach Lucknow officially only after he had ensured the irreversibility of the conversion of the masjid into a temple. He wanted the crowds to swarm Ayodhya from all around before officially taking note of the incident.'[26]

Nair's official radio statement too underplayed the situation and after stating that '[a] few Hindus entered (the) Babri Masjid … and installed a deity there,' added that the situation was 'under control'. The first directive that Nair received was a written message from UP chief secretary Bhagwan Sahay, which was personally delivered to him by the deputy inspector general who reached the spot at 2.30 p.m. This provided the first indication of the state government's immediate response, or 'policy', on the crisis. The first instruction to Nair was that he was to 'maintain status quo' and not revert the shrine to its previous state. Second, Nair was allowed to 'use force (to the minimum necessary) if required'. But Sahay asked him not to 'use force such as firing' although he could make 'large scale arrests'. Lastly, in the bundle of conflicting directives, Nair was given a free hand and the 'actual handling of the situation is entirely left to your choice'.[27] This order to Nair was typical bureaucratese and open to interpretation either way. Nair chose to follow the first directive most diligently. The chief secretary would not have written a note on such a sensitive matter without consulting the chief minister, and given Pant's political orientation, certainly he would have influenced the instruction to maintain the status quo. Pant made no effort at removing the idol and reversing alterations inside the mosque—after all, his loyalist legislator Baba Raghav Das had backed all programmes at Ayodhya prior to the mosque's occupation. In fact, later in 1950 when the Centre, at Nehru's directive, was pressuring the state government for action, Raghav Das threatened to resign from the assembly and the party if the idol was removed.

*

Whenever an act of gross illegality is committed and the government makes little effort to turn the clock back, a scapegoat has to be found to pin the blame on. For Lucknow, Nair was the obvious person as he was the officer on the spot. The blame game and search for the proverbial whipping boy began only after outrage at the developments spread and political pressure for restoration of the mosque mounted on the Centre as well as the state. After meeting a delegation of Muslim leaders which included Maulana Abul Kalam Azad and Maulana Hussain Ahmed Madani, Nehru 'issued instructions for the removal of the idols'. Pant acted hereafter and went into a huddle along with state home minister Lal Bahadur Shastri and senior officials including the chief secretary and home secretary. It was decided to shift the idol to the Ram Chabutra. It was also decided to inform Nair about this decision. It was the district magistrate's turn to act according to the plan he had been part of—to ensure that the idol was not removed and the Babri Masjid's status was not reversed.

By the time the state government's instructions were relayed to Nair, more than forty-eight hours had passed. Meanwhile, Visharad's pamphlets and posters ensured that not just in Ayodhya but even in the countryside and neighbouring towns and cities, people became aware of the theory of *'Ramji prakat hue'* or Lord Ram had manifest himself. As a result, and also because of information spread by word of mouth, thousands of Hindu devotees and curious onlookers were drawn for a darshan of Ram Lalla. Citing this was convenient for Nair, and eventually the state government too accepted his plea that removing the idol and restoring the mosque would make the situation volatile and was highly avoidable.

In a letter dated 26 December, Nair provided explanations for two pointed queries that were put to him. One, why did he not take precautions to 'prevent planting of the idol in the mosque'? Two, why was the idol 'not being removed' in the aftermath? On the first point, the district magistrate claimed that he had no prior information as CID reports on this were silent. Nair conveniently glossed over the fact that he did not require any information or intelligence reports regarding the plan because he was part of it. On the more important query, regarding non-removal of the idol, Nair wrote that 'removal without careful consideration of consequences would … have been a step of administrative bankruptcy and tyranny', an argument which reveals his stance on the issue. Specifically, he said that the removal could result in communal riots 'in places remote from headquarters' and that any such act of the administration could 'instead of solving the problem have created a bigger one'. Smart that Nair was, he put the onus on higher-ups, saying that he could not have embarked on such a course 'without clear orders from government'.[28]

In response, the district magistrate was provided an 'outline of a scheme' to remove the idol 'surreptitiously'. Nair refused to order any such action for it could lead to 'conflagration of horror unprecedented in the annals of this controversy'. He said Hindus were 'ready to kill and die' and that he was even unable to identity a priest who would agree to remove the idol (due religious procedure had to be followed vis-à-vis installation or praan prathistha although this was not done by Das). Paradoxically, Nair accepted that the planting of the idol was certainly an 'illegal act, and it has placed not only local authorities but also government in a false position'. He thereafter proposed a 'solution' which was accepted by the state government promptly. Nair suggested that the Babri Masjid be 'attached' and Hindus as well as Muslims be kept out. But puja must be allowed to continue and access should be provided to designated pujaris and other staff. Ironically, Nair accepted that his solution 'perpetuates an illegal possession created by force and subterfuge ... [and] does not immediately restore status quo'. But Nair justified this illegality by hoping for a civil court decision in 'favour of Hindus' even before the judiciary was petitioned to hear the matter.

Nair's guile was further exposed when he wrote that he hoped Muslims could be 'induced to give up the mosque voluntarily in return for another mosque built for them at no cost'. When the Supreme Court pronounced its verdict in November 2019 and stated that Muslims would be given land for a new mosque, it became evident that many an old proposal were being accepted in altered situations and with new reasoning.

Nair argued that even the magistrate who ordered the mosque's attachment could not be directed to restore the status quo which although an 'ideal objective, but it cannot be allowed to become a fetish to be assuaged with a crown of glory'.[29] After arguments pleading for the idol to remain beneath the central dome of the mosque were completed, Nair added in direct threat, if the government still ordered the idol's removal, he should be 'relieved and replaced by any officer'. The warning and warped reasoning worked. The next day, Sahay called and asked him to proceed although 'impression should continue to be publicized that the government could not accept the correctness of the position which has been created'.[30] On 28 December 1949, the shrine was attached and placed under the control of Babu Priyadatta Ram, chairman of the Faizabad-cum-Ayodhya Municipal Board. The executive had done its job and now it was the turn of the judiciary to lend a 'helping hand' to Ram Lalla while the legislature, although expressing disapproval of the decision, did little beyond exchanging notes, darting memos and trading charges.

*

As part of this exercise in make-believe, Sardar Patel spoke to Pant while Nehru sent a telegram expressing concern over the developments. Patel's 9 January 1950 missive to the UP chief minister ambiguously warned that 'any unilateral action based on an attitude of aggression or coercion would not be tolerated'. Pant was equally platitudinous in his reply that 'efforts to set the matter right peacefully were continuing and there is a reasonable chance of success'.[31] No one asked 'aggression' against whom and what the contours of success were for which the chief minister exuded hope.

Nair's proposal to Sahay was part of the 'efforts' that Pant mentioned to Patel but these were not aimed at restoring status quo. Rather, it was intended to ensure permanence of the Babri Masjid's occupation in a phased manner. The first step in this direction was taken on 29 December by Nair who secured a preliminary order from the attaching magistrate appointing the municipal board chairman as the custodian of the shrine and entrusted with maintenance of the property. This magistrate's order cunningly referred to the dispute (reason for the attachment) as emerging from differences 'between Hindus and Muslims of Ayodhya over the question of rights of proprietorship and worship in the building'. The magistrate ruled that the gate of the mosque be locked, although the 'receiver' and priests and other staff appointed by him could enter the mosque to offer prayers to the idols at specified hours. Hindus were prevented entry to the mosque but could offer obeisance from outside the iron-grilled gate. Muslims were directed not to come near the precincts of the Babri Masjid. This order did not take note of the fact that the shrine had a different status before the intervening night of 22-23 December and made it implicit that it was the receiver's duty to ensure status quo as it was at the time of taking charge.

Priyadatta Ram took control of the now erstwhile mosque on 5 January 1950 and immediately asked the district magistrate for a monthly allowance of Rs 1,057 (fairly high for those times) to maintain the shrine and pay salaries to the pujari and other staff. The Gita Press promoter, Hanuman Prasad Poddar, a long-time friend of

Digvijaynath and the Hindu Mahasabha, offered another Rs 1,500. The new custodian of the shrine drew up a detailed daily schedule and stated that the 'number of pujaris (priests) cannot be less than three' and they would also get food in the form of bhog. Further, two people were needed to 'keep constant watch to prevent the depredations of monkeys who snatch away the flowers'.[32]

Despite the appointment of Priyadatta Ram, the judiciary was still outside the realm of the legal dispute. The courts were drawn into this dispute on 16 January 1950 when Visharad filed a petition before the Faizabad civil judge. For the Mahasabha, this was an important day. An important national leader, V.G. Deshpande, was in Ayodhya to assess the gains his party had made as a consequence of its involvement in the episode. In his plea, Visharad asked permission for 'worship and visit without obstruction and disturbance'.[33] He also pleaded for a permanent injunction against any move to remove the idols. In his petition, Visharad named eight defendants which included the state of Uttar Pradesh, the deputy commissioner, the superintendent of police of Faizabad, and five local Muslim residents. The judge, while issuing notices to the defendants, issued an interim injunction against the removal of idols. The second step to safeguard Ram Lalla's new site of enthronement was taken, this time by the judiciary after Nair's first step on 29 December.

In three days, the notices were returned and one of the defendants filed an application questioning the injunction. The judge said the injunction against the removal of the idols and continuation of puja had been delivered because what was going on inside the Babri Masjid was merely 'limited puja'. The same day, the judge confirmed the order against removal of the idol. The court reiterated that 'opposition parties [meaning government and Muslims] are hereby restrained by means of a temporary injunction to refrain from removing the idol in question from the site in dispute and from interfering with puja etc, as at present carried on'. The order was issued by the civil judge, Bir Singh, the same person who was named by Nair as his 'collaborator' in one of his candid moments.[34] In less than fourteen months, on 3 March 1951, the interim order of January 1950 against removal of the idol and continuing with the puja was converted into a permanent one (judgement of S.U. Khan, UP High Court, September 2010).[35]

The judiciary endorsed the steps of the executive even though Nair was removed from his position within days of the permanent injunction. His fate did not impinge on his wife's preparations to contest election for the first Lok Sabha. Her victory from Gonda was more than just a symbolic reward for the couple for enabling the 'liberation' of Ram Janmabhoomi. In Ayodhya, the permanent injunction against the removal of idol was met with joy. An organization, Shri Rama Janmabhumi Sewa Samiti, was formed with its reins entrusted in the hands of Visharad, Ramchandra Paramhans Das and Guru Datta Singh. It collected large funds and in time, this became the reason for clashes between them. But as far as the Babri Masjid was concerned, a new spell of darkness had enveloped it barely fifteen months after the night which changed its fate.

*

If exchanges between government officers at various levels and proceedings of courts were examples in feigning seriousness, missives between principal political players within the Central and state governments were little different. These letters, memos and telegrams were exchanged between Nehru, Patel, Pant and Shastri, with the lone Gandhian standing in Ayodhya, Akshay Brahmachari, firing the odd epistle which did little more than triggering pangs of guilt in Nehru's heart. Despite anguished missives, Nehru's colleagues were driven by the sentiment that Tandon and Pant articulated during the Faizabad–Ayodhya by-election which obliquely contended that India's 'oneness' had to be reciprocated by Muslims. Patel wrote on 9 January 1950 to Pant that the events had taken place in the backdrop of Muslims 'just settling down to their new loyalties (sic)', and that if the matter had to be 'resolved amicably' it can only be done 'if we take the willing consent of the Muslim community with us'. Not very dissimilar views were held by Pant or Tandon. Undoubtedly, several influential colleagues of Nehru were of the opinion that Muslims would have to make a gesture to meet aspirations of Hindus to build a Ram temple.

Nehru declared his intention to visit Ayodhya on more occasions than one. Yet he never made the trip. On 17 April 1950, his frustration was evident in a letter to Pant. He wrote that the reason for not visiting the temple town was because he did not wish 'to come into conflict with my old colleagues and I feel terribly uncomfortable there, because I find that communalism has invaded the minds and hearts of those who were the pillars of the Congress in the past. It is a creeping paralysis and the patient does not even realise this.'[36]

Nehru had the foresight to see the long-standing and widespread impact of events in Ayodhya. On 5 February 1950, barely ten days after India became a republic, he spoke about its 'repercussions on all-India affairs and more especially, Kashmir'.[37] Despite the haunting sense of failing his principles, Nehru had a wider framework to set in order.[38] The lament was uttered less than three months after the adoption of the Constitution, and its inclusive spirit was nowhere near being the norm in the country. It was not just a matter of the Babri Masjid. There were other shrines too which were under threat. The prime minister was also besieged by Hindu traditionalists within his own party. In time, the Babri Masjid became collateral damage in Nehru's wider struggle to secure a firm foothold for a nation that drew on the composite heritage. Did he choose to lose a battle to win the war? This was the uncomfortable question as the Babri Masjid faded into oblivion in a few years only to resurface on new shoulders in the 1980s.

4
Getting Started

'God and Country are an unbeatable team;
they break all records for oppression and bloodshed.'

—Luis Buñuel

Till the death of its second sarsanghchalak, M.S. Golwalkar, in June 1973, the RSS had limited mass contact. The next chief, Madhukar Dattatreya Deoras (Balasaheb Deoras), was less driven by political moralism and conservative Hindu spiritualism. Under him, the organization embarked on expanding its social base and increased direct engagement with electoral and party politics. Roots of the RSS's active role in electoral politics, pursued unabashedly since 2013 under Mohan Bhagwat's stewardship, can be traced to 1974 when the organization placed key functionaries and cadre to the Navnirman and Total Revolution movements. Despite forming the government in 1977, the Janata Party imploded due to the rising presence of the RSS. When leaders of the erstwhile Jana Sangh regrouped as the Bharatiya Janata Party, they felt stigmatized because of their overt association with the RSS. As a result, the new party's programme was branded as an amalgam of Gandhism and socialism, distinct from its Hindu nationalistic or religio-cultural roots. The reluctance of Messrs Atal Bihari Vajpayee and co. to publicly own up association with the ideological fountainhead implied that the RSS was on its way back to being the pariah of Indian politics.

These leaders' strenuous effort at marking several degrees of separation between the new party and the RSS was paradoxical. In numerical terms, the RSS membership rose as a result of its reorientation under Deoras. Home ministry reports recorded a significant growth, around 100 per cent between 1977 and 1980. By 1981, the number of regular RSS activists were assessed at close to 1 million. Along with sympathizers, they brought in more than ten million rupees every year.

Purists within the BJP, however, opposed the turn away from its ideological roots. Vijaya Raje Scindia, the only woman leader of standing, was an important voice of criticism. But her opinion, articulated at the party's first plenary session in Bombay in December 1980, that the avowed policy of Gandhian Socialism was making the BJP a virtual 'photocopy' of the Congress was dismissed.[1] Consequently, the RSS had little option but to explore other means of amplifying its presence in spheres outside electoral politics.

Deoras evolved a three-pronged strategy. His first initiative was to take the RSS outside its cloistered Hindu upper-caste world and draw the backward castes and Dalits into the fold, although the task was daunting, and success would not be easy. His second tactic was aimed at giving a greater political thrust to the RSS's engagement with the tribal population, constituting a significant demographic group in several states in north India. Since 1952, the RSS, through its affiliate, the Vanvasi Kalyan Ashram, had striven to draw tribals into the Hindu fold and provide them with a sense of belonging to the Hindu religio-cultural collective. Its programme acquired greater urgency at Deoras's behest. The third step was to reactivate the Vishwa Hindu Parishad, started in 1964 but with little to show after the inaugural World Hindu Conference in 1966.

Of the three paths that Deoras chose to walk almost simultaneously, the most noticeable initiative initially was the third. Moreover, the first two plans did not create headline news and were tracked by just a handful of non-believers. The RSS and most of its affiliates remained shadowy and as a result the potential impact of manoeuvres made under Deoras's stewardship remained unevaluated. What, however, got noticed was the second edition of the World Hindu Conference held by the VHP under Deoras's guidance in Allahabad between 25 and 27 January 1979. By then, factional feuds within Janata Party had intensified and it appeared that sooner or later, one of the groups would break away, reducing the government to minority and throwing the country into political turmoil.

The conference was attended by Hindus from eighteen countries besides India. The convention revived efforts at forging a pan-Hindu unity and creating a Hindu diaspora network. The event aimed at generating the sense that Hindus were a 'global' community with common concerns. Furthermore, the VHP event was attended by a large number of Buddhists from outside India. The conference received an immense boost when the Dalai Lama agreed to inaugurate the three-day affair. In his address, he explained his 'awkward' presence by contending that it was 'not impertinence' because 'Hindus and adherents of all those Bharat-originated religions are participating in this Sammelan'.[2]

Although the Tibetan leader merely restated Article 25(2)(b) of the Indian Constitution, which specifies 'Hindus shall be construed as including a reference to persons professing the Sikh, Jaina or Buddhist religion', his depiction of Buddhism as an Indic-religion and indistinct from Hinduism was straight out of the RSS vocabulary. The Dalai Lama's presence was enormously significant and he was accorded top billing alongside the Shankaracharya of Jyotish Peeth, head of one of the four cardinal seats of Hinduism. Vedic mantras were chanted by specially commissioned priests from Varanasi at his arrival. The Shankaracharya's presence was effectively a formal endorsement of the VHP's effort at mobilizing all sects of Hindus from across the world. It provided the organization with the locus standi as representative of Hindus and the moral authority to discuss religious matters and raise demands on their behalf. With the RSS's backing through 'handlers', the VHP began to emerge as the spokesperson for political Hinduism.

Once Hinduism was accepted as representative of all 'Bharatiya' religions, the field was clear for Deoras to lay the basis for religio-cultural mobilization by preying on fears and bolstering prejudices. Predictably, he was a keynote speaker in one session and he asked Hindus to 'awaken themselves to such an extent that even from the election point of view, the politicians will have to respect the Hindu sentiments and change their policies accordingly'.[3] Deoras's assertion was the first forthright bid from the apex of the Hindu nationalistic pyramid to create a Hindu vote bank. The intention was to exert pressure on political parties to shape their policies to the satisfaction of the 'awakened' Hindu. Asserting 'electoral politics to be of crucial importance',[4] the speech marked Deoras's first step in moving away from the RSS's abhorrence to state power, a principle set by his predecessors, Hedgewar and Golwalkar, who considered politics 'impure' and contended that it was necessary to keep the cadre away from its 'corrupting influence'.[5]

Driven by this sentiment, Deoras added, 'Muslims and other minorities usually vote en bloc while Hindus are divided.' This contention, however, was a red herring and aimed at 'othering' Muslims because no religious community in India has ever been electorally homogeneous. Yet, the claims of a 'Muslim vote' guided by a clergy that shut doors on religious reforms yielded two-pronged benefits. First, it fanned Hindu anxiety. Second, it laid the ground for political and electoral mobilization of Hindus at the clarion call of sadhus or an appropriate representative body like the VHP or RSS. The reasoning was simple: if Muslims could be asked to vote for a particular party by the ulema, so could the Hindus be advised by sadhus and sants.

The World Hindu Conference adopted a six-point charter: Minimum Code of Religious Conduct.[6] This included accepting the Sun as the eternal god to whom daily obeisance must be paid, wearing a talisman (insignia of Om around the neck which was stated to be the 'universally accepted symbol of divinity'), placing a copy of the Bhagavadgita in every home irrespective of caste for it was a 'non-sectarian scripture', compulsorily growing a tulsi plant, displaying personal deities at a prominent space inside Hindu houses, and lastly, attending regularly, as far as possible, the centres of faith for darshan and prayers. Several of these practices were already in vogue but this was the first time that instructions were issued to publicly display Hindu-ness. With this code, the VHP made a push towards semitizing Hinduism, or taking it closer to being a 'religion' in the Western sense of the word, away from dharma which surpassed religion. Gradually, the RSS and its affiliates undermined Hinduism's pluralism and weakened the idea of religion in the country. This was done by converting it to the pursuit of a 'unidimensional' truth as different from the oft-repeated Vedic saying: *Ekam sat, viprah bahudha vadanti* (Truth is one, wise men describe it variously).

*

Deoras had been keen on direct political participation for long. After becoming the chief of RSS, he concluded that he had to make the organization more socially inclusive. Within a year of assuming charge, Deoras delivered a watershed lecture in Poona where he unveiled his intention of forging Hindu solidarity across castes. In the spring of 1974, he delivered a lecture at a decades-old annual event, Vasant Vyakhyanmala or Spring Lecture Series. In his talk, titled 'Social Equality and Hindu Consolidation', he argued that 'Hindu consolidation is a must for the welfare of the nation'.[7] Deoras contended that India's history showed how 'just a handful of Muslims and even fewer Englishmen could rule over us and could forcibly convert many of our brethren to their religions ... We have to admit that social inequality amongst us has been a reason for our downfall. Fissiparous tendencies like caste and sub-caste rivalries and untouchability have all been the manifestation of this social inequality.'[8]

Although scathing in his criticism of the leaders of Hindu organizations for paying mere lip-service to dharma and sanskriti (religion and culture), he did not spare Muslim or Christian efforts at proselytization. Yet he claimed that responsibility lay at the doorstep of the varna vyavastha or caste system. Despite his urgent pleadings, Deoras could not alter the thinking of others in the leadership. He had to bide his time.

Deoras's second initiative to expand the Sangh Parivar's socio-political footprint did not threaten social status quo within Hindu samaj or society. As a result, there was no impediment to this programme. As stated previously, the RSS had engaged with India's tribal community for decades. Although tribals were chiefly animists and not ethnographically Hindus, the RSS had consistently worked among the community especially in central and eastern India. This was initially the effort of individual swayamsevaks. India's tribal population at independence according to the 1951 census was 5.6 per cent. This had grown to 7.6 per cent by the time of the 1981 census. In 1952, Golwalkar facilitated the formation of the VKA ostensibly to engage with the tribal community, but in actuality to counter the rising influence of Christian missionaries who were providing identity and dignity to a forsaken community. Golwalkar and others were of the view that tribals had to be initially provided a sense of belonging to the Hindu society and in time, the VHP established a separate tribal-outreach wing to secure their participation in religious programmes. But this effort made little headway insofar as results were concerned.

After assuming the chief's position, Deoras concluded that it was necessary to draw the burgeoning tribal population into the sangh fold not merely to prevent unchecked growth of India's Christian population, but also to broaden the social base of Hindu society. Accordingly, Deoras ordered expansion of the VKA in 1977 and renamed it Akhil Bharatiya Vanvasi Kalyan Ashram (All-India VKA [AIVKA]). The VHP's tribal unit too was merged with the new all-India body. Efforts of the national leadership enthused fieldworkers. As a result, when Indira Gandhi returned to power in 1980 and the RSS no longer wielded power and influence as it did during the Janata Party years and even after the BJP signalled its drift away from the RSS, Deoras and others were not worried. Their preparations to change gears were complete and merely half a chance was required.

*

They did not have to wait long. India awoke on 20 February 1981 with the stunning news of mass conversions of nearly 800 Harijans to Islam in an obscure village called Meenakshipuram in Tirunelveli district, Tamil Nadu. The event permanently etched the village's name in the annals of Indian political history and was the result of continued harassment of Dalits by the upper castes. The village not only had separate drinking water wells (for Harijans) but also 'three tea-stalls at Panpoli (a bigger village nearby) run by a Moopanar, a Thevar and a Muslim. Harijans can get tea at a shop run by the Muslim but not from the other two stalls.'[9] A state government report stated: 'From the discussions with the converted Scheduled Castes it was obvious that a longstanding social discrimination based on untouchability and indifference of Hindu society at large towards them was the major cause for the conversion.'[10]

Yet, instead of examining the causes which triggered these conversions and preventing continued ostracization of the Scheduled Castes across India, several groups alleged 'conspiracy' and 'Gulf money'. Even the Union home ministry doled out data selectively, suggesting that conversion had not been a one-time affair, but was going on unnoticed for more than a year.[11] Accusations of a 'foreign hand' behind the conversions were made by a diverse lot—from Tamil Nadu chief minister, M.G. Ramachandran, to the RSS. After a visit to the village, a VHP team claimed that 'temptation for financial gain and assurance of protection from police appear to be the main reasons for conversions in Tamil Nadu'. The RSS promptly began reconverting these Harijans.

Ironically, the RSS campaign emphasized on 'conspiracy' and not on the 'unfulfilled task' as spelt out by Deoras seven years ago at Poona. Lower castes were being discriminated against and the result was there to see. This reflected not just the duplicitousness of the RSS, but Deoras's inability to get his organization on board apropos his reformist idea. Outside the RSS fold, many non-affiliated Hindu religious leaders took independent initiatives to embrace Harijans. For instance, at New Delhi's Lakshminarayan Mandir, 100 Harjians were anointed as priests in August 1981. In Meerut (UP), the local Arya Samaj body conducted a yagna in a colony inhabited mainly by Jatavs, a Harijan sub-caste. More importantly, Swami Karpatri, one of the most orthodox Hindu preachers in north India and who was consulted prior to the installation of the idol in Ayodhya in December 1949, asked for removal of every restriction on Harijan pilgrims at Varanasi's Kashi Vishwanath temple.

Still, instead of campaigning to end caste-based segregation and maltreatment, the RSS stuck to the 'influence of vast amounts of money, coercion and such illegal and anti-religious methods'. It alleged that 'Muslim proselytisers' had given the 'lure of so-called equality in Islam' while making 'promises of security in the Muslim fold because of political favouritism and dangling of lucrative jobs in oil-rich Muslim countries'.[12] The Meenakshipuram incident, however, provided the RSS with the perfect opportunity to fortify the Hindu community and stigmatize Muslims (and Christians). Deoras directed the VHP to post-haste mount a nationwide campaign against mass conversions. Several other anti-conversion initiatives too were kick-started in Tamil Nadu, namely, the Hindu Ottrumai Maiyum (Centre for Hindu Unity) and the Hindu Munnani (Hindu Front). These publicity and mass mobilization drives secured widespread support as reflected in the Hindu Munnani candidate winning a Tamil Nadu state assembly seat in 1984 from Padmanabhapuram, former capital city of the erstwhile Hindu kingdom of Travancore.

The incessant Sangh Parivar campaign against religious conversions, especially the Meenakshipuram incident, coincided with a spurt in communal incidents since the beginning of the 1980s. Social scientist Ashutosh Varshney, who tracked communal violence and riots in India over a forty-five-year period from 1950 to 1995, recorded a spike in the number of deaths in communal incidents from the beginning of this decade. In north India, between mid-August and November 1980, 'Muslims in Moradabad experienced the most bloody orgy of violence'.[13] The 1980s was the decade when religion emerged as a major factor in electoral politics and statecraft. Indira Gandhi eyed the emerging political Hindu. She began by enlisting this constituency to her party's benefit during the Jammu and Kashmir assembly elections in 1983.

One of Indira's confidantes, Karan Singh, scion of the one-time Kashmir royal family and a minister in her government on several occasions, cast his net in troubled waters. He started to act as a 'bridge' between Hindus who were anxious about the Meenakshipuram incident having a spiralling effect, and those who shared some of these concerns but found the RSS narrative too coarse for their liking. 'The Hindu opinion was divided, even before independence into two streams, one of the RSS parivar and the other is the Congress parivar … I, having been in the Congress all my life, felt that there were people who may be turned off, who may not go to the RSS parivar but who would come here,' Singh told social scientist Christophe Jaffrelot years later in February 1994.[14] The 'bridge' that the Congress leader raised was the Virat Hindu Samaj (VHS), which had 'RSS and BJP (and VHP) men as its leading figures' despite Singh's association with the Congress party.[15] Within a month of its formation, the VHS organized several public meetings in north India. At one of these big gatherings in Delhi in October 1981 where Singh, the Sanskrit scholar and Gandhi loyalist was the star, the VHP's Ashok Singhal was among the *nepathya nayaks* or backstage heroes.[16] The Sangh Parivar had started infiltrating organizations outside its fold and collaborations were being planned for specific projects and programmes.

*

If these developments firmed up a political launch pad for the Sangh Parivar, the year 1983 marked the genesis of the agitation for the Ram temple at Ayodhya. At that time, however, no formal announcement was made of a plan that would, in time, raise a framework within which the Indian political discourse is now conducted. Paradoxically, the first steps to revive the Hindu demand for the Ram temple, which lay forgotten in public memory after the initial enthusiasm of the early 1950s, were not taken by the RSS, but by two former Congress leaders. The proposal to put it on the national agenda was first mooted by Daudayal

Khanna, an ageing one-time UP minister. In May 1983, he wrote to Indira Gandhi asking for the restoration of not just the Ayodhya temple, but even the two in Varanasi and Mathura. He also met cabinet minister in the Union government, Kamlapati Tripathi, who 'told him that they [Khanna and his associates] were trying to ignite *barood* [gunpowder] and Congress policy of Hindu-Muslim unity will lose its significance'.[17] Barely weeks prior to Khanna despatching his letter, Gulzarilal Nanda, one time Union minister who also acted as interim prime minister for two short durations (after the deaths of Nehru and Shastri), founded the Shri Ram Janmotsav Samiti (Society for the celebration of Shri Ram's birth anniversary) on the occasion of the festival of Ram Navami (the date according to the Hindu lunar calendar that is believed to be the day when Ram was born).

To mark the occasion, Nanda hosted a feast, as traditionally organized during such festivals. He also succeeded in gathering leaders from several organizations, including the RSS. The BJP White Paper on Ayodhya released in 1993 states that the movement was 'conceived' at a 'meeting at Muzaffarnagar, attended among others by the former Union Home Minister Gulzarilal Nanda and Professor Rajendra Singh [he became sarsanghchalak after Deoras relinquished office] of the RSS, [where] the question of the liberation of Ram Janmabhoomi was raised by Shri Daudayal Khanna'. With the advantage of hindsight, it is evident that several initiatives were taken almost simultaneously and these arose from the Hindu disquiet over the Meenakshipuram conversions.

Yet, the RSS did not devote its energies to the demand for the Ram temple immediately. This was due to two reasons. First, the RSS and VHP were already working on a plan to mobilize Hindus nationally with a programme emphasizing religious identity. The programme, given the name of Ekatmata Yatra (literally one-soul pilgrimage but essentially conveying oneness among Hindus), used elements of yatra (religious pilgrimage) and Hindu iconography involving two powerful symbols—the River Ganga and Mother India—as objects of divinity. In this programme, preparations for which were made through 1983 before its launch on 16 November, the VHP partnered with Karan Singh's outfit. This programme mirrored Deoras's viewpoint that the RSS world view should eventually become part of daily social discourse of the 'samaj' or society, or as they often say '*sangh hee samaj hai*' (RSS is the society and vice versa).

Lavishly mounted, the yatras drew unprecedented crowds. Chariots carried giant urns with water from rivers considered holy by Hindus. *India Today* reported:

> ...dark Harijan women lined up with fair and fat Thakur wives to worship not any deity but an eight-foot-high brass vessel mounted atop a truck and containing 400 litres of water. The water was drawn from Gangotri, the Himalayan cradle of the Ganga; the plywood canopy, looking rather theatrical against the backdrop of the dusty and barren fields in winter, depicted a goddess astride a lion. No, she is no familiar goddess. She is Bharatmata or Mother India, admitted last fortnight into the Hindu pantheon of 33 crore divinities and currently trundling her way from the famed Pashupatinath Temple in Kathmandu to Rameswaram, the temple town on the Bay of Bengal in distant Tamil Nadu.[18]

There were three main processions: from Kathmandu to Rameswaram, the temple town on the shores of the Bay of Bengal; from Gangasagar in coastal West Bengal to the Somnath temple in Gujarat; and the last one from Haridwar, the pilgrim town in the Himalayan foothills, to

Kanyakumari, the southern tip of India where three oceans meet. There were as many as ninety smaller marches, each of which joined any one of the main marches. The month-long campaign had a rousing impact on people. The VHP estimated sixty million citizens participating and the yatra traversed 85,000 km through the country.

Political yatras were not new to Indian politics. In post-Independence India, however, this tradition had petered out after the Bhoodan Andolan. In 1982, just months after N.T. Rama Rao founded the Telugu Desam Party, he launched the Chaitanya Ratham. This was India's first political motorized chariot. NTR's initiative caught the imagination of the people and contributed immensely to his massive victory in the assembly election a few months later. In January 1983, Chandra Sehkhar embarked on his Bharat Yatra which was immensely successful. Yet, it failed to make headway after its conclusion because of the absence of organizational network and an alternative idea of polity to what existed. The RSS–VHP drew from the successes of NTR and Chandra Shekhar but projected its political campaign as a Hindu pilgrimage.

During the yatra, the VHP sold Ganga water in 50 ml plastic pouches (at Rs 10 each) and an estimated one-and-a-half million such pouches were sold, adding to the coffers of the VHP (it had already raised rupees five crore for programmes in the aftermath of the Meenakshipuram incident). The processions congregated at Nagpur, the central Indian city where the RSS headquarters is located, before going ahead to complete the preordained routes. Each motorcade was accompanied by numerous portraits of 'Bharat Mata', the deity that, according to the VHP, symbolized the 'holy motherland'.[19] Many of these processions were also led by cow-pulled carts at times to establish the link between three objects revered as mother goddesses by Hindus—Ganga, Bharat and Gau Mata. K.S. Sudarshan, who later went on to become the sarsanghchalak of the RSS in 2000, commented: 'When people were told that Ganga Mata is coming, thousands of people came there. It was a thing to be seen to be believed … Even in Kerala which is Leftist ideology … even if they could get just a few drops on their body, they thought, "we shall definitely go to heaven" … All these things evoke a nationalist sentiment.'[20]

When the three main processions arrived at Nagpur, an Ekatmata Yagna or integration rite was conducted. The yatra was a grand success as a religious ritual. Something of this nature and dimension had no precedent in public Hinduism and was not exclusive to any sect. Consequently, it witnessed the participation of an estimated eighty-five sects among Hindus. The 'fat Thakur' woman who may have rubbed shoulders with a Dalit woman to have a darshan of Bharat Mata was not incensed at the violation of her exclusive spiritual space because this public space had no tradition of being restrictive. The yatra and the yagna at Nagpur were a public show of religio-cultural nationalism, choreographed to rousing hymns with 'Har-Har-Gange' as its refrain.

Not surprisingly, small and big religious as well as political leaders accompanied all the yatras. Speeches were made at regular intervals in important towns, cities and rural centres. Because this programme was not politically partisan, leaders of almost all hues joined it. Such was the popular appeal of the yatra that even Indira Gandhi considered attending a public meeting when the procession reached Delhi on 17 November 1983, but decided to give it a miss at the last minute. Those who addressed the assembled gatherings made 'rousing religious speeches which often bordered dangerously on the political … The speakers had one central theme: Hinduism is in danger. They ranted against "politicians" who, they said, had "pampered" the Muslims because the Muslims were their vote-banks.'[21] As social scientist Neeladri Bhattacharya described, the rituals, hymns and the images or tableaux atop trucks or cow-pulled carts and at the head of processions primarily acted as a 'ritual of communal mobilisation' and as 'rituals of confrontation' because it was made amply evident that the raison d'être of the yatra was 'threat' to Hindu society.[22] People who turned out for the yatra, to walk along or offer prayers to Bharat Mata and purchase a pouch of Gangajal, secured a sense of having participated in a non-violent movement, albeit belligerent, to rejuvenate Hindu society. Rituals associated with the Ekatmata Yatra enabled the RSS–VHP to enrol new volunteers, and this stood them in good stead during the Ram Janmabhoomi agitation. In later years, the VHP used consecrated bricks, fire and human blood to fire people's imagination and commitment. Each ritual conveyed the message that Hindus were no longer meek and were willing to make sacrifices to protect Hindu society. In time, protecting Hindu samaj became synonymous with protecting the nation and any attempt to challenge one meant an affront to the other.

*

The second reason why the RSS did not immediately follow up on either Khanna's missive to Indira Gandhi or Nanda's initiative and the meeting at Muzaffarnagar was that the leadership was unsure of the resonance the Ram temple issue would have. They were uncertain if the issue would be a big draw among all sections of Hindus because different sects deified diverse gods. By the late 1950s, the RSS had emerged as the principal Hindu nationalistic outfit, as the Hindu Mahasabha had been marginalized. The Ram Rajya Parishad founded by Swami Karpatri no longer featured in the race for the support of the Hindu constituency after winning some assembly seats in Hindi-speaking states in 1957. A resolution adopted by the Akhil Bharatiya Pratinidhi Sabha of the RSS in 1959 was indicative of the organization's prioritization of the Ram temple issue. This extremely significant document, rarely noticed, was the first in which the RSS formally adopted a position on 'temples converted into mosques' by 'intolerant and tyrannical foreign aggressors and rulers in Bharat'.

Titled, 'Issue of Temples Turned into Mosques', the resolution did not mention the Ayodhya shrine and limited a direct reference to the Kashi Vishwanath temple in Varanasi. The RSS falsely claimed that 'an intense desire to resurrect these places of worship was ever present at the heart of the freedom movement'. It accused independent India's government of remaining 'totally callous to the legitimate rights of the Hindus over such temples'. For the RSS these shrines were a 'reminder of the continuing foreign aggression' and that it was 'but natural that discontent among Hindus will remain acute'. Non-restoration of these 'temples' to Hindus would not make it 'possible to bring about emotional integration of the Muslims with the main [sic] national society of the land'. The RSS demanded that the government, guided by the 'view of creating an atmosphere of mutual tolerance and goodwill, should take steps for the return of all such desecrated temples and ensure their renovation'. Only the Varanasi temple was mentioned as holding an 'unique position as the centre of devotion and faith of all Hindus throughout the country'.

This validates the aforesaid contention that prior to the agitation, Ayodhya was not among the most important pilgrimages.

Another illustration of the Ram temple issue losing its initial attraction, this time in Faizabad itself, was evident three years later during the 1962 general elections. The Jana Sangh fielded candidates for the parliamentary as well as the assembly seat and released a ten-point charter of promises exclusively for Faizabad–Ayodhya (Guru Datta Singh, the city magistrate during the idol installation, was the party candidate for the state Vidhan Sabha seat). There was no mention of either building a Ram temple or throwing open the Babri Masjid to Hindu devotees in this local manifesto. The closest that the Jana Sangh came to bringing up the matter of the temple was item number nine of the manifesto, pledging 'religious places to be kept pure'. At point number eight was another promise from the religious realm—'the preservation of Hindu laws'[23]—demonstrating that the Ram temple issue had dropped off the electoral agenda to be replaced by more general demands and promises. The party in those years was focussed on establishing that the Congress made a wrong choice by industrializing India and governing it on principles of secularism. In its place, the party talked of modernisation and development of the Hindu spirit and not by 'imported' ideas, as, it asserted, was being done by the Congress. Although no specific mention was made of temples that required to be handed back to Hindus, Deendayal Upadhyaya argued in a 1962 article in *Seminar* magazine that the contribution of Muslims and Christians 'in the fight for national emancipation has not been credible. They can be both good Christians and Muslims and patriotic Indians. It requires decommunalizing our politics.'[24]

It was not surprising that two decades later, in 1983, the RSS concluded that the Ram temple matter could not be used overnight as a religio-political device to mobilize Hindus. In addition to this, RSS leaders were also reluctant to take up a matter that had the potential of triggering large-scale communal conflagration. Deoras and others feared this would draw the Centre's wrath which had tempered past animus towards the RSS after Indira Gandhi began testing the boundaries of Nehruvian secularism to play ball with Hindu communal sentiments in several states, especially Punjab and Jammu and Kashmir. Additionally, RSS leaders were unsure if people would accept the mythical version of Ayodhya being the site of Ram's birth and his depiction by the RSS as a historical character and not a mythical one. In time, the Sangh Parivar put out the argument that on matters pertaining to religious opinion, faith was of paramount importance. But in 1983, the RSS leadership did not have the confidence to push this belief among Hindus.

As a result, although the *Organiser* brought out a special issue for Diwali devoting half a page to Ayodhya, no claim was made on the Ram temple. In fact, it made the startling assertion, although this was on the side of truth, that all belief regarding prior existence of a temple at the site of the Babri Masjid was based on hearsay. The resounding success of the Ekatmata Yatra however altered this and by the end of the year, the VHP was given the go-ahead to consider ways through which the Ayodhya issue could be foisted on the political centre stage.[25] Soon, plans started being drawn for what later became one of the largest religio-political and cultural nationalistic mass movements in independent India. Significantly, in just two years and ten months since the mass conversions at Meenakshipuram and months after the conclusion of the Ekatmata Yatra, the VHP had stepped from obscurity to national limelight.

The Sangh Parivar zeroed in on the Ram temple issue over several phases but the final decision was taken after an assessment of the success of the Ekatmata Yatra. Onkar Bhave, an important RSS functionary and a hard-core organizational man who held numerous positions in the five decades of his association with the RSS, and who passed away in 2009, told me in July 1989 how the issue was finally picked up. According to him, a VHP zonal meeting was held in Lucknow in early 1984 and this was attended by several RSS leaders including Moropant Pingle, the man who could have become sarsanghchalak after Deoras if he too had not been a Maharashtrian. Bhave had been deputed to the VHP and had coordinated one of the three main Ekatmata Yatras from Haridwar to Kanyakumari. He told me that till this meeting, most leaders of the RSS–VHP had only hearsay information regarding the ground situation in Ayodhya and barring a handful, no one had visited the disputed and locked shrine. Absence of awareness regarding the simmering conflict among frontline leaders of the Sangh Parivar is revealed in a significant admission by L.K. Advani. In his autobiography, he wrote that till 1986 when the gates of the disputed shrine were unlocked, he 'never had an occasion to speak on this matter, even though I had been a political activist since 1952'.[26] According to Bhave's version, the RSS leaders decided to visit to Ayodhya at the conclusion of the meeting and when they had darshan and 'saw the plight of Ram Lalla, tears came to their eyes'. That was when they vowed to build a magnificent temple for Ram.

*

Despite gains in introducing religio-cultural nationalism as a modern idea necessary to ward off challenges India faced, the leaders of the RSS and the VHP were hamstrung by the absence of weighty Hindu saints in their fold. This deficiency was realized more acutely after the Meenakshipuram incident and the VHP decided to make amends immediately. Within a month the VHP constituted a Kendriya Marg Darshak Mandal (Central Guiding Council) in March 1981. This body consisted of religious leaders from various Hindu sects and was handed the brief of advising the VHP leadership on matters relating to 'Hindu philosophical thought and code of conduct'.[27] These saints with no prior political affiliation were drawn to the VHP-linked set-up, because of 'threat' to Hinduism from 'Islamic' money.

The Kendriya Marg Darshak Mandal was the VHP's link to religious leaders and assumed importance in the next few years. These leaders in the Mandal enlisted other religious patrons and in 1982 constituted yet another body. This bigger assembly was given the name of Dharam Sansad, a name carefully chosen to make it appear a truly representative religious body at par with the Indian Parliament. The Dharam Sansad was positioned as the apex Hindu institution, general body of sorts, while the Kendriya Marg Darshak Mandal acted as the executive committee, deciding on issues between Sansad meetings. Yet, there was no ambiguity that while the VHP allowed itself to be 'guided' by the priesthood, its office-bearers were the actual decision takers.[28] Prior to every meeting of these bodies, senior members were intimated by the VHP brass regarding 'decisions' they had to 'take' and they did the needful to get these endorsed.

The VHP, like every affiliate of the RSS, remains largely oligarchical. In the years immediately after its revival, real power within the VHP remained in the hands of two or three senior functionaries and the RSS 'handler'—Bhaurao Deoras (younger brother of Balasaheb) to begin with, and Moropant Pingle subsequently. Both worked in consultation with the sarsanghchalak. Not surprisingly, the VHP is the only RSS affiliate in which the sarsanghchalak is a trustee of the governing board or Nyasi Mandal. After Golwalkar's death, Balasaheb had joined the board, but towards the latter part of his tenure, when his health begun deteriorating, he deputed Moropant Pingle to the Mandal.

At a time when RSS–VHP leaders were weighing options on future programmes, their visit to Ayodhya was triggered by a development in the temple town. From 1950-51 onward, local residents, especially those connected with the akharas and court cases, observed Ram Prakat Utsav, the celebration to mark Ram's appearance, every year. The date was chosen on the basis of the Hindu lunar calendar to mark the December night in 1949 when the idol was installed. In the initial years, there was considerable enthusiasm but as time passed, it became a ritual or a routine event.

On 4 January 1984, however, the day was commemorated with greater gusto. People went inside the inner compound of the disputed property even though only the priest was permitted by the old court order. Unknown numbers of men also climbed atop the central dome and hoisted the Hanuman Pataka or the flag of Hanuman. As in December 1949, the news spread like wildfire and on getting to know about this, 'massive crowds' began gathering outside the shrine.[29] Several prominent mahants of Ayodhya too arrived and performed a yagna inside the sanctum sanctorum. For the first time after December 1949, so many religious leaders had gathered inside the Babri Masjid to conduct a religious ritual. News of this reached RSS leaders and they unsuccessfully tried to co-opt the local organizer of the event, a retired air force official. The RSS's endeavour was aimed at assessing if the issue had the potential to be converted into a major rallying point. The Hindu community that the RSS and its affiliates had tried to raise as an electoral constituency for several decades after independence, now appeared to be integrating into a single block. The RSS leadership hoped that while the process had been initiated by the Ekatmata Yatra, the Ram temple agitation would ensure its permanence.

Consequently, before the Dharam Sansad met for two days in Delhi during 7-8 April 1984 at the government-owned Vigyan Bhavan, there was buzz of excitement that the temple demand would be included in the charter and a definite timeline for an agitation would be announced. The moot point was if the campaign would provoke violence or remain restricted to being another exercise in 'knitting' Hindu society like the Ekatmata Yatra. The meeting was attended by nearly one thousand religious leaders from various Hindu sects. The meeting adopted a resolution 'unanimously' calling for 'restoration' of the three religious sites, first featured in the August 1949 Hindu Mahasabha resolution: Varanasi, Ayodhya and Mathura. The Dharam Sansad, however, decided to initially take up the demand for constructing the Ram temple after 'shifting' the mosque. It is worthwhile to recall that the idea to get Muslims of Ayodhya to hand over the shrine to Hindus was first made in the immediate aftermath of the forcible installation of the Ram Lalla idol in December 1949.

The three arguments for reinforcing the demand for the Ram temple, which had done the rounds in the years preceding 1949, were resurrected. Several new generations of Indians who had never heard of these arguments were impressed. The three points were: that Lord Ram was born at the precise spot where the disputed shrine was located, that an ancient temple stood at the site for several centuries and was greatly venerated by Hindus, and finally, that Babur ordered construction of the mosque after demolishing this temple. The juxtaposition, in various speeches made at the Dharam Sansad, was between Ram, the ideal king or Maryada Purushottam, literally meaning 'the man who is supreme in honour', the trait of a perfect man, as against the god of an 'alien' religion whose *punya bhoomi* or Holy Land was located in another country.

The second contention of the VHP was that the Ramjanmabhoomi was one of the foremost Hindu pilgrimage centres while the Babri Masjid was a ramshackle and obscure mosque over which Muslims had no control for decades. The final comparison that people were asked to make was between Ram and Babur. While the former was projected as a righteous Hindu deity, the latter was depicted as an invader king who built a mosque in place of a temple to assert religious hegemony. Similar juxtapositions were easy to frame for Varanasi as well as Mathura, and with more substantive 'proof'. So why were Ayodhya and the Ram temple prioritized by the VHP and not the other two? I had put this question to Bhave during my conversation. He explained that the shrines in Varanasi and Mathura were located in heavily populated localities and Muslims were also in physical occupation of the mosques in both places. In contrast, the shrine in Ayodhya was situated in a desolate spot with little human habitation. Moreover, Muslims had already lost de facto possession and the shrine was already a functional temple—it was just that devotees needed to be allowed entry.

Furthermore, Ram was presented not just as a deity but

as a 'unique symbol, the unequalled symbol of oneness, of our integration, as well as of our aspiration to live the higher values. As Maryada Purushottam, Sri Ram has represented for thousands of years the ideal of conduct, just as Ram Rajya has always represented the ideal of governance.' This notion of Lord Ram provided the cultural nationalistic ideology with a religious basis.

Once it was decided that the demand for the Ram temple would be prioritized, a new organization was established on 18 June 1984. It was named Shri Ram Janmabhoomi Mukti Yagna Samiti. Daudayal Khanna was appointed coordinator. Three months later, when the samiti was formally structured in Ayodhya, Mahant Avaidyanath, Hindu Mahasabha leader and head of the Gorakhnath peeth, was nominated its president. Two local saints, Mahant Paramhans Ramchandra and Mahant Nritya Gopal Das, were appointed to the chiefly ornamental position of vice-president, while executive powers were vested in the hands of Bhave and two other RSS leaders as secretaries.

Mahant Avaidyanath was elected to the Lok Sabha in 1989, 1991 and 1996, the first time as a Hindu Mahasabha member, thereafter as a BJP nominee. Besides being the successor of Digvijaynath, Avaidyanath had made a name for himself in the wake of his participation in the vigorous agitation against cow slaughter in 1966. For more than a decade, limelight had eluded him, and he seized the opportunity. Soon, the samiti announced its first programme, an awareness-building yatra from Bihar's Sitarmarhi to Delhi via Ayodhya. Called Shri Ram Janaki Rath Yatra, it was flagged off on 23 September 1984 and the Ayodhya movement had taken off. The yatra was to conclude in Delhi on 31 October and reached Ghaziabad a day before. Despite being forced to abandon its plans after Indira Gandhi's assassination, the Ram Janmabhoomi movement had announced its arrival on the Indian political scene. While violence erupted after the prime minister's assassination and political focus shifted elsewhere, it was only a matter of time before the Ayodhya dispute became a dominant theme in Indian polity.

*

The year 1984 was a momentous one in Indian history. The year had its moments of jubilation, but despondency and threat to national security were the dominant themes. The deteriorating situation in Punjab kept making headlines, eventually resulting in Operation Blue Star and the prime minister's assassination.

RSS–VHP leaders concluded that in such a political milieu, an agitation for the Ram temple would provide fearful Indians, especially the Hindu majority, a greater sense of purpose. It is not happenstance that the Shri Ram Janmabhoomi Mukti Yagna Samiti was established less than a fortnight after the completion of Operation Blue Star. The RSS-VHP brass believed that once the demand was placed before the prime minister, it would resonate during parliamentary polls due later that year. The meeting with Indira Gandhi at the conclusion of the Shri Ram Janaki Rath Yatra Yatra was scheduled for 31 October, by when the countdown for elections to the eighth Lok Sabha was about to start. The Sangh Parivar was not alone in its conclusion that the time for raking up the Ram temple matter had come. Indira Gandhi too was of the view that the issue had electoral potent. Narasimha Rao, then the home minister in her government, claimed that in the period preceding her assassination, Indira Gandhi 'asked [colleagues and officials] to prepare various plans for the development of Ayodhya. The political potential of this emotive issue was not lost on Mrs Gandhi.'[30] Her strategy was, however, different from the Sangh Parivar's. She wished to first develop the mostly desolate temple town as a major pilgrimage destination replete with modern tourist infrastructure, paradoxically pursued with unprecedented zeal by Modi and his potential challenger from within the Hindutva fold, Adityanath. Back then, the Ram-ki-Pauri project, to be developed on the lines of Har-ki-Pauri in Haridwar, was given a fresh start and long-delayed funding was cleared. A facelift was ordered for the decrepit tourist guest house of the UP State Tourism Development Cooperation, Saket, situated adjacent to the entrance of the Ayodhya railway station.

Indira Gandhi's death forced the election to be held in the background of discourses on national security and enhanced threat perception. Consequently, there was no opportunity to raise the temple demand, especially as the Bhopal gas tragedy further elevated national trauma. Not just the VHP agitation, but all government projects for developing Ayodhya were put on hold.

The BJP performed miserably in the 1984 parliamentary polls, winning just two seats. Even its charismatic president, Atal Bihari Vajpayee, lost from his old hometown Gwalior to Madhavrao Scindia. The erstwhile royal had begun his political career with the Jana Sangh in the early 1970s but jumped ship during the Emergency when opposition leaders were being detained.[31] The BJP's debacle in 1984 was attributed in parts to the widely circulated political rumour that the RSS cadre backed Congress candidates. Speculations apart, the Congress too fanned people's anxiety of national security issues with a high-blitz advertising campaign that raised fears of the country's borders reaching one's 'doorsteps'. The advertisements also liberally used images of turbaned men, albeit unrecognizable, which enabled the Congress to cast male Sikhs as the visible 'enemy within', sardonically providing temporary 'breathing space' to Muslims. The Akhil Bharatiya Karyakarini Mandal (ABKM) of the RSS had not been critical of Operation Blue Star, terming the assault as 'inevitable' and arguing that 'many of our Sikh brethren have tended to overlook the fact that the religious precincts had already been defiled'.[32] Although critical of the government, the RSS labelled sections of Sikhs as 'misguided' and being in league with 'pro-Pakistani elements'. This was paradoxical as the RSS traditionally blurred lines between Hindus and Sikhs and never lost an opportunity to remind people that under the Constitution, Hindus are also construed as persons professing Sikhism, Jainism or Buddhism.

The 1984 resolution went ahead with a contentious claim: '…the Khalsa panth had been created' for the 'protection' of the 'parent Hindu society'. In the resolution adopted by its Akhil Bharatiya Pratinidhi Sabha (ABPS) after the Lok Sabha polls, the RSS noted that 'people had accepted the argument (of the Congress) that unity and integrity was under threat seriously'. The RSS had accepted the Congress thesis that the challenge to national security stemmed from Sikh militancy. Although still flagging 'the divisive and explosive nature of anti-national activities such as the politics of conversion being carried on under the cover of the right of religious freedom', the RSS pressured the government to first solve the Punjab crisis. It reposed faith in Rajiv Gandhi and hoped his decisions and actions would reflect 'the implicit trust reposed in it by the people by undertaking prompt and effective steps'. The Sangh Parivar intended to revive the campaign on the Ram temple but were awaiting an opportune opening. Few knew this would come within months of Rajiv Gandhi's landslide victory. It was once again the judiciary which opened, this time unconsciously, the door for the RSS and its associates.

*

The Shah Bano issue was one of the biggest factors behind the BJP's emergence as India's principal party of governance in 2014. Even after decades, this criminal case involving a Muslim woman, filed in 1978 when she was sixty-two years old, continues to be cited as the most glaring instance of Muslim 'appeasement' by the 'pseudo-secular' Congress government. In many ways, ten years after her death in 1992, it was the political agitation arising from it, incubated in the wake of the Supreme Court verdict, that was at the root of the Godhra carnage on 27 February 2002. The Sabarmati Express, it must be recalled, was returning to Gujarat from Ayodhya with exuberant VHP activists spoiling for a confrontation after participating in a programme to take the temple project ahead. The massacre outside the station triggered the Gujarat riots, completed the process of Muslim 'otherization' in the state and enabled the BJP to storm back to power with Modi at its helm. Had Rajiv Gandhi's government not yielded to Muslim conservative sentiment and nullified the Shah Bano verdict, it would not have been easy for the Sangh Parivar to mobilize people on the rebound. Consequently, Modi may well have remained a mere footnote in history.

Back in 1985, opposition to the Supreme Court verdict from traditionalist Muslim quarters provided ammunition to the VHP to revive the campaign for a Ram temple. It has been wrongly believed by most that the Rajiv Gandhi government's decision to unlock the gates to the disputed Babri Masjid–Ram Janmabhoomi shrine was a quid pro quo gesture in return for overturning the progressive apex court verdict on the rights of a divorced Muslim woman. But a granular and in-depth recreation of the developments in 1985-86 shows that both decisions were near simultaneous and part of a grand Congress plan.

As mentioned, Indira Gandhi was sympathetic to the VHP demand. Unfortunately for the Congress party and its leader, the balancing act backfired and Rajiv Gandhi was personally accused by communalists among Hindus, as well as Muslims, of appeasing the other. Instead of taking decisions which would reflect India's secular foundations, Rajiv Gandhi's strategy was aimed at assuaging traditionalists in both communities. As a result, he had no option but make concessions to hotheads in the two communities to overcome the twin political challenges in 1985-86: rising Muslim anger against the Shah Bano judgement and the Ram temple agitation which was being revived.

Compromise on religious matters by political leaders had deep roots in India. As noted, even Nehru was forced to balance secular laws and politics with religious sentiment. Leaders were perpetually in a bind: neither could constitutional commitment to secular values be abandoned nor could one ignore that most citizens were often Janus-faced; despite commitment to India's constitutional principles, they often prioritized religion as the basis of social identity.

First capturing national attention on 23 April 1985 as a Supreme Court confirmation of the High Court of Madhya Pradesh judgement of 1 July 1980, deliberations on the Shah Bano verdict within the Muslim community 'evolved into a confrontation well beyond the immediate concern of providing financial security for an old woman'.[33] Within months, the judgement triggered 'an unprecedented Islamic resurgence not seen in the country for decades'.[34] Muslims in India were torn between two warring camps—vocal traditionalists of multiple hues on one side and a liberal minority on the other. The Shah Bano matter had no interconnection with the national preoccupations of the time, national security and minority profiling during communal riots, but involved questions of law and constitutionalism.

Arrayed against Muslim liberals was an emerging spectrum of Muslim leaders ranging from those couching arguments within the framework of law and Constitution to those looking at the issue solely through the keyhole of threat to Muslim identity and the community's right to exclusively interpret personal law. Syed Shahabuddin emerged as a representative of Muslims. He stepped beyond his role as Janata Party general secretary and confidant of party president, Chandra Shekhar. One-time radical student leader and member of the All India Students' Federation (AISF), the students' wing of the Communist Party of India (CPI), he could join the Indian Foreign Service only after Nehru secured his clearance after the intelligence department flagged Shahabuddin's past involvement in political radicalism. The prime minister noted in the concerned file sent to him that the highlighted incident—the firebrand youngster had led 20,000 angry protestors waving black flags in 1955 when Nehru arrived in Patna three years earlier—was 'merely an expression of youthful exuberance'.

As career diplomat, Shahabuddin served numerous positions and was working on the personal team of India's first non-Congress foreign minister, Atal Bihari Vajpayee, when he decided to resign from government 'while I still have fire left in my soul and strength in my shoulders, I would like to do something for the country and its people which can be done best by joining the public life'. Within a year he returned to Delhi's power corridors, but as Rajya Sabha member representing the Janata Party. He had joined the party to pursue his objective, articulated poignantly in 1971 after working passionately for securing international recognition for Bangladesh. Shahab, as his college-mate, Muchkund Dubey—who eventually became foreign secretary—called him, considered 1971 as 'a watershed year for Muslim politics in India'. Hereafter, 'Indian Muslims realised that Pakistan offered them no hope, no future and itself had no future. Muslims of India were and are convinced that the fulfilment of their aspirations depends entirely upon their standing in their own country, India.'[35]

The transformation of a foreign service officer who resigned from the service because he believed that he would be able to 'bridge the gap between the Muslim community and national politics'[36] into the polarizing antagonist of the Sangh Parivar, is more a tragedy than a paradox. Within months of the Shah Bano judgement, Shahabuddin became equally adept at explaining his standpoint among the intelligentsia as in arousing passions of the hoi polloi. At a consultative meeting with a citizens' group in November 1985 in Delhi organized by Swami Agnivesh to discuss the SC judgement, which I attended, he said: 'After the judgement every Muslim was saying that the state had already taken away everything valuable to his faith. Now, I will not let you take away the last of my valuable possessions, my personal law. It is the basis of our religious identity and we shall safeguard this at all costs.' The diplomat was soon to head for Kishanganj in Bihar as the Janata Party had nominated him as a candidate for the Lok Sabha by-election.

*

Ironically, Muslim liberals disconcertingly found their position being endorsed by Hindu nationalists for whom the opposition to the apex court judgement by conservatives provided an opportunity to vilify all Muslims. Shah Bano was championed as an unfortunate woman whose survival depended on Rs 154.20 (her original plea in the High Court of Madhya Pradesh was to enhance her maintenance from Rs 25 to 179.20) whereas the truth was quite different, because as Salman Khurshid pointed out, the origins of the litigation lay in a property dispute between the two families. Amid rising religious polarization in India in the mid-1980s, Justice Y.V. Chandrachud's words sounded like music to Hindu nationalists: 'A common civil code will help the cause of national integration by removing disparate loyalties…'

The judges argued against the viewpoint that reforms in personal laws were best left to the community. They contended that the judiciary and the legislature had a role to play in the event of no initiative from representatives of the community. Unavoidably, the 'role of the reformer has to be assumed by the courts, because it is beyond the endurance of sensitive minds to allow injustice to be suffered when it is so palpable'. Hindu nationalist discourse had argued for decades that the Nehru government enacted laws—collectively called the Hindu Code Bills—regulating personal matters of Hindus in the mid-1950s, but allowed Muslims their own personal laws.

The Shah Bano judgement rejigged India's established

political equations and alignments and, in time, created a new fulcrum in electoral politics. Although Muslim traditionalists gathered in strength and gave several rousing calls to up the ante after hitting the streets through the summer of 1985, Rajiv Gandhi remained ambivalent. Khurshid claimed in his book that there was little evidence that Rajiv took a position, either in favour or against the verdict for several months. His government had to weather a storm that was more turbulent than the one his mother braved after she amended Section 125 of the CrPC in 1973 and earned the wrath of Muslim conservatives. Finally, in August 1985, during the monsoon session of Parliament, Rajiv allowed his ministerial colleague Arif Mohammed Khan to defend the judgement and state that the government had no intention of introducing a law to nullify it.

Within months, the situation altered. Pressure was brought on the frail illiterate woman who ignited the political minefield and in November 1985 she put her thumbprint on a document proclaiming that she 'disavowed the Supreme Court' verdict.[37] Shah Bano also refused her maintenance money and opposed judicial interpretation of matters pertaining to personal laws. She obviously did not want to live the rest of her life as a pariah within the community.

Silence in politics is often counterproductive. In December 1985, Rajiv Gandhi learnt the bitter way that his silence or inaction on the apex court verdict was beginning to hurt his party electorally. In by-elections to several parliamentary and state assembly seats, Congress nominees were defeated as Muslims who were previously loyal turned hostile. Besides the constituency from where Shahabuddin contested, the party lost many crucial seats, most importantly in Assam where simultaneous parliamentary and assembly polls for the entire state were held for these were delayed due to the anti-foreigner agitation in the state. In a stunning blow to the Congress, the newly formed United Minorities Front (UMF) won eighteen assembly seats. Almost all these constituencies were Muslim majority. UMF campaigners in Assam made merely two points: the threat to immigrant Muslims due to the recently signed Assam accord and the loss of identity owing to the Shah Bano case judgement which simultaneously opened avenues for interference in personal laws. Congress nominees lost by-elections in Gujarat, Bengal and Odisha.

The elections had taken place almost eight months after the Supreme Court judgement and the Congress was yet to formulate a formal stance. For a leader with a 400-plus majority in the Lok Sabha, this indecisiveness was unfathomable. Rajiv allowed conflicting opinions in the community to be articulated not just within the party, but in public too. Arif Mohammed Khan's statement in Parliament was argued against by his senior in the government, Z.R. Ansari. Rajiv had hoped that the wall of opposition to the judgement among Muslims would crumble under self-contradictions. But the by-elections demonstrated this was unlikely and Rajiv Gandhi had to act.

*

The VHP chose the backdrop of government indecision and inaction in the face of rising Muslim assertion to restart yatras for the Ram temple. Six yatras were flagged off from Bihar and one in UP on Vijaya Dashami or Dussehra on 23 October 1985. Paramhans Ramchandra raised the bar by announcing he would immolate himself if the gates of the shrine were not opened by Ram Navami in 1986 (falling in mid-April). Enthused by the fervour these yatras generated on the ground, the second Dharam Sansad that met at Udipi in November 1985 decided to upscale the agitation. Going beyond the call for unlocking the gate of the Ayodhya shrine, to permit unhindered access for Hindu devotees, the saints asked for the shrine to be handed over to the Ramanandi sampraday, the Vaishnavite Brahminical sect which emphasizes worship of Ram.

Not to miss out on possible gains from the escalation of the agitation, the Congress chief minister of UP, Veer Bahadur Singh, visited Ayodhya in the third week of December to inaugurate the government-sponsored Ramayan mela. VHP leaders immediately lined up to hand over another petition to him pressing for their demands. During the interaction, Singh made a pledge, one that he would go on to fulfil to direct legal experts to study the title dispute and opine if the locks could be opened without attracting contempt of court. There was no ambiguity that the Congress had become a party in the process of throwing open the Babri Masjid to Hindu devotees. A VHP account of the meeting states that the chief minister 'listened to all that was said before him in an impassioned plea for the removal of the said locks'.[38]

According to Advani's claim, after Congress candidates were defeated in this round of elections, Rajiv Gandhi firmed up his mind to nullify the Shah Bano judgement. In December 1985, Advani's father, Kishinchand D. Advani, passed away. Advani claimed that in early 1986 the prime minister visited him at his New Delhi residence to offer condolences. According to the BJP stalwart's version, the prime minister queried: 'What do you think should be done in the case of the Supreme Court's judgement in the Shah Bano matter?' Advani wrote in his autobiography that he was 'taken aback by the question and quickly realised that he [Rajiv] had made up his mind to backtrack on the issue and was probably seeking my party's support for his move'. Advani added that the conversation continued for several minutes and Rajiv Gandhi said that 'opposition is building up fast. There could be a serious situation if something is not done quickly.' Advani wrote he was blunt and without mincing words said that if Rajiv nullified the judgement on the basis of his majority in Parliament, he 'would be doing a disservice to the nation'. Rajiv Gandhi 'went down several notches in my esteem that day,' Advani wrote.[39]

The conversation provided the BJP leader with an indication that Rajiv was contemplating steps to invalidate the Supreme Court verdict. It is possibly mere coincidence that within days of this meeting, a conference of Hindu religious leaders was held in Lucknow on 19 January 1986. That the endgame on the demand to open the disputed shrine to Hindu devotees had begun became evident when assembled delegates announced they would forcibly break open the locks on the day of Mahashivratri festival, in early March. This advanced the deadline set by Paramhans Ramchandra and forced the government to redouble its efforts to find a way to meet the VHP demand. According to Narasimha Rao, after Indira Gandhi's assassination, Rajiv Gandhi 'and another colleague of his took command of the Ayodhya matter'. Adding a spin of his own, he added: 'From then on, a series of disastrous steps followed.'[40] Although Rao did not name the ministerial colleague who helped Rajiv Gandhi untangle the Ayodhya knot, it is widely presumed that Arun Nehru, close aide, minister and cousin, was this associate.

By this time leaders of the Dharam Sansad had begun lobbying with Congress ministers and other party leaders to secure support for the temple. The meeting of Hindu religious leaders in Lucknow added to pressure on the government. The VHP claimed that 'close search of the (historical and legal) records appears to have been ordered'.[41] The effort met with success and on 21 January 1986 a previously unknown young Faizabad-based lawyer, Umesh Chandra Pandey, moved an application in the regular suits praying that the locks on the grill be opened and unrestricted puja and darshan be permitted. Unwilling to wait for the plea to come up routinely, he moved another application in the ongoing title case on 25 January before the local munsif. When this was rejected, he filed an appeal on 30 January before the district judge of Faizabad. On 1 February, the judge examined the district collector, whereupon he ordered the lock to be opened without allowing Muslims to be impleaded as a party in the case. The local administration abided with the order the same day in 'as much time as it took a police officer to reach Sri Ram Janmabhoomi at Ayodhya from the courtroom of the district judge at Faizabad'.[42] The lawyer, district judge and the collectors were all Brahmins with Pandey as their surname.

State complicity in the opening of the gates and handing over the shrine to Hindu devotees needed no greater proof as news of the unlocking was broadcast within hours on the state broadcaster Doordarshan, the only television channel at the time. The VHP did not secure possession of the Babri Masjid, but its leaders knew that a major hurdle had been cleared and they could plan the next move.

*

Unlocking of the gates enraged Muslims and civil society. A day after the dramatic development in the temple town, the working committee of theAll-India Muslim Personal Law Board (AIMPLB) expressed 'deep sense of shock at the virtual handing over of the Babri Masjid to the Hindu community'. Not only were Hindus allowed entry into the mosque, but the judge had not followed the basic principles of jurisprudence. He acquiesced to the prayer without settling 'the substantive question of origin and title'. The judge altered the status quo of the property without ruling on the legal dispute—whose land was it? The AIMPLB asserted that the 'unilateral seizure will only serve to undermine the faith of the Muslim community in the political order and the judicial system', but nevertheless asked Muslims to maintain calm.[43]

But not every response of Muslims was laid out on the same principles of non-confrontation. On 4 February, the Majlis-e-Mushawarat, another representative body of the Muslim leadership, with Syed Shahabuddin as its acting president, asked the community to observe 14 February 1986 as a black day, hoist black flags and sport protest badges. A call for protest was also given in the Aligarh Muslim University (AMU).

Shahabuddin and other leaders required time to mobilize public opinion in several cities, but the Shahi Imam of Delhi's Jama Masjid, Abdullah Bukhari, required no such preparation; a captive audience was ensured every Friday after the afternoon namaz at Jama Masjid. The imam had used the Jama Masjid as a political proscenium since the mid-1970s, especially on Fridays. After the unlocking of the gates in Ayodhya, sections of the Urdu media created a stir by publishing photos of the idol inside Babri Masjid. These were widely distributed in the walled city and generated anger. Bukhari's Friday sermon on 7 February was an unabashed exercise in rabble-rousing. The imam 'warned the government that if Babri Masjid was not given back to Muslims, he would start a mass movement'.[44] He also endorsed the call for observing 14 February, also Friday, as black day and asked people to congregate at the Jama Masjid. A bigger crowd assembled and Bukhari spoke lucidly and eloquently, making his address the first 'public "performance' in the Babri Masjid case'[45] and enhancing his standing among Muslim leaders.

The protest on 14 February in Delhi took a violent turn when police opened fire to disperse crowds returning from Jama Masjid when they began threatening public order. Two Muslim youth died and several localities in the walled city were placed under curfew. Violence spread elsewhere soon, in 'six towns across four northern states and the Union territory of Delhi'. Twenty people died. Clashes related to this also erupted in five towns in Jammu and Kashmir.[46] In other parts of the country, too, the situation was highly charged as the VHP and the emerging Muslim political leadership locked horns in competitive provocation. There was also intense rivalry among different Muslim leaders.

Few were inclined to explore options of moderation. Maulana Ali Hussain Naqvi, president of the AIMPLB, issued a statement calling for restraint. Although he was not alone in his opinions, most remained reluctant to air their views because of fears of marginalization and being labelled as a stooge of the majority. Upping the ante by stoking the rising siege mentality among Muslims was the only way to steal a march over others in the race to emerge as representative leaders of the Muslim masses. These voices fanned fears of being minority in a country where many secular politicians camouflaged majoritarian instincts. These Muslim leaders campaigned within the community, stressing that not just personal laws, but even places of worship were being 'taken away'.

Almost simultaneously and as if fuelling one another, the RSS–VHP leaders kept saying that Hindus could no longer forgive and forget the past and that the unlocking of the Ayodhya shrine was a step towards 'avenging' past 'indignities'. Campaigns of the VHP propped up 'lost' masculinity of Hindu men with the objective of triggering the emergence of a new stereotype—the angry Hindu.

Not just the VHP, even the RSS adopted a formal position on the state of affairs. In the meeting of its Akhil Bharatiya Pratinidhi Sabha after the unlocking, it stated that the event had 'opened the flood-gates of jubilation among all our countrymen and lovers of our culture abroad'. It took note that 'Muslim fanatics are going about inciting the Muslim masses' and that this is 'bound to cause grave concern to all lovers of emotional integration of our country'. The resolution went on to specify that 'faith and veneration for one's great forbears [meaning Lord Ram] is an essential aspect of nationalism' and that 'had Muslims here too welcomed the court's decision vis-à-vis Ram Janmabhoomi and honoured Shri Ram as their great ancestor that would have strengthened our emotional bonds'. Clearly, Muslims could become part of the national mainstream only if they adopted the ideas and ideals of the majority community. The RSS also demanded that the Rajiv Gandhi government must 'hand over the Janmabhoomi place and adjacent land to the Ram Janmabhoomi Trust created for the purpose of developing that hallowed spot in a befitting manner'.[47]

At another important RSS conclave in Gwalior on 11 November 1986, RSS sarsanghchalak Deoras claimed that a robust and united Hindu community was essential for Indian political ideals to flourish. The argument was that 'democracy, socialism and secularism can be achieved only "if Hindus are united, strong and in a majority in the country". If the Hindus are reduced to a minority, the Hindu nation would meet the same fate of Bangladesh, Pakistan and Arab countries.'[48] Such reasoning was politically immoral for it posited that only a dominant and politicized Hindu community would permit constitutional ideals to flourish.

In later years, as majoritarian sentiment gained ground, Hindu animosity and aggression refused to be moderated even if Muslims 'stayed quiet'. Even after the November 2019 Supreme Court verdict, Muslim 'non-reaction' to or 'acceptance' of the Centre's decision on Article 370 did not in any way lead to scaling down of Hindutva goals and the law on citizenship was still amended. On the contrary, the BJP regime remained focussed on majoritarian pursuits and this appeared to be its main electoral instrument. Several states embarked on passing new laws from late 2020 onwards to proscribe religious conversions of any kind with intention to prevent interfaith marriages. In July 2021, the UP government followed the state of Assam to initiate steps to legislatively control population and disincentivise people with more than two children. Previously, in January 2021, the intrusive month-and-a-half-long campaign to seek donations for the Ram temple was started. This arms the Sangh Parivar with a countrywide database of those who did not contribute, and in this manner they will be profiled accordingly.

In 1986, for the Muslim community, it was a choice between the proverbial devil and the deep sea. Not protesting the judicial 'handover' of the Babri Masjid to the Hindu community would have been interpreted as a sign of weakness and made the majoritarian offensive more belligerent. Yet, opposition to the developments benefited VHP in its drive to enlist Hindus in its agitations. Although the Muslims were not a homogenous community and there were sharp divergences on responses to the events, the Sangh Parivar was able to depict the community as united and backed by secularists. It must be noted that Muslims had been active in various political parties from the dawn of independence—barring the Jana Sangh and others of its ilk. Although these leaders were not unified by common concerns, they were consistently treated as 'Muslim' leaders within their parties. From the first Lok Sabha election onward, almost every party fielded them only from constituencies with significant Muslim voters. After the Babri Masjid's gates were opened, different Muslim leaders cutting across party lines began deliberations among themselves to examine if they could come on a single platform to lobby the government to file an appeal against the Faizabad court order. Although the efforts came to naught, these discussions were painted as evidence of Muslims 'ganging up' against a 'genuine' Hindu demand.

*

Syed Shahabuddin had by the end of 1985 begun emerging as the 'modern' Indian Muslim, mainly in Western attire. He convened a meeting of Muslim members of Parliament on 20 February 1986. He was locked in a direct conflict with Bukhari for leadership of the community. He formed the 'Tehrik-e-Bazyabi-e-Babri Masjid' (Movement for the Restoration of the Babri Masjid). He also edited a monthly journal called *Muslim India*. Its March issue termed the unlocking as 'unilateral seizure' and added that 'for all practical purposes the Indian state has been transformed into a Hindu state. The transformation had been going behind the facade of secularism for quite some time ...

no pretence is any longer necessary ... the mask is off ... the Muslim community ... prepare itself for a long and hard struggle.' Although his invitation letter to fellow Muslim lawmakers called for 'calm appraisal', the meeting was anything but tranquil as thousands of activists owing allegiance to the Hindu Sangharsh Samiti (HSS), an organization backed by the VHP, stood outside the venue to heckle parliamentarians gathered inside. They raised slogans, which became vocal signatures of the temple agitation: *ab koi Babur paida naheen hone denge* (we shall not let another Babur be born).

The HSS was stewarded by B.L. Sharma 'Prem', a little-known rabble-rouser then, but who became a BJP member of the Lok Sabha from East Delhi constituency in 1991. An official release of the HSS claimed that 'foreign invaders had demolished Hindu temples and hammered our nationhood'—the first instance in the agitation of Ram being equated with Indian nationalism, with loyalty to the mythological hero becoming the yardstick for patriotism. A 1988 VHP publication, *Musalmanon Ko Kya Karna Chahiye* (What the Muslims should do), described Muslims protesting against unlocking the gates as people who did not 'believe in the Indian Constitution, and did not accept the judicial process of the country'. This proved, it further added, that 'Muslims did not believe in the country's tradition, culture, society and law'.

Muslim leaders who trod the path of legalism and constitutionalism did not oppose the opening of the lock per se, but merely argued that Pandey's application should have been rejected because hearing on the ongoing title suit was still under way. Yet few were inclined to appreciate the nuanced stance. The VHP publicized that Muslims were opposing the unlocking and were by default anti-Ram and hence anti-nationals. Muslims leaders became aware of what they were up against. Shahabuddin wrote in April 1986, 'Try as we might to project the Babri Masjid question as a question of democracy and secularism, of Constitution and rule of law, of progress and development, the needle finally gets stuck in the groove of Hindu-Muslim interaction. It becomes a Hindu-Muslim question.' He was aware of what to stay away from yet was sucked into that maelstrom because silence was not an option in a democracy.

*

Ram Navami is an important Hindu festival and is considered as the day of Ram's arrival or birth. Traditionally, tens of thousands of devotees congregate in Ayodhya for a dip in the Sarayu and pay obeisance at temples. It was obvious that the newly 'restored temple' and the idol inside would be the chief attraction in 1986. VHP leaders called for a Ram Janmabhoomi Mahotsav on this day in the town. Several Muslim leaders called for a parallel event in Faizabad. The district administration, under instructions from the state and Centre, attempted to seal entry points to the city but still an estimated 10,000 Muslims sneaked in and held a public rally. The unlocking of the Babri Masjid had become a major threat to peace and intercommunity relationship, and the RSS–VHP was benefitting from communal polarization.

Yet the government of the day believed it could successfully ride the rival waves simultaneously. The plan that Advani claimed was already brewing in the prime minister's mind in January 1986, when the latter paid him a visit to condole his father's passing, had taken concrete shape. After consultations with the AIMPLB, Rajiv had made up his mind to address popular Muslim sentiment on the matter. He concluded that it was necessary to work with the AIMPLB if he intended to regain support among Muslim masses. He met Tahir Mehmood, acknowledged scholar of Muslim personal law who later became chairperson of the National Minority Commission, and Salman Khurshid, then known mainly as a Cambridge-educated Supreme Court lawyer and son of Khurshid Alam Khan, a senior Congress leader and Union minister.

Rajiv's decision to get his law minister to move the Muslim Women (Protection of Rights on Divorce) Bill in Parliament on 25 February 1986 provoked adverse reaction from most quarters although for different reasons. Secularists, led by eminent jurist and former Supreme Court judge, V.R. Krishna Iyer, wrote to the prime minister within seventy-two hours, dubbing the legislation sinful and having dangerous consequences for the nation. On the other hand, proponents of the religio-cultural perspective termed the law as another proof of Congress appeasement of Muslim conservatives. Girilal Jain, editor of *The Times of India*, often considered the first articulate English-speaking (and writing in that language) Hindu nationalist with mass readership, wrote in a signed editorial dated 28 February that the bill was 'a wholly retrograde piece of legislation and that its introduction in the Lok Sabha represents a violation of the assurance the Prime Minister had given'. Further, he argued that it was 'shocking beyond words that the Prime Minister, who had made "march into the 21st century" his battle-cry, should have endorsed a march into the seventh century for one-eighth of the Indian people'.[49]

Arif Mohammed Khan's resignation the day the bill was tabled was just the shot in the arm the VHP needed to mobilize support. Having achieved the objective of 'liberating' Ram Janmabhoomi, the next target was set:

building a magnificent temple in place of the existing structure. The Centre did not impose restrictions on the VHP's programmes because it believed the 'balancing act' between Hindu and Muslim hardliners would succeed. The reasoning was that Muslim conservatives had been satisfied by the Muslim Women (Protection of Rights on Divorce) Act that was passed in March and became law on 19 May after receiving President Zail Singh's assent. Correspondingly, Hindu chauvinists were assuaged by the opening of the Babri Masjid.

Days before the process of nullification of the Supreme Court's Shah Bano verdict was completed with the presidential decree, another significant development took place. The BJP effected a change of guard—Advani in place of Vajpayee as president. But more significantly, the party junked the middle path it had adopted in 1980 and returned to its Jana Sangh roots with closer linkages to the RSS, ideological as well as in manpower.

*

In October 1985, while deliberating on an internal report to examine reasons for the debacle in the 1984 polls, the BJP opted for a policy of 'back to the roots'. The executive, still under Vajpayee's stewardship, acquiesced with two hypotheses. One, that the proclamation that 'BJP is a party with a difference means that the party, amongst other things, possesses an ideology which is not fully shared by others'. Two, that 'adherents of the political movement which culminated into the BJP have not been able to identify the BJP ideology as a derivative of the political philosophy that they so assiduously formulated … incorporation of Integral Humanism as an ingredient of the party ideology would go a long way to fill this void.' By accepting that henceforth the party should 'work for the rebuilding of our country on the basis of Indian Culture and tradition', the party leadership accepted their error in not doing so since April 1980.[50]

Prior to Advani assuming charge, the BJP had already firmed up its mind to pursue Hindu nationalist politics. In his acceptance speech, the new president reiterated old demands of the RSS and the Jana Sangh; abrogation of Article 370 of the Constitution would certainly be on the priority list. Additionally, the demand for Uniform Civil Code was listed, besides calling for proscription on cow slaughter. Advani adroitly spoke about the BJP ideology, but couched its exclusionary character in genteel vocabulary. Advani emerged as the first leader groomed within the RSS stable who successfully communicated with the English-speaking intelligentsia, till then the dominant opinion makers of the country. He added new words to the political lexicon which were lapped up by the media and passed on to the people. His first coinage after becoming party president was 'minorityism' in January 1987 at a party convention, dubbing constitutional guarantees and safeguards for minorities as appeasement. He listed the decision on the Shah Bano judgement as an example of the 'dangers of minorityism', when a progressive judicial verdict was overturned to mollify the conservative sentiment. Although the BJP and other Hindu nationalists took up cudgels on behalf of Muslim women, they did not advocate the community's anguish at rising alienation and threat to their identity.

The BJP under Advani's helmsmanship also began reconvening regular meetings of the Samanvaya Samiti or coordination committee in which leaders of the BJP and RSS held consultations on political issues. Another significant tradition, abandoned after BJP's formation in 1980—deputation of RSS pracharaks to the BJP—was revived. This system was started in 1951 when Deendayal Upadhyaya was the first preacher 'loaned' to the Jana Sangh after its establishment. The first group of RSS pracharaks deputed to the BJP in early 1987 included the man who eventually led the party to its overarching dominance: Narendra Modi.

Despite its unequivocal shift to the right, the BJP remained silent on Ayodhya although it highlighted India's 'unity, integrity, security, and honour of India' being in 'more danger than at any time since Independence'.[51] Criticism of the government for nullifying the Shah Bano judgement was listed as a major failure.

Insofar as the Ayodhya dispute was concerned, the VHP was unwilling to settle for what it had achieved; now it asked for the 'handover' of the site to construct a Ram temple. This was obviously intended to keep the social temperature soaring. Across north India, Muslim leaders responded by organizing regular public meetings and submitting memoranda. The Centre was reminded to direct the Uttar Pradesh government to seek judicial review of the Faizabad district judge's order. They organized a confrontational all-India conference in Delhi in December 1986 by when leaders were locked in competitive brinkmanship. Eventually, Shahabuddin joined hands with the 'several other political players'[52] by giving a provocative call: Muslims should not celebrate the Republic Day in January 1987. He also asked the community to prepare for a march, later in 1987, to Ayodhya to 'claim the mosque for themselves as the government was doing nothing on the matter'.[53] To mobilize people for this 'long march', it was decided to hold a public rally on 30 March 1987 in Delhi. The Republic Day boycott call was provocative and evoked the response Shahabuddin wanted. Articulating the BJP's anger at its executive meeting in Vijaywada over the year end, Advani said the threatened boycott was 'anti-national, inflammatory and irresponsible' and speeches were an 'unabashed attempt to intimidate the nation by threats of violence'.[54] The VHP added: Shahabuddin and other Muslim leaders had put 'religion over the nation'. Shahabuddin realized the explosive nature of his move and withdrew his call but the damage was done and the VHP and other constituents of the Sangh Parivar received another boost. Hereafter, it was merely a matter of time and tactics that the ultimate objective of demolishing the Babri Masjid and building a new temple would be realized.

5
The Giant Leap

'Mob law is the most forcible expression of an abnormal public opinion; it shows that society is rotten to the core.'

—Timothy Thomas Fortune

Competitive rhetoric and efforts to outdo rivals in the sweepstakes for Muslim leadership—Shahabuddin's call for boycotting Republic Day functions, for example—provided the BJP–VHP–RSS a tailor-made opening to politicize the temple issue without formally committing to the demand for building a Ram temple. The Independence and Republic Days are the two most significant secular national celebrations. Asking for a boycott bordered on being treasonous. In the resulting din, few had time for the fact that the Muslim leadership had opposed the unlocking of the disputed shrine on legal basis—that the order was issued without settling the title suit. This provocative act, besides providing justification for the vilest depictions of Muslims, also laid the ground for the Hindu nationalistic combine to leverage the reverence for Lord Ram in the typical Hindu psyche. This was the first time that the VHP demand was stated to be a national aspiration. It was claimed that anyone obstructing the programme to construct a Ram temple in Ayodhya before legal resolution of the dispute—Muslims and secularists alike—who wished the matter to be resolved according to legal principles, was against 'national' interests.

Contentions of leaders of the Sangh Parivar that Muslims opposing the Ayodhya agitation were putting Emperor Babur at par with the deity were accepted by a large number of Hindus. This provided additional opportunity to give shape to the argument that Muslims live on 'our land' yet were unwilling to respect 'our ideas and ideals'. For Advani, the Ayodhya dispute was 'not just a legal issue, nor is it merely a question of history. It is essentially a question of a nation's identity. Whom must this nation identify with; Ram or with Babur?' The BJP formally joined the debate over the Ayodhya imbroglio and Advani's statement asked if people like the former diplomat would 'like Hindus to identify with Ram, and Muslims with Babur. BJP rejects this perverse and separatist approach and holds that all patriots, Hindus and Muslims, cannot but identify themselves with Ram and recognise Babur for what he was, a foreign invader.'[1]

Almost three-and-a-half decades later, this contention was further expounded by Narendra Modi: 'The basic argument [in the course of the Ayodhya agitation] was that Muslims too must accept Lord Ram as the symbol of national identity, that he was a Mahapurush [great man] of this country. And that everyone [living] in this country should believe in this.'[2] It was a tough call for Muslim leaders and others asking for law to run its course. The worry in accepting the Ayodhya shrine as a one-off case stemmed from previous resolutions of the Hindu Mahasabha and the RSS which talked about 'restoration' of other Hindu temples which were allegedly 'converted' into mosques. Silence on their part in leaving the unlocking of Babri Masjid unchallenged would have encouraged the VHP and its affiliates to seek immediate possession of other 'disputed' shrines, especially the two in Varanasi and Mathura. But opposition to the Ayodhya campaign could have been tackled more adroitly instead of going into a headlong collision which achieved little but the moniker of *Babur ke aulad* (descendants of Emperor Babur) for almost the entire Muslim community. The VHP successfully constructed a stereotype within months and the argument that Muslims did not 'belong' here and had to be 'put' in their place gained currency. For the RSS–VHP–BJP combine the Ayodhya issue was merely part of a larger political project. Its adversaries, however, were yet to see through this.

*

Meanwhile, other political developments from the last quarter of 1986 started to shake the foundations of the Rajiv Gandhi government despite its emphatic majority in Parliament. The finance ministry under Vishwanath Pratap Singh had earlier that year hired American investigator Michael J. Hershman's Fairfax Group to probe alleged violation of currency control laws by several wealthy Indians. This was among the first of the accusations of financial embezzlements by people connected with Rajiv Gandhi. As a result, Singh was shunted out from the finance ministry and deputed to the defence ministry.

The finance and defence ministries were at the time housed in colossal colonial buildings cast in red sandstone on opposite sides of the road which was known as King's Way during the Imperial Rule. These heritage buildings that have been witness to much of modern Indian history are to become mere relics of the past, courtesy Modi's self-aggrandizing Central Vista project pushed through rapidly amid the Covid-19 pandemic. That, however, is a different story altogether except for underscoring that the obsession with grandiosity was not limited to temple, statues and bathing ghats. It was merely a hundred metres or so that Singh had to walk across from North Block in January 1987 to take his new position as defence minister in South Block. These strides may have taken him in closer in physical proximity to Rajiv Gandhi and the Prime Minister's Office (PMO), also housed in the same building, but the distance between the two grew manifold. By then, Singh was already the 'second-most popular politician in the country' and *Euromoney*, the prestigious English-language monthly magazine, had termed him 'one of the best finance ministers in the world'.[3] Singh's abrupt transfer fuelled allegations that Rajiv Gandhi's administration had spawned a web of corruption and promoted cronyism in government. By the time of the next general elections in November 1989, Rajiv Gandhi's Mr Clean image had taken a beating in people's perception and 'corruption in high places' became a frequently used phrase in the Indian political theatre.

There were allegations of financial irregularities in defence purchases, first the long-delayed submarine-to-submarine killers (SSK) acquired from the West German company, Howaldtswerke-Deutsche Werft (HDW). Singh was sought to be blamed for this but he struck back and precipitated a political crisis by quitting the government on 12 April. The second and more scandalous allegation was in regard to the purchase of Swedish field guns from howitzer manufacturer, Bofors AB. In a legendary journalistic scoop, Swedish Radio sensationally reported on 16 April that kickbacks were paid to several people to secure the $285 million contract. Allegations of links of middlemen with Rajiv Gandhi became the dominant narrative thereafter. V.P. Singh resigned from the Congress party and eventually emerged as Rajiv's primary challenger at the head of another anti-Congress political conglomerate. Due to these dramatic developments, which fundamentally altered India's political narrative, the Ram temple issue receded from the headlines.

*

From early 1987, saffron flags—symbol of ascendant Hindu society—were met by black flags hoisted by politicized Muslims. Street rallies and provocative slogans were the order of the day. The situation became alarming in Uttar Pradesh, with the 'state intelligence bureau constantly feeding reports to the Home Ministry that the threatened show of force over the never-ending Ram Janmabhoomi-Babri Masjid issue could precipitate communal trouble in sensitive districts, particularly in Meerut, Rampur, Moradabad, Kanpur and Allahabad'.[4]

The situation in Meerut was particularly alarming, thanks partly to the rally in Delhi called by Muslim organizations in the month of March. This rally is recognized as the 'largest ever Muslim gathering for any political cause in post-colonial India'.[5] Although the meeting was peaceful, speeches were fiery. 'Militancy among the Muslims was growing on this question. The Hindus were by no means less aggressive, perhaps a degree more. If Muslims raised the slogan: "We Muslims are 30 crores, we will wring blood out of you", the Hindus shouted "Hindus and Sikhs are brothers, where did the Muslim community come from", and "If you want to live in India, you have to live like a Hindu". These slogans

. Advani, Kedarnath Sahni and others huddled in Ayodhya on the morning of demolition, 6 December 1992 (above); and (below) rehearsing the demolition: P activists practising how the Babri Masjid was to be demolished, Ayodhya, early cember 1992. Photos: Praveen Jain.

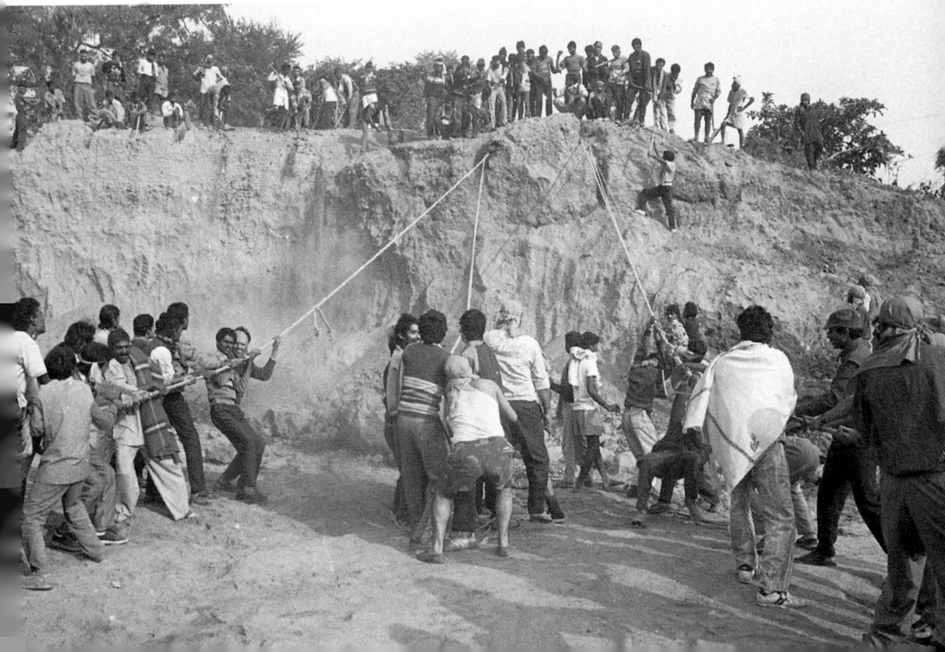

(Top right): VHP activists practising how the Babri Masjid was to be demolished. Photo: Praveen Jain.

(Below): The final charge: VHP activists making the final assault to demolish the Babri Masjid with no police to stop them, 6 December 1992. Photo: Sanjay Sharma © IPN

Fist of fury: Mahant Ramchandra Paramhans Das and Mahant Avaidyanath, key leaders of the Ram temple agitation (above) and (below) Mahant Ramchandra Paramhans Das (centre) flanked by Mahant Avaidyanath and Acharya Dharmendra of the Ram temple agitation walking on a Ayodhya street, December 1992. Photos: Sanjay Sharma, © IPN

VHP President Ashok Singhal readying to address a gathering in Ayodhya, December 1992 (top left) and (top right) L.K. Advani and Uma Bharti waving to supporters after being detained at Akbarpur, UP following the demolition. Photos: Sanjay Sharma © IPN

Much to smile about (below): L.K. Advani being welcomed by his wife Kamala while a young Narendra Modi looks on. Photo: Praveen Jain.

A tonsured VHP Kar Sevak with Ram inscribed on his head (above) and (below): When pilgrimage and political agitation merged: Hindu devotee on way to join Kar Seva in December 1992. Photos: Sanjay Sharma © IPN

The idols placed inside the makeshift structure constructed after the demolition of Babri Masjid (above) and (below): Mahant Ramchandra Paramhans Das receiving a Ram Shila, a consecrated brick, as part of the VHP's Shila Pujan and Yatra programme, Ayodhya, November 1989. Photos: Sanjay Sharma © IPN

Reduced Scale 0.6"= 10' or 1" = 16.66'

A.F. =97' E.F. = 140'

B.C.= 9' C.D.= 21'

(A.F. X E.F.) - (B.C. X C.D.) = 1482.5 Sq. Yd.

G.H. = 66' H.J. = 89'

K.L.=21' L.D.= 40'

(G.H. X H.J.) + (K.L. X L.D.) = 746 Sq. Yd.

Exact Dimensions and area has been calculated from the original map with the help of scale. They are not given in the original map which is on the scale of 1"=10'

The original site plan of the disputed shrine with the three domes, Ram Chabutra and Sita Rasoi clearly marked out separately.

(Top Left): Uttar Pradesh Sunni Central Waqf Board chairman Zafar Ahmad Farooqui (Source: UP Sunni Waqf Board website) and (top right): Oldest Muslim litigant Mohd Hashim Ansari addressing the media before his death in July 2016 (Photo: courtesy Rediff.com); (below): A Sufi shrine on the land allotted in Dhannipur village to construct a mosque. The project includes a mosque, hospital, museum, library, community kitchen (Photo: Courtesy *The Print*)

Chief Justice of India Ranjan Gogoi flanked by CJI-designate Sharad Arvind Bobde and Justices Dhananjaya Y Chandrachud, Ashok Bhushan and S Abdul Nazeer after delivering the verdict on 9 November 2019. (Photo: Wikipedia Commons)

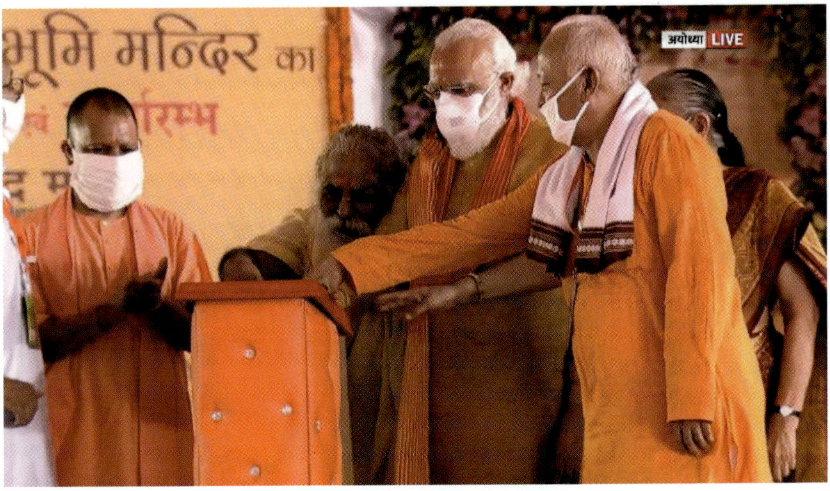

Prime Minister Narendra Modi, UP Chief Minister Yogi Adityanath and RSS Sarsanghchalak, Mohan Bhagwat after the Bhoomi Pujan ceremony, Ayodhya, 5 August 2020, and (below): Narendra Modi with Yogi Adityanath holding up Ram statue. (Source: @BJP4India, official Twitter account of the Bharatiya Janata Party.)

PM Narendra Modi performing Bhoomi Pujan in Ayodhya, 5 August 2020.
Photo: Wikipedia Commons

(Left): Model of the R
temple displayed at th
VHP office in Ayodh
(below): Sculpted
sandstone
for use in the Ram
temple; and (far belo
The workshop of
the VHP trust that
functioned in Ayodhy
from 1989 onward.
Photos: Courtesy
Newsclick

were painted on the walls of Meerut.'[6] A large number of Muslims who participated in this protest rally returned to their cities, including Meerut from where they came in large numbers, wearing shrouds to further provoke Hindus. Things came to a head in Meerut on 14 April while Muslims were celebrating Shab-e-barat. Although ten Hindus and Muslims died, this bout of violence was contained, but the worst was to come.

Beginning 16 May, Meerut became a communal cauldron again. It started with the murder of a Hindu youth in a property dispute. It was the month of Ramzan and in Muslims localities, people gathered for the ritual breaking of the day's fast. On 18 May, in one of these colonies, Hashimpura, the Provincial Armed Constabulary (PAC) arrived to arrest a Muslim, allegedly involved in the land dispute and the killing. His associates rushed to block his arrest. The skirmish escalated and drew more people from both communities. A shop belonging to a Muslim was burnt and the Hindu tenant was stabbed to death. The narrative still had nothing to do with the Ayodhya dispute. Soon, loudspeakers from a local mosque beseeched 'believers of faith' to come out and protect Islam. There was retaliatory action from Hindus and a full-blown riot was in hand.[7]

When the police and the infamous PAC moved in to make arrests, they were pelted with stones by Muslims. Eventually the PAC personnel had their way and detained almost one hundred of them. Muslim anger spilled on to the streets over the next couple of days but each act of violence was reciprocated by Hindus and police alike. The economically weaker sections among the Muslims faced the brunt of these attacks although Hindus too suffered fatalities and injuries. On 22 May, the PAC personnel took Muslims arrested from Hashimpura in trucks to Muradnagar, shot forty-six of them in cold blood and threw the bodies into the Upper Ganga Canal. Decomposing corpses were later recovered floating several kilometres downstream. The state government belatedly ordered investigations and the case limped along in various courts before the Delhi High Court convicted sixteen surviving PAC personnel in October 2018. The convicted thereafter challenged the decision in the Supreme Court but the policemen remain in jail. But the principal trial in a Meerut sessions court on the Maliana massacre, in which seventy-two Muslims were killed, is at a standstill and a petition has been filed against denial of justice in the Allahabad High Court.

Another major incident where the PAC joined forces with local Hindus was in Maliana and other nearby villages. This area had an estimated population of about 35,000 of whom about 4000 were Muslims and they were attacked by policemen in collusion with Hindus from the neighbourhood. The violence was macabre and at the end of the offensive, 'nothing stirred in Maliana as people sat huddled together, gripped by fear as the stench of smoke and human bodies rose about them'.[8] On the surface, the violence in Meerut had nothing to do with the Ayodhya conflict, but the ghost of the dispute cast its shadow on the city.[9]

*

Communal violence in Meerut triggered riots in the Indian capital on 19 May. These clashes in Delhi first broke out in an urbanized village in the southern part of the city. Though this locality had a significant Muslim population dating back to the twelfth century, it did not have a tradition of conflict between the two communities. The violence spread to other localities in the city and reports of the fatalities in the media varied from eight to fifteen. Eid was due on 28 May and two days prior to this, the Shahi Imam decided it was time for grandstanding on his part. He instructed Muslims not to offer congregational prayers at big mosques, including the Jama Masjid. On the day of the festival, after he finished offering namaz along with the chosen faithful, Abdullah Bukhari dramatically announced the closure of the Jama Masjid from 4 June to protest 'against extreme atrocities and barbarism' and declared that it would remain shut 'till guilty police officials [involved in the Meerut violence against Muslims] are severely punished, all innocents arrested are immediately released. Not verbal, but practical assurance for the security of life and property for future is made.'[10]

The closure of the Jama Masjid to protest violence against Muslims during communal riots was highly provocative. This was the first time in its history that the mosque was shut down by its management—it had been closed by the British after the rebellion in 1857 for five years. The imam even ordered that parts of the mosque visible from outside should be draped in black cloth. The shutdown was undoubtedly a public statement of dissent and a media event. Although he received a lot of flak from several quarters, even from within the community, the imam remained firm and forced the government to accept his demand. The mosque reopened immediately after the government ordered an inquiry on 13 June.

The incident boosted Bukhari's stature in the community as he was seen as a person capable of extracting concession from the regime. He developed proximity with V.P. Singh who was reaching out, separate from Shahabuddin, to create a personal political constituency among Muslims.

Significantly, while appearing alongside Singh, the imam did not mention Babri Masjid in his speeches. Other parties, however, warned the government that the shadow of the Babri Masjid dispute could not be ignored. C. Rajeshwar Rao, general secretary of the Communist Party of India, reminded Rajiv Gandhi in a letter dated 25 May 1987 that the 'background of the present wave of communal violence is, of course, the Babri Masjid-Ram Janmabhoomi controversy ... I must say that the Central government and the UP government cannot escape responsibility'.[11] Several leading intellectuals of the time issued a statement recognizing the fact that the Ayodhya 'syndrome has been exploited by both sides to rouse passions. This must stop and the issue be settled by negotiations, arbitration or judicial process. In the meantime all demonstrations must be banned.'[12]

These incidents provided the VHP an opportunity to up the ante and it threatened to give a 'fitting answer' to those calling for the law to take its own course.[13] However, Rajiv Gandhi was preoccupied with a number of corruption charges exploding in his face and merely appointed a three-member cabinet subcommittee—comprising Home Minister Buta Singh, P.V. Narasimha Rao and P. Shiv Shankar—to devise a 'line of action' but the trio displayed little sense of urgency. The Congress's assessment was that Muslims were already placated by the Union government's capitulation on the Shah Bano case, and hard-line Hindus had been assuaged by the unlocking of the Ayodhya shrine. Those who were still protesting would never back the Congress party and little purpose was served by engaging with them.

Non-communist opposition parties were focussed solely on weakening the Congress and adopted no position on the Ayodhya matter. Furthermore, they had no qualms about partnering with the BJP to weaken the Congress regime. Devi Lal of the Lok Dal was the first one to sew up a political alliance with the BJP for the 1987 assembly elections in Haryana. This election was startling for another reason: the BJP and the two communist parties, CPI(M) and CPI, entered into an opportunistic, albeit indirect, alliance with one another which provided the template for the 1989 Lok Sabha elections. In order to minimize the split in the anti-Congress vote, Devi Lal decided that his party would put up candidates in sixty-nine of the ninety seats, while the BJP was allocated eighteen seats and the two communist parties were handed one each with one being farmed out to an independent candidate. While the BJP and the communists did not put up candidates against the Lok Dal, they were free to contest against one another, which they did in one seat. There is no doubt that the communists and other non-Congress opposition parties contributed immensely to the BJP's spectacular performancc in the general elections in 1989 where the party won eighty-five seats as against just two in 1984.

The 1987 assembly polls in Haryana were held in the middle of efforts to form another opposition front on the lines of Janata Party in 1977. This time, however, the BJP decided to stay out and bask in what it termed its splendid isolation. Advani explained that his party had opted not to merge into another anti-Congress umbrella outfit because it believed that 'mere aggregation of disparate groups without a coherent set of policies and programmes to hold them together, cannot inspire confidence in the people ... far more important than opposition unity is opposition credibility'.[14]

Yet the party was not averse to joining opposition platforms and entering into informal electoral tie-ups. The alliance between Devi Lal and the BJP was firmed up in June, when the embers of the riots in Meerut and Delhi were still smouldering. No common position was taken by the alliance partners on Ayodhya. As expected, the alliance was victorious and the BJP joined the coalition government. It stopped being a political untouchable without giving up its pursuit of politics based on religious identity. For tactical reasons, however, the BJP did not embrace the demand for a Ram Mandir till fairly late. Instead, it positioned itself as protector of India's unity and integrity as against the Congress which was dubbed in a 1986 'charge sheet' prepared by the party as endangering 'unity, integrity, security, and honour of India'.[15] The underplaying of the Ayodhya issue by the BJP provided other non-Congress parties with the veneer of staying aloof from sectarian forces and the Haryana electoral arrangement provided the template for the 1989 Lok Sabha elections.

The other constituents of the Sangh Parivar continued harping on the Ram temple. The VHP formally demanded that the Babri Masjid be handed for constructing the temple as the 'question was a matter of prestige and dignity for the entire Hindu samaj'. Another prominent rabble-rouser, B.L. Sharma 'Prem', reiterated that Ayodhya was 'just the first milestone'. There were several other Hindu shrines that had to be 'liberated from the clutches of Muslims'.[16] The formal VHP petition was submitted to the government by Mahant Avaidyanath and Daudayal Khanna, office-bearers of the VHP-propped affiliate Ram Janmabhoomi Nyas whose brief was the construction of the temple as against the VHP's charter of waging an agitation. The decision to form the Nyas or trust in late 1986 was part of the ploy to establish multiple organizations to ensure multiplicity of voices although key decisions were always made by the VHP brass.

The Sangh Parivar strategy during this period was three-pronged. The VHP, the belligerent arm of the Hindu nationalistic edifice, launched campaigns, held meetings and organized rallies to garner greater support for the Ram temple. In a calculated strategy, the organization escalated its activities in 1989 as the elections for the ninth Lok Sabha that year came closer. It assumed that on the eve of elections, political parties would find it tough to oppose the demand for the Ram temple because of its emotive content. Furthermore, after the Bofors disclosures, public sentiment was more focused on the anti-corruption campaign. As a ploy, the VHP chose to sneak the temple programme into the election campaign.

The second prong of the Sangh Parivar strategy involved the BJP. As part of the strategy to back V.P. Singh, while refusing to be a party to any unity talks among opposition parties, Advani issued a public statement backing the Jan Morcha leader when he was physically roughed up by Congress activists in 1987. The BJP president raised the dark spectre of a decade-old repressive era when he stated that events of the 'past few weeks should serve as an ominous warning to all democrats that this government would have no qualms in repeating 1975, and clamping a second Emergency'.[17]

The third spear in the campaign was the RSS itself. Although Advani and Ashok Singhal were the most visible public faces of the effort to catapult the political Hindu on to the centre stage through the late 1980s, the most crucial role was played by Balasaheb Deoras for it was under his aegis that the VHP and BJP became resurgent organizations. As previously elaborated, Deoras shepherded the expansion of the RSS's socio-political engagement through coordinated action of its affiliates. From 1986 onward, Deoras redoubled his efforts. Part of this vigour stemmed from a deep-seated frustration with the RSS's social stagnation. Speaking at a function to mark the RSS's diamond jubilee in 1985, he bluntly asked: 'We have done thousands of works of social significance. And still RSS has no effect on the society as a whole.'[18]

Deoras had already started taking a personal interest in the fortunes of key affiliates and realized it was necessary to directly influence people who had unshakable control or 'ownership' of the affiliate organizations. Consequently, Advani and Singhal became Deoras's conduits for creating a pyramid of leaders and activists committed to breaking status quo and catalysing fundamental change in societal thinking on emergent situations as well as routine developments. Soon, the Ram temple agitation was no longer limited to the Ayodhya dispute or at best including the other two shrines in its embrace. It instead became the opening move of a complex manoeuvre that would challenge the political consensus built after Independence.

The so-called Nehruvian agreement was unflinchingly articulated by Manmohan Singh at a National Development Council meeting in December 2006, although two decades had elapsed since Deoras made the move to challenge this and initiate the process of altering the fundamental assumptions of Indian polity: 'We will have to devise innovative plans to ensure that minorities, particularly the Muslim minority, are empowered to share equitably in the fruits of development. They must have the first claim on resources.'[19] Deoras did not say so in as many words, but his thoughts were implicit in the vocabulary of Hindu nationalists thereon: Instead of the minority having 'first claim', it should be the majority community that should enjoy the status of 'rights holder'. Following which, the minority must accept its 'secondary' position in social hierarchy.

With his intention and organizational strategy spelt out, the question was what programme the RSS under Deoras would conceptualize to make Hindus more assertive and begin instilling among Muslims the sense of being part of a 'larger whole' and not mark out their distinctiveness. An opportunity arose in 1988 and the RSS grabbed it without a second thought, although it was in contrast to values practised by the RSS since its inception. The organization, it must be recalled, was established by Keshav Baliram Hedgewar, a migrant Telugu Brahmin settled in Nagpur, who paradoxically raised the RSS as a Maharashtrian-Brahmin-centred organization. Hedgewar was born in April 1889 and Deoras was quick to seize the opportunity to organize a year-long birth centenary. The political situation did not permit the launch of an agitation to demand handing over the site of the Babri Masjid to enable construction of a Ram temple, and the centenary celebrations came in handy to keep the Sangh Parivar in the news.

The decision to organize a year-long celebration was against past traditions of the RSS because Hedgewar was opposed to self-congratulatory rituals like anniversary celebrations.[20] Deoras, after assuming charge as sarsanghchalak in 1973, had forbidden *vyakti-puja* or glorification of individuals. He even directed his aides to ensure that his remains were not entombed in Nagpur's Hedgewar Smriti Mandir as had been done for Golwalkar, whose ashes were kept in the same compound. But because the Hedgewar centenary would enable the RSS to spread its message far and wide across India and even among the Indian diaspora, Deoras, despite failing health, 'imaginatively and meticulously' choreographed the centenary and also 'undertook a whirlwind tour of the country'.[21] Deoras was completely focused on the centenary plan, mirroring the Sangh's working style of being systematic and methodical: 'It never takes for implementation more than one major programme at a time.'[22] As a result, from early 1988, the Sangh shifted its attention from the Ayodhya agitation, although the VHP ensured that the fire did not die out. Likewise, the BJP had little to do with the organization and planning of the Hedgewar centenary celebrations. This was in sync with 'another organizational tenet followed by the Sangh leadership ... every worker to focus only on the work entrusted to him'.[23] Every affiliate was directed to remain engaged only on its essential work or brief.

To spread the idea of Hindu nationalism, the RSS leadership established a special purpose committee, Dr Hedgewar Janmashatabdi Samiti or Committee for the Celebration of the Birth Centenary of Dr Hedgewar. This committee provided the RSS with the opportunity of expanding its footprint: shakhas spread to new towns and villages and the number of swayamsevaks grew phenomenally. 'In addition 50 lakh people are connected with its activities through 38 front organisations.'[24] As part of the drive to raise awareness for the centenary, an estimated 'two crore slick leaflets were distributed all over the country to highlight the social work done by its 10,585 [affiliated or symbiotically connected] institutions. Another blatantly communal pamphlet titled "Warning: India in Danger" was a frontal attack on Muslims and Christians. Through its network of volunteers, it reached two crore people across the country. About 50 lakh inland letter cards and envelopes—which show India, Afghanistan, Pakistan, Nepal, Sri Lanka and Bangladesh under a saffron flag—were sold by the Delhi unit alone.'[25]

In his formative years, when Hedgewar was a medical student in Calcutta, he learnt the benefits of engaging with the community through *sewa* or service programmes. The experience of time spent as a volunteer with the Ramakrishna Mission after floods in Burdwan gave him the idea of utilizing sewa as an entry point into the community and publicizing the political agenda after he formed the RSS. Likewise, in 1988, the RSS established Dr Hedgewar Janmashatabdi Sewa Samiti with Maharashtra's Chandrapur as its headquarters. Its founding president was an important RSS leader but his significance is greater in the contemporary context. His name? Madhukarrao Bhagwat, father of current sarsanghchalak Mohan Bhagwat and an early mentor of Prime Minister Narendra Modi. The RSS left no stone unturned in its efforts to popularize Hedgewar's name and secure support for its religio-cultural definition of the nation. In Rajasthan's capital Jaipur, a sporting event—Dr Hedgewar Olympics—was coordinated by a former ABVP leader who later became an important state BJP leader, Satish Poonia.[26]

In the era when there was no social media, graffiti was a powerful medium of publicity. A massive project of wall writing was undertaken throughout India. There was hardly a town or city where the slogan '*Garv se kaho, hum Hindu hain*' (Say with pride that you are a Hindu) was not visible on the walls. There were other slogans too, each aimed at bolstering the 'sagging morale' of Hindus. But none had the resonance of the one-liner stating that being Hindu was a sufficient reason to be proud, either individually or collectively. The crafty slogan was aimed at bolstering Hindu confidence and make them assert their Hinduness which, it implied, had been 'taken away' during the dark medieval years. The slogans valorised the Hindu sense of being and provided a basis for the VHP to step up the Ram temple campaign.

*

The VHP benefited from the Rajiv Gandhi government's sheer ineptitude in devising a coherent plan to prevent political benefit accruing to the Hindu nationalists. The champions for the Ram temple were also boosted by continuing declarations of motley Muslim groups who threatened to organize a 'long' march to Ayodhya for the restoration of the Babri Masjid. A meeting of one of the groups, the Babri Masjid Movement Coordination Committee (BMMCC), was first held on 24 January 1988 at which it resolved that because the VHP had started preparations to 'take over other mosques and shrines, adding to our [the Muslims'] sense of religious insecurity', there was little option for the Muslims but to 'undertake the march to Ayodhya'. Although it did not act on this resolution, it enabled the VHP to crank up support among Hindus. The BMMCC once again adopted its confrontational stance in May 1988 and announced a 'mini' march on 12 August and a 'long' one on 14 October, both Fridays. It only helped the VHP to bolster support in its constituency. Although the BMMCC postponed the first march days before it was scheduled to be flagged off, 'in response to a call of the Home Minister for a negotiated solution',[27] it only ended up playing into the VHP's hands.

The call for a political accord on Ayodhya by the home minister was at the initiative of the cabinet subcommittee and involved the UP chief minister too. This was the first effort at mediation and it became clear that there could never be a negotiated solution because of extreme postures:

Muslim parties would settle for nothing less than the eviction of the idols and the Ram Janmabhoomi Mukti Yagna Samiti ruled out negotiation as Ayodhya was one of the three most sacred places of Hindus. There were political groups—ironically this included the rump of the Janata Party that was left with only Subramanian Swamy as a noteworthy leader—that called for conversion of the disputed shrine into a national monument, and handing it over to the Archaeological Survey of India. In 1988, political polarization was still limited in India. Consequently, we can merely speculate if at that time the shrine could have been officially declared a protected monument and handed over to the Archaeological Survey of India to provide access to visitors irrespective of faith.

This argument gains strength from the fact that in 1988, the Ram temple issue was yet to become a mass movement dominating national political agenda. The BJP too had not expanded its social and regional footprint. But the opportunity was lost, as the Centre asked for 'documents' from the VHP and initiated an acrimonious exchange by forwarding these to Shahabuddin. He correctly contended that these papers did not 'contain an iota of evidence on the two basic issues seen in a larger perspective: (a) Whether the Babri Masjid stands on the birth site of Shri Ramchandraji? (b) Whether a pre-existing temple on the site was demolished to construct the Babri Masjid'. He added that the documents 'do not take us any further. The onus still lies on the claimant.'[28]

The Ayodhya dispute may not yet have become cause célèbre nationally, but there were sufficient reasons to trigger Hindu–Muslim riots once again, especially in north India. The pro-Babri group in the city of Muzaffarnagar gave a call for a demonstration on 14 October. To preempt this, Hindu communal groups called for a citywide bandh or general strike on 8 October and when a few Muslim traders refused to down their shutters, violence ensued. In this round of conflict an estimated eighty-seven people were killed, the majority of them Muslims. The riots occurred almost on the eve of the 'long march' to Ayodhya that Shahabuddin and other Muslim leaders had planned to launch on 12 October. Naturally, Buta Singh was worried that this march would trigger violence in other parts of UP. He convened a meet of a few BMMCC leaders and secured a postponement of the march by promising that he would expedite the legal process 'after the festival season'.[29]

The Shahi Imam of Delhi's Jama Masjid, who had been waiting for an opportunity to discredit Shahabuddin, used this postponement as a pretext to accuse Shahabuddin and Ibrahim Sulaiman Sait of the Indian Union of Muslim League,[30] not to be confused with the original Muslim League which secured India's partition, of 'compromising' Muslim interests.[31] The schism within the Muslim groups, evident for several months now, surfaced, and on 26 November 1988 many of them parted with the group led by Shahabuddin. They held a two-day convention in the Jama Masjid and announced the formation of another organization, the All India Babri Masjid Action Committee (AIBMAC). Speakers derided the former diplomat for not being 'sincere to the cause of the *qaum*' and instead 'having vested interests'.[32]

Buta Singh was aware of the implications of this split. In his note to Rajiv Gandhi, he termed this development as 'noteworthy' and forewarned that the 'protagonists of the Ram Janmabhoomi' were adopting 'a more aggressive stance'.[33] This was a reference to the week-long Ram Janki Rath Yatra in the first fortnight of December 1988 that the

VHP organized in Madhya Pradesh to 'awaken' Hindus. Despite being aware that the VHP was beginning to up the ante, the government did not ramp up its counter-measures to diffuse the situation. In one of the interactions with Buta Singh, VHP leaders were intimated that Shahabuddin had said that the VHP's documents did not substantiate the case for the Ram temple at Ayodhya. This was the first time the VHP unveiled its argument that questions of faith were beyond negotiation, and 'need not be proved'. Instead of contesting this, Buta Singh merely played the role of messenger and passed on the VHP response to the Muslim leadership. It was the election year and the VHP's plans were beginning to appear ominous.

*

Announcements on successive days by the warring self-styled community representatives unveiled the likely turn of events in 1989, insofar as the dispute over the shrine in Ayodhya was concerned. The newly formed AIBMAC declared in the Indian capital on 31 January that it was forming *hifajati dastas* or 'defence squads' to protect the mosque from attempts of the VHP activists to demolish it. Their leaders announced that secret squads would be 'trained adequately to sneak into the inner ring' of the shrine and 'maintain a vigil' to prevent 'assembly of VHP activists with the aim of demolishing the mosque'.[34] Undeniably, the plan, if allowed to go through by the government, had the potential of setting off nationwide violence. But even before a coherent response could be articulated to this announcement, the other, and unambiguously more potent, declaration was made by the VHP at Allahabad where the Maha Kumbha Mela was being held. In hindsight, there appears little doubt that the calendar of events was planned in advance by the dramatis personae on both sides and they merely went through preordained motions at formal meetings.

On 1 February 1989, not just the VHP's, but the entire Sangh Parivar's most ambitious religio-political campaign since the stormy anti-cow-slaughter agitation in 1966 was announced. Leaders declared they would conduct the *shilanyas* ceremony to symbolically lay the foundation of a new Ram temple at Ayodhya on 9 November 1989. The chosen date coincided with the annual festival of devothan ekadashi, the day when gods are believed to rise from slumber. The foundation-laying ceremony was a novel ritual in the Indian political theatre and it was scheduled right in the middle of the election season so as to extract maximum political benefit for the BJP by ensuring that the Ram temple matter became a significant talking point in electoral discourse. Pilgrims in tens of thousands traditionally gathered in the temple town during devothan ekadashi. The VHP was thereby assured of a base level of crowds in Ayodhya for the ceremony. Yet, it left no stone unturned to mobilize support and eventually succeeded in assembling a sea of humanity.

This was done by a mass campaign, called Ram Shila Pujan, for which specially manufactured bricks, with Shri Ram written on them, were consecrated in religious rituals performed in hundreds of thousands of cities, towns and villages following which they were eventually transported to Ayodhya in processions to be used for constructing the temple. The two programmes, the shilanyas and the Ram Shila Pujan, appeared ludicrous initially, because the VHP was apparently jumping the gun by laying the foundation of the temple much before a judicial verdict. Moreover, the land around the Babri Masjid was also disputed because the legal cases involved multiple plots of land. Furthermore, the brick consecration ceremony had no precedence and there was no certainty that people would get enthused with it.

Shahabuddin was one of the few who foresaw the likely impact. It was dusk on a cold February evening when I parked my bike in the driveway of his modest official Janpath residence. Those days reporters could walk in on politicians known to them during 'civil' hours. Shahabuddin, as usual, peered at me through piles of newspapers, magazines, books and official reports while sitting on his CPWD chair. Pleasantries over, I informed him about the VHP announcements. His face turned ashen when I told him about the shilanyas and Ram Shila Pujan programmes, providing further details about the Ram Shila Yatras to Ayodhya. 'With this programme, the VHP has ensured that it will never have to look backwards on their road to Ayodhya,' he said softly. I must have had a quizzical look on my face for he explained, the shila pujan would give Hindus, even in remote reaches of India, a chance to 'participate' in the agitation. Shahabuddin was not alarmist in his response for the VHP too believed that successful execution of the Ram shila programme would 'give a sense of belonging to the Hindus at large'.[35]

It turned out exactly as the VHP had predicted. The very act of 'touching' the bricks gave people a sense of participation without even stirring from their homes. The token money they paid as offering provided a sense of having contributed to the cause of the Ram temple. VHP reports later recounted that during the shila pujan programme specially printed coupons in denominations of Rs 1.25, Rs 5 and Rs 10 were sold. These coupons were often proudly displayed by people as noted by this writer and several other reporters. The VHP was clear that this was another reach-out and the intention was to ensure that every person participating in shila pujan rituals contributed at least Rs 1.25.[36] The campaign was replicated in early 2021 with the door-to-door nationwide fund-raiser from 15 January till the end of February to raise further resources for the cash-rich Shri Ram Janmbhoomi Teerth Kshetra Trust. The campaign led to communal violence in some states although fortuitously not on the scale of 1989. Following instructions of RSS chief Mohan Bhagwat that not a 'single house' should be missed, VHP activists went from house to house, amid the pandemic, seeking funds. RSS leaders declared they 'expected' every Indian family, regardless of religious faith, to donate for the temple. The Indian media reported that stickers were pasted in houses of families who donated.[37] Absence of donor-stickers marked those who did not contribute for the temple. In history, there are numerous instances of mobs targeting homes that were previously marked out.[38]

People's response to the two mass-contact programmes, separated by almost thirty-two years, highlights the dramatic rise in the support for Hindutva over this period. The shila pujan campaign was to seek support for a demand that had the backing for just one section of Hindu society. It was partisan in nature and there was no socio-political consensus on the demands of the Ayodhya agitation. Several parties and groups of people who principally supported the claim for a Ram temple at Ayodhya, did not back the confrontation set up with this drive.

In contrast to the sectional backing for shila pujan, the fund-raiser in 2021 was not opposed by the majority of mainstream political parties. The campaign was given legitimacy by the state when the President of India became the first donor, albeit in his personal capacity. Several other public personalities who held public offices followed. This marked a blurring of lines between religion and state on the one hand and religious activity and political campaigns on the other hand. The entire fund-raiser was treated as a national programme with the tacit backing of the state.

In 1990, a few scientists from the Central Building Research Institute in Roorkee (then in Uttar Pradesh, now Uttarakhand) clandestinely tested consecrated bricks to assess if they could be used in a single structure. In 2020-21, this institute, and other premier scientific national establishments were involved with the temple trust on a quasi-formal basis with no eyebrows being raised, almost as if it was national duty. Within three decades clandestine collaboration had become officially 'approved' collaboration.

On the eve of the first anniversary of Bhoomi Pujan performed by Modi in August 2020, a senior temple trust functionary briefed journalists on the progress made on the construction of the temple. This person, presumably male, declared that the garbha griha, where idols are installed, would be opened for devotees in December 2023 (it cannot be missed that parliamentary elections are scheduled between March and May 2024) even though the construction will not be completed till at least 2025. As is the norm, the idol of Ram Lalla will have to be ritualistically installed after shifting from the makeshift temple where it is currently placed since March 2020. This ceremony, given the past practice, will certainly be carefully choreographed for maximum political and religious impact, and possibly performed by Modi, the way he laid the foundation and followed it with a speech packed in political content.

Significantly, the unnamed spokesperson of the temple trust also told a journalist that Ram Shila bricks and almost

30 per cent of almost 1.25 lakh cubic feet of special stone carved in the VHP workshop in Ayodhya since 1990 would not be used in construction of the temple. The 'bricks do not have the composite strength required',[203] it was stated. This makes it evident that the Ram Shila programme, as well as the pre-construction activities in Ayodhya from 1990 onwards, were essentially means to mobilize public support and keep people enthused about the agitation.

As it had done for the Ekatmata Yatra programme, the RSS network of cadres fanned out through the country for the two campaigns. Making the Ram shila programme successful was necessary because it was the first mass-contact drive in the agitation and because it was the election year. Senior leaders like Moropant Pingle and H.V. Sheshadri personally coordinated with tehsil-level point persons. Manufacture and transportation of bricks to Ayodhya were supervised by designated RSS–VHP leaders. In these interactions, it was stressed that the novelty of the two rituals should be emphasized just as the ritual of kar seva was used for the first time in a modern political context in the aftermath of Operation Blue Star to rebuild the demolished Akal Takht. The intention was to connect present actions with past rituals. The idea of the nation as God(dess) had already been reiterated into a socio-political campaign with the Ekatmata Yatra. Now, the shila pujan programme, although a political programme, was given the veneer of what Jaffrelot termed 'nationalist devotionalism'.[39]

For the VHP, 1989 was an important year, as it marked its silver jubilee. This was considered as the 'take-off year for the VHP for expansion, growth and creating Hindu consolidation and energisation'.[40] The organization was certain that the Ram temple agitation would enable it to significantly expand its following. The challenge was to convert this into 'permanent infrastructure'.[41] But how could the large number of neo-converts be drawn into the Sangh Parivar fold permanently? How could the basic value system, ethos and ideology be inculcated in them?

*

After considerable deliberation, the leadership drew a plan built on 'three pillars: 'assembly regularity'; 'the temple'; and 'Dharmacharyas'.[42] Assembly meant creating a system of regular interaction between neo-converts and either the old guard or those who had already been initiated into the clan. As part of this effort, regular meetings were to be held at different times—'afternoon for ladies and night for men'. The objective was to develop these gatherings as platforms to refurbish 'children's *sanskar* [culture] activity, youth exercises, *satsang* [religious gatherings] and social service nuclear'.[43]

Focus on 'the temple' was meant to convey that 'temples have been the forts of Hindu society's corporate existence'.[44] However, the problem, as seen by the VHP, was that some of them had 'shrunk to worship function only', and this decline had to be 'reversed'. Temples had to become places where people went not just for personal devotion but also for religio-cultural, nationalistic renewal. On the third plank of the programme, the VHP noted with a certain amount of satisfaction that 'traditional recluses have now come into the towns and are leading the Hindu society. They have bypassed their individual differences and identified the areas of common contribution for the well-being of Hindu society.' Certainly, there was satisfaction that sadhus had been enlisted and were participating in deliberations and programmes putting aside divergences of sects and mutts. This VHP plan was to engage with Hindu society at various tiers—the masses at the assembly level; the purely religion driven, who saw temples only as institutions of deliverance, were encouraged to see these as political symbols of Hindu dominance; and finally, the saints were provided with greater space than what they hitherto had as conductors of rituals on specific occasions from birth to death of an individual.

The VHP was aware that rigidity and stratification of Hinduism were impediments to Hindu consolidation. This explains its forceful and sustained post-Meenakshipuram campaign against religious conversion and repeated calls for social inclusion within Hindu society. Yet, even after more than four decades of efforts beginning with Deoras's lecture in Poona, mentioned previously, this remained a daunting matter for the Sangh Parivar. In July 2021, after expanding the central council of ministers, BJP's spin doctors emphasized how under Modi, the OBC-karan or OBC-fication of the BJP had taken place. This effort followed successful efforts to enlist support of non-dominant Dalit sub-castes. Yet, these efforts still remain a work in progress. After changing gears on the Ram temple issue, the intention was also to utilize this agitation to convert the organization into a cadre-based network on the lines of the RSS and BJP. The objective was to appoint VHP workers in 'every up-khand [sub-area] and noting that such a vast network would require meticulous organisational backup, listing, documentations, registrations, and particulars of committee members and in-charge karyakartas [officials]. Invitees' lists and mailing lists will be maintained. Visits, contacts, correspondences will require a high degree of promptness and regularity.'[45] The task VHP set for itself underscored its commitment to the religio-cultural cause. This was also the first indication of entities within the Sangh Parivar being run as corporatized units with verticals to plan and manage multiple tasks coming their way (after 2014, the BJP has appeared more like a corporate behemoth and less a cadre-based political party).

The VHP also decided to work with other Hindu organizations and win them over for the Ram temple agitation. It advised cadre that these 'organisations must be co-opted and VHP workers should collaborate with them'. Individual units were tasked to ensure that halls (to act as venue for these campaign events) are 'made available in all districts where 200-250 people can gather'. On occasions when VHP did not have connections to secure these halls gratis, activists were directed to rent these. 'The hall must bear the name board of VHP, to be used in the morning for physical exercise of youth, the yoga-shiksha kendras [centres for training in yoga] for adults, sanskar kendras [cultural centres] for children, for ladies in the afternoon and assembly in the night.'[46] In each of these programmes, local units were directed to distribute 'literature, stickers, pictures, lockets, etc.'. Certainly, the VHP was not just preparing for the Ram shila programme but gearing up for a war of sorts. This level of advance planning, networking and resource generation was unmatched in India in 1989. It played a vital role in pitchforking the Sangh Parivar into a pivotal position by the end of the year. The Sangh Parivar also consistently drew other men of god or spiritual leaders to back the demand for the Ram Temple. While Sri Sri Ravi Shankar was controversially named to be part of the mediation committee by the Supreme Court in 2019, Jaggi Vasudev became an ardent backer of the temple. In the earlier decades, popular revered saints and Shankaracharyas were involved with every programme.

As the conclusion of the Hedgewar Centenary Celebrations neared in 1989, the vocabulary of accusations against adversaries expanded. RSS leaders started accusing its critics of 'appeasing' minorities, a common refrain in contemporary politics. Even the moderate-faced Vajpayee claimed that while in the 1984 parliamentary elections, 'the Congress played the Hindu card, this time we are going to play it better'. Vajpayee followed this comment made at Udaipur during the National Executive meeting during 3-5 March, with more strident assertions. On 2 April 1989 while addressing the Hedgewar birth centenary rally in the capital's Ramlila maidan, 'Vajpayee used all the slogans of RSS and declared that Ram Janmabhoomi-Babri Masjid issue is an election issue. Apart from voicing his support for virtual Hindu Rashtra (in the name of consolidating the principle of Hindutva) he issued a warning to the minorities to either give away their distinct identity, or face the worst.'[47]

The 'warning'—conveyed relatively mildly by Vajpayee as compared to demagogues of the VHP and some affiliated organizations—was an expression of the 'anger' among Hindus that the RSS–VHP tried to amplify with the Ayodhya agitation. From Ekatmata Yagna to the Ram Shila yatras and the shilanyas, the effort was all about assertion of Hinduness which was 'long suppressed', so ran the argument. Leaders of the political Hindu constellation articulated in speeches that Lord Ram was not just a god in the Hindu psyche but instead symbolized much more. These arguments were suitably assisted by the government's decision to telecast the TV serials *Ramayan* and *Mahabharat* on the state broadcaster, Doordarshan. It must be noted that the festival of Dussehra was entwined with the mythological tale of the goddess Devi, different forms in different regions, slaying the monster or asura, Mahishasur, in a battle that depicted the victory of good over evil. The public enactment of the Ramayana as Ramlila was a phenomenon restricted chiefly to north India. The TV serial gave it a pan-Indian coverage. By the time the shilanyas ceremony was conducted, the RSS–VHP had successfully elevated Ram as the 'hero of significance to Hindus of all sects' and the Ramayana as the fifth veda.[48]

*

The VHP meticulously planned the shila pujan campaign and the yatras. An estimated four lakh bricks were manufactured in various brick kilns in India and distributed for consecration across India. The final figures of mass participation in these two programmes were indeed impressive: shila pujan took place at 297,705 places and an estimated 110 million people joined the rituals or participated in the yatras.[49] Likewise, for the fund-raiser in 2021, 900,000 volunteers of the Sangh Parivar divided into 175,000 teams reached out to 100 million households. The VHP officially stated that it raised Rs 2500 crore physically. In addition, hundreds of thousands of people donated online, a process still under way during writing. The VHP claimed that to ensure transparency during the process, forty-nine control rooms were set up across India while a group of twenty-three senior activists, backed by chartered accountants kept a hawk's eye on the drive.[50]

Back in 1989, as the programme drew near, adversaries voiced apprehensions regarding the possible fallout of the processions with the bricks. Yet the government made no effort to declare the programme unlawful and stop it. The VHP successfully enlisted the support of the Shankaracharya of Badrinath who performed shila pujan at his Himalayan hermitage on 27 August. This was followed by similar consecration rituals conducted by the Shankaracharya of Kanchi and several other important Hindu religious leaders. The consecration ritual started throughout India on 30 September for which preparations had reached frenzied pace by the beginning of the month.

The entire RSS network of cadre was deployed to make the programme a stirring success. Special care was taken to ensure that southern states too participated in the functions. Reports of shila pujan conducted abroad by the Hindu diaspora poured in to add to the fervour. The international wing of the VHP was instructed to kick-start the programme earlier to ensure that these bricks could be used to publicize support for the Ram temple movement within the global Hindu community. These specially inscribed bricks started reaching the capital by the middle of September and were immediately displayed to the media. Later, these were kept in vantage offices of the VHP and taken out in processions through important cities.

Finally, the shila pujan programme began on a cautious note on 30 September in, as the VHP eventually claimed, five-and-a-half lakh villages and localities in India. However, with elections round the corner, trouble started surfacing as the bricks wended their way from villages to the collecting centres and were later taken to the urban centres from where they were to head for Ayodhya. In the initial phases of the shila pujan programme, people turned out primarily out of curiosity because they had never witnessed such a religious ritual. Ordinary bricks wrapped in the symbolic red silk scarves with vermilion marks smeared on them were venerated. Offerings were made in front of the bricks. For the lakhs of devotees who assembled in temples where the rituals were being conducted, the bricks symbolized the temple at Ayodhya, although these were never used for constructing it.

These processions were escorted or led by hordes of VHP activists, mobilized in the course of months of planning, and they ensured smooth completion of the newly conceptualized ritual. These activists also acted as 'minders' of these bricks that were taken out in processions before being loaded in specially hired trucks to be transported to Ayodhya. This ceremony provided the first appearance of the 'angry Hindu'. They sported saffron bandannas, shouted aggressive slogans and, in many cities and towns, doubled up as agent provocateurs when processions passed through Muslim-dominated localities. In these situations, these youngsters, incited by the local VHP leadership, did what they always did in riotous situations—ridiculed and provoked the Muslims. This time, however, there was a vital difference—these processions carried consecrated bricks purportedly to be used to construct a temple to deify the mythological hero who was now projected as the epitome of the Indian spirit and soul. Every person who opposed the programme was depicted a traitor and descendant of the 'villainous' Mughal emperor, Babur—*Babur ke aulad*.

The vilification of Muslims was also greatly aided by Ayatollah Khomeini issuing a formal edict calling for the execution of the celebrated author, Salman Rushdie. Even though the Indian government had bowed to Muslim pressure and banned *Satanic Verses* in October 1988, some Bombay-based groups joined a transnational campaign against the book. For the developing constituency of the political Hindu, the ban by the Rajiv Gandhi government was another instance of Muslim appeasement. Muslims in some other cities too joined this global assertion against the book, an act which fuelled Hindu anger against them. On 24 February 1989, the first Friday after the fatwa was issued, the police intervened to disperse protestors in a 'great stigmatised Muslim locality' in Bombay.[51] Eleven people reportedly died in these disturbances. This gave the VHP an opportunity to mount a campaign contending that if Muslims could unite for a pan-Islamic cause which 'hurt' their religious sentiments, it was not only justified but essential for Hindus to unite and back a movement for seeking rights to construct a temple to deify Lord Ram who embodied Indian nationalism or Bharatiyata.

The ban on Rushdie's book came in handy for the VHP when the police in Hazaribagh (then in Bihar) turned down the demand for the shila yatra procession through the road on which the local Jama Masjid was located. In response, the VHP staged an angry demonstration which made the administration relent. But fears that the procession through a sensitive area would be provocative were not unfounded. As the procession made its way through the winding streets, a bomb exploded and nineteen lives were lost. The incident was used by the VHP as well as other pro-Babri groups to incite communal tensions. Riots erupted in similar fashion in several others cities, most notably in Kota, Badaun, Indore and Bhagalpur, the last one being among the goriest conflagrations between the two communities. Everywhere the story was almost the same: the Ram shila yatra would slow down when crossing a Muslim-dominated locality, the slogans would get more provocative and violence would erupt. In the long run, it mattered little whether someone threw a crude bomb or cracker from one of the overlooking parapets, or if someone in the procession knifed a local trader or a resident of the locality.

A home ministry internal report stated: 'No single

issue has so adversely affected communal harmony between Hindus and Muslims as the Ram Janmabhoomi-Babri Masjid controversy.'[52] The twin shila pujan and shilanyas ceremonies had a direct correlation with the rise in incidence of communal riots: The average number of communal riots jumped from 400 between 1980 and 1985 to almost 700 between 1986 and 1989 and from 1000 in 1990 to 2000 in 1993. Of the eighty-five seats the BJP won in the parliamentary polls in 1989, as many as forty-seven constituencies were ravaged by communal riots triggered by the Ayodhya dispute. Buta Singh claimed in a subsequent interview that the government had attempted to 'save the situation'. As home minister, he had tried to 'defuse the situation which had surcharged every village in the country'. He conceded that the programme involving the consecrated bricks had been a runaway success and as the date of the shilanyas programme approached, the government was in no position to put a stop to it as 'there would have been a worse situation'.[53]

*

Once the RSS lent its full weight to the shila pujan programme and shilanyas ceremony, it was a matter of time before the BJP would embrace the cause of the Ram temple as its own too. In June 1989, the nondescript hill station of Palampur in Himachal Pradesh was chosen as the venue for a crucial meeting of the BJP's national executive. The most important resolution adopted at this meet was the one on the Ram Janmabhoomi issue. It started with strident criticism of the Congress and other parties for 'callous unconcern ... towards the sentiments of the overwhelming majority in this country, the Hindus'.[54] The party resolution thereafter made the following significant points: The Ayodhya dispute cannot be resolved by a court of law; no court can adjudicate if Babur actually invaded Ayodhya, destroyed a temple and built a mosque in its place; secularism in India had come to be equated with an allergy to Hinduism, and a synonym for minority appeasement; secularism, according to our Constitution makers, did not mean rejection of India's cultural heritage; sentiments of the people must be respected and Ram Janmasthan (or Janmabhoomi) handed over to the Hindus through a negotiated settlement or by legislation—litigation certainly being no answer.

Peculiarly, while calling for negotiated settlement, the BJP also demanded that the Rajiv Gandhi regime must 'adopt the same positive approach in respect of Ayodhya that the Nehru Government did with regard to Somnath'. The BJP, however, while saying that the 'the site in dispute should be handed over to the Hindus', added that a new mosque could be 'built at some other suitable place', a suggestion mooted decades earlier that was eventually endorsed by the Supreme Court more than three decades later in their November 2019 verdict. But for the Congress accepting this suggestion in 1989 ran the risk of similar demands being made on other shrines already on the VHP 'list', besides of course the ones in Varanasi and Mathura, long part of the demand of Hindu nationalists. This possibility became a reality when immediately after the final verdict, the challenge to the Places of Worship Act, 1991 was revived and court cases expedited, not just on the Mathura and Varanasi shrines, but also a mosque in Lucknow that was, like before, claimed to have been built after demolishing a mythologically linked temple.

The BJP's decision to come out openly in support of the Ram temple in 1989 created problems for the nationwide anti-Congress alliance that required to be strung together to defeat the ruling party in the imminent parliamentary elections. Advani was aware of this and acknowledged that the problem arose because the Janata Dal was 'not a single, homogeneous party. It is a condominium of diverse factions.' What further complicated matters was that while some of the factions 'appreciate BJP's role in Indian politics, and are keen to cooperate, some others can hardly conceal their animus towards us'. Advani cautioned his party colleagues that given the animosity of a certain section of the Janata Dal to the BJP, it had to 'move ahead with cautious optimism', while working out an electoral relationship with it. In its 1993 White Paper on the issue, the BJP termed the Palampur resolution as the 'turning point' in the agitation for the Ram temple as by the 'middle of 1989, the Ayodhya movement had reached a state and status in Indian public life when it was no more possible to ignore its effect in politics, including electoral politics'.

Paradoxically, according to the BJP White Paper of 1993, none of the non-BJP parties recognized that the Ayodhya movement had the potential to 'become a powerful expression of the disapproval of the post-Independence distortion of national politics' and remained concerned with their own targets. The Congress was convinced that damage to its electoral prospects could be limited by allowing the shilanyas. The party started exploring ways to declare the site chosen for this ceremony as undisputed. Such a declaration would prevent violation of the Allahabad High Court order to maintain status quo of the disputed site. Non-Congress opposition parties were chiefly driven by their objective of ousting Rajiv Gandhi and remained willing to partner the BJP. They certainly were not looking beyond the impending elections. The communist parties articulated the danger of electorally allying with the BJP, but even they were more keen on ousting Rajiv Gandhi and did not stress on the necessity to isolate the BJP. The result was that when the results of the November 1989 elections were declared it was evident that the Ram temple issue had emerged as the 'central issue in national politics and set the political agenda of the nation in the years that followed'.[55]

While attacking the Congress and raking up the Ayodhya issue during the election campaign, BJP leaders systematically questioned notions on which there was political consensus even among its allies—secular, communal and national. When the polls were called on 17 October 1989, especially after the BJP became part of the anti-Congress bandwagon, it was evident that it would perform creditably 'but even for the biggest optimist, the party's showing (85 seats) had come as a surprise'.[56] The RSS general secretary, H.V. Sheshadri, declared in an interview that the RSS had been stressing for several years that 'it is the Hindus, awakened and made conscious of their national responsibilities who can give a healthy turn to the degenerated political culture. From this angle there appears to be quite a distinct improvement, which is reflected in the vastly improved position of the BJP.'[57]

There was no doubt that a new political vocabulary was in the offing and this would irrevocably alter the jargon of the past. The 1989 results, coupled with the verdict of 1991 when Advani famously declared, 'the victor came second', heralded the unfurling of 'unapologetic Hinduism'[58] and the BJP finally '[catching] up with its identity, spelling out its ideological position, without a trace of compromise and expediency'.[59] A pro-BJP commentator was delighted that after '42 years of independence, the Hindu worm was turning, and wisdom demands that the Hindus' aspirations to be masters in their own country are fruitfully and constructively channelised'.[60] It took almost a quarter of a century before this sentiment came to fruition but a foundation had been made.

The shilanyas ceremony, which undoubtedly announced the BJP's coming of age in Indian politics, was ironically conducted on the day the Berlin Wall fell. For Hindu nationalists, this coincidence was reason for much comment, and it was contended that this too, like the installation of the idol in December 1949, was an act of divinity. For Jay Dubashi, the happenstance underscored that while history had its quirks, 'there was a method in its madness'. It was contended that with the laying of the 200-odd bricks in the pit dug at the spot where a Muslim graveyard was located, 'a temple was going up in Ayodhya', while 'a communist temple was being demolished five thousand miles away in Europe. If this is not history, I do not know what is.'[61] For another journalist who became a BJP member of the Rajya Sabha, the coinciding of the two events could not be dismissed: 'Ayodhya, too, was a movement for change and it too was energised by a staggering participation of youth.'[62]

The fall of the Berlin Wall marked the collapse of communism. Its fall and the digging up of a historical graveyard could hardly be compared even though efforts were made to convey the latter event as being equally important. The shilanyas ceremony represented the complete failure of the state to prevent the desecration of a historical site. It was after all 'permitted' by a panic-stricken Centre without clearance from the Ayodhya Special Development Authority after, at a meeting convened by Rajiv Gandhi and attended by the chief secretaries along with the home secretary and the directors general of police of all states (another of chief ministers was held later), 'no one was willing to take on this campaign of shila pujan and shilanyas. Everybody said that it was beyond us, we cannot help...'[63]

A galaxy of political leaders of different shades flocked to Faizabad–Ayodhya prior to the shilanyas. Not just Buta Singh, but even the tottering Congress leader Kamlapati Tripathi, CPI leader C. Rajeshwar Rao, V.P. Singh and Syed Shahabuddin had reached the twin towns. On 2 November the VHP had suo motu identified a spot where it intended to conduct the shilanyas and hoisted a saffron flag to mark the place. This action presented the government with a fait accompli and thereafter, it became imperative on the Centre to find ways to declare that the shilanyas ceremony at the chosen spot did not violate any law or judicial order. Time was running out and influential Hindu saints were contacted by the government to get the VHP to either postpone the function or give it another shape.

When this failed, the Centre moved the Allahabad High Court on 6 November asking it to clarify its order of 14 August whereby it had asked for status quo to be maintained insofar as the disputed shrine was concerned. The Court was also astute and did not want to rule if the spot selected by the VHP for the shilanays was outside the disputed area or not. It merely ruled on 7 November that the previous order for maintaining status quo was for areas within the limits of EFGH in the site plan lying before the court. The next day, the home minister sat with a motley crowd that included the sub-registrar of the Allahabad High Court and the advocate general of the state government. The law officer ruled that the site of the shilanyas was clearly outside the aforesaid area. Even Shahabuddin acquiesced in this because, as he said in a later conversation, 'Objecting at that stage would have caused mayhem.'[64] The BJP was aware that legal clearance for the shilanyas was a mere smokescreen. It noted in its White Paper that 'the Uttar Pradesh government and the Central government caved in, under mass pressure and could not stop the shilanyas'.

The ceremony was a long-drawn affair, starting close to noon on 9 November and continuing till the next day. The foundation of the first brick was symbolically laid by Kameshwar Chaupal, a Harijan member of the VHP who was later shifted to the BJP and became a member of the state legislature in Bihar before being appointed as member of the Ram temple trust. His choice had the signature of the RSS sarsanghchalak who had mandated social inclusion in RSS activities almost a decade-and-a-half ago. At a press conference in the evening after the ceremony concluded, Ashok Singhal, flanked by Vijaya Raje Scindia, declared: 'We have today laid the foundation stone of a Hindu Rashtra.' The VHP announced that the next phase of the movement would be discussed at a meeting of religious leaders in Allahabad on 27-28 January 1990.

The new Janata Dal government assumed office on 2 December 1990 and in the ensuing euphoria—which had to be cut short after Home Minister Mufti Mohammed Sayeed's daughter, Rubaiyya, was kidnapped—the government lost sight of the important date in the VHP timeline. Like the previous government, V.P. Singh's regime too did not act in time and remained complacent. It turned out to be no smarter than the regime it had replaced and would pay for this slip in less than a year.

6

Demolition Day

'No human heart is denied empathy. No religion can demolish that by indoctrination. No culture, no nation and nationalism—nothing can touch it because it is empathy.'

—Dayananda Saraswati

The word 'egregious', which means 'extremely bad in a way that is very noticeable', is used predominantly to add negative characteristics to a violation of norm, convention or law. In November 2019, the Supreme Court of India used this word to describe the Babri Masjid's demolition in December 1992. It further added that the infringement of the rule of law had been 'in utter violation of the order passed by this Hon'ble Court' and required to be seen in conjunction with 'damage to the mosque in 1934, its desecration in [on 22-23 December] 1949 leading to the ouster of the Muslims'. Despite concluding that the two events in post-Independence India, spread over forty-three years, first altered and later obliterated the Babri Masjid, the apex court awarded the entire land in Ayodhya to Hindu parties.

Seldom has a single day in the history of a city or town

impacted a nation's politics the way events in Ayodha on 6 December 1992 did. Till that time, hope existed, however slim, of the mosque either being restored to the Muslim community, or at least its status quo being maintained as it had been since 1949. The then BJP general secretary, K.N. Govindacharya, while speaking at the launch of my first book in January 1994, hypothesized that the demolition of the Babri Masjid was as significant as the storming of the Bastille. His claim appeared a tad overstretched, given that his party had only weeks ago suffered an unforeseen defeat in assembly elections in Uttar Pradesh, Madhya Pradesh and Himachal Pradesh, the first after the demolition. The results demonstrated that despite overwhelming Hindu support for the Ram temple agitation, the BJP could be electorally humbled by forging strategic caste alliances—the consistent obstacle to Hindu political consolidation.

Emmanuel Joseph Sieyès, the French Roman Catholic abbot, clergyman, political writer and, most significantly, one of the chief theorists of the French Revolution famously remarked: 'What is the Third Estate? Everything. What has it been up till now in the political order? Nothing. What does it desire to be? Something.' The Third Estate in eighteenth-century France was the commoner who was not part of the clergy or the nobility. In separate statements, following tumultuous events on 6 December 1992, many religio-cultural nationalist leaders regretted the demolition. This was not how the day was planned, they claimed. But the people had taken it on themselves to 'correct' a historical 'wrong' or 'avenge humiliation' in the past.

Although the RSS–BJP–VHP took ownership of the agitation and aimed to harness political benefits accruing from it, the 'spontaneous' destruction of the mosque was stated to be the handiwork of Sieyès's 'Third Estate'. The parties ignored the fact that this mass of people had not lined up to destroy the mosque of their own volition but were enlisted by these organizations in the course of an epochal movement. When it came to taking responsibility, however, it was pinned on 'anti-social/anti-national elements'. (This was stated by Justice S.K. Yadav, judge of the CBI court in the Babri Masjid demolition criminal case. The verdict was publicized to claim that leaders of the agitation were not involved in act.) Yet pointers exist to a prior plan, known to a networked band of leaders and activists who had the full-throated support of people who had been aroused sufficiently enough to risk life and spare time to 'restore' Hindu dignity. The thousands who assembled in Ayodhya that day were testimony to the Sangh Parivar's success in recruiting a new economic and social class of people who had previously maintained an arm's length from it.

*

The events of 6 December 1992, leading to the Babri Masjid's demolition, cannot be deciphered merely by reconstructing the chronology of the day. The conduct of dramatis personae on both sides—agitators and state machinery—their speeches, acts of commission and omission over a considerable period of time, require detailing for a comprehensive appraisal of the day. In hindsight, it became clear that the state and a large section of the political system collaborated to demolish the mosque. Over a period of almost a decade prior to the demolition, these public figures successfully converted an issue, which initially did not motivate people, into an emotive one with the capacity to mobilize masses in tens of thousands repeatedly. The central characters in this national-spirit-altering episode are ironically not just those who waged the agitation but even the ones who could have quelled it and find a solution within the framework of the law and the Constitution.

There are manifold narratives to the events leading up to the demolition and the conclusions are often contradictory. Most starkly, the CBI's special court judgement on 30 September 2020 is at complete odds with the Supreme Court's view that the vandalism that led to the destruction needed 'restitution to the Muslim community for the unlawful destruction of their place of Worship'. The CBI judge's verdict, however, was strange for it remained blind to evidence that was available while the trial was going on. In her deposition to the Liberhan Commission of Inquiry,[1] Uma Bharti, one of the accused, 'categorically took responsibility' for the demolition. This admission made it amply clear that 'it was not an unseen force that demolished the mosque, [but] human beings did it'.[2] Yet, Justice Yadav said that 'nobody could be blamed', adding blasphemously that 'administration and police had so many things to do other than taking care of the security of the "structure"'. A reading of the judgement makes it evident that Justice Yadav chose to rely on exhibits that were handiwork of partisan institutions like the local intelligence unit which, almost without fail, acts as the state government's handmaiden, displaying none of the autonomy that is required of intelligence agencies.[3]

Additionally, Justice Yadav based his conclusions on assumptions that defy common sense. For instance, he asserted that 'since there was a mandate from the highest court that status quo should be maintained there, no one would have wanted to go against the Supreme Court as it is held in reverence and obeyed by all'. It is no secret that orders of various courts, the apex one included, are routinely violated and questioned by all and sundry, especially those from the political class. In contrast to the peculiar reasoning of Justice Yadav—'Advani could not have been party to the crime as "he had expressed sorrow over the demolition of the mosque"', and that 'Kalyan Singh had given a commitment to the Supreme Court that the status quo in Ayodhya would be maintained, he could not have been part of a conspiracy'—Justice Liberhan was more meticulous, although the delay in submitting the report played a role in the fact that there was little follow-up to his findings.

The report of the Liberhan Commission of Inquiry was of the 'considered opinion that the security apparatus was non-existent in Ayodhya on 6 December 1992 … The police and other personnel deployed had been bound down into an ineffective role and had specific instructions against any substantive action. They were to ensure that the (state) government (of the BJP) achieved its election manifesto. The state administration was there to appease the political executive by helping it in consolidating their hold on the general public.'[4] This observation established that the state BJP government ignored its constitutional obligations to maintain law and order. Instead of taking pre-emptive action to prevent breach of security measures and judicial directives, it was a willing partner in the destruction of the medieval mosque. Justice Liberhan's remarks also substantiated the commonly held belief that the Centre, with P.V. Narasimha Rao as prime minister, did little to prevent the BJP's free run. As such, while the BJP and its affiliates in the Sangh Parivar were directly responsible, the Union government was complicit in the destruction.

The Union government was aware from mid-November 1992 that events in Ayodhya were heading for a flashpoint and this would imperil the shrine. Acknowledgement of this is established in a noting in the official file,[5] in which the Union home minister, Shankarrao Bhavrao Chavan, expressed 'apprehension about the generation of religious frenzy at the proposed karseva and again held out a veiled threat of imposition of President's rule'.[6] The Centre, however, did not take any action despite reports with it that the local administration had arranged for extra hospital beds and ambulances, and had erected adequate barricades to regulate crowds likely to range between one and two lakh people. Besides this, tens of thousands of kar sevaks were to camp in nearby cities, ready to march at short notice. The Centre estimated in late November that between four to five lakh kar sevaks were expected to reach the temple town before 6 December.[7]

Ample evidence exists to demonstrate that the Centre did not take note of its own intelligence reports regarding plans to demolish the mosque. Instead, it 'relied on the assurance given by the Uttar Pradesh government'.[8] Additionally, the prime minister 'had great faith in the ability of the RSS leadership to prevent the immediate demolition of the shrine, a trust that few besides him even in the RSS clan shared'. This trust emerged from Rao's proximity 'with several senior leaders of the RSS clan [which] lulled him into complacency and he believed in their assertions that the Supreme Court order would not be violated'.[9] Yet, his cabinet ministers did not share his optimism. A senior journalist, then working in *The Telegraph*, met the human resource development minister, Arjun Singh, on 4 December after his return from a meeting with Kalyan Singh in Lucknow. Singh had no doubts that 'anything may happen any day'.[10]

Narasimha Rao had become prime minister in June 1991

in the backdrop of an economic crisis and the balance of payment emergency which forced the previous government to pledge gold. Consequently, Rao drafted in Manmohan Singh as finance minister and backed economic reforms which he embarked on. The BJP was keen not to be seen as a 'single issue party'. It was also in power in UP, MP, Rajasthan and Himachal Pradesh and was committed to de-escalate communal tension. This compelled moderation of its stance on the Ayodhya conflict. The party also broadened its religio-cultural nationalistic plank by launching its then president, M.M. Joshi, on an Ekta Yatra (Unity March) from Kanyakumari, the southern tip of India, with plans to hoist the Indian flag in Srinagar on Republic Day 1992. By then, the internal security situation in the Kashmir Valley had turned unstable with frequent instances of violence. As a consequence, Central rule had been imposed in the state and the flight of Hindus had begun. Rao thereby believed that BJP leaders would play the game of brinkmanship but 'sober' elements within the party would eventually prevail over belligerent sections of the saffron fraternity, as in the past, to either push back the planned assemblage in Ayodhya on 6 December, or disperse after a token programme.

In the weeks preceding the demolition, leaders of the Sangh Parivar spoke with a forked tongue. Kalyan Singh assured Rao that 'karseva would consist of singing bhajans and kirtans'. On the other hand, during his yatra from Varanasi to Ayodhya to drum up support for the gathering, in an address to a raucous audience, Advani emphatically stated that the programme 'would be performed with bricks and shovels and not by merely singing devotional songs'. Rao went by private pledges that status quo would not be disturbed, dismissing assertions like Advani's as rhetoric. Although an incisive political leader, he went by the chief minister's assurance while disregarding the more weighty Advani's public claims. It is also possible that Rao was guided by his judgement that demolition of the mosque would 'deprive' the Sangh Parivar of a 'hate symbol' for use in future, and they would thus safeguard it. However, this turned out to be Rao's biggest political miscalculation and added to several blunders of the Congress party in the handling of the Ram Janmabhoomi movement.

*

After being elected to government in UP in June 1991, the BJP claimed that the verdict was a 'mandate to build the Ram temple'. The same was reiterated by the RSS. Chief Minister Kalyan Singh moved swiftly and in the first week of October his government acquired 2.77 acres of land in front of the disputed shrine. Although ostensibly done to 'promote tourism and provide amenities to pilgrims', the real intention was to transfer this land to the VHP-controlled trust. The plan was to allow this body to begin construction on undisputed land, while the legal case continued. This was a ploy to unhinge the construction process from the disputed shrine and served two purposes. First, it appeased belligerent Sangh Parivar activists. Land acquisition was aimed at providing a sense of 'progress' in attaining the goal. Second, the saffron combine believed that once construction of the temple commenced, even if on undisputed but contiguous land, no government, even an adversarial one, would be able to stop it later because this would cost Hindu support.

The state government's decision was challenged in the Allahabad High Court which ruled that during the pendency of the case, the state government could neither transfer the land to any party nor build any permanent structure on it. Although this upset the plans of the BJP and the VHP, the state administration ingenuously began destroying existing buildings, many of them small temples, on the plea that the court had merely prevented construction, not demolition. The Centre was within its powers to step in but chose not to. Arjun Singh, also challenger to the prime minister from a secularist position, stated 'the (Rao) government lost its chance by not acting the moment the demolitions started'.[11] Kalyan Singh's regime additionally granted 42.09 acres of land in the vicinity of the disputed complex to the VHP trust to implement a long-standing project of designing and building a Ram Katha Park. These land transfers took place through late 1991 and the first half of 1992.

In early May 1992, the VHP ratcheted up its plans on the Ram temple. It organized a meeting of religious leaders associated with the VHP in Ujjain. At its conclusion, leaders announced resumption of kar seva from 9 July. The Rao government did not act with alertness but casually parleyed with VHP leaders. The kar seva was started on the ground in front of the Babri Masjid which was previously levelled by the state administration after tearing down pre-existing buildings. VHP activists started raising a three-tiered platform, contending that although cast in concrete, this was not a permanent structure. Construction activity continued for more than a fortnight but the Centre took no action. The local administration turned out in full strength to help VHP activists when 'nights merged into day in the temple-town as thousands of kar sevaks would lie huddled together in the massive tents that were erected in the acquired land. Concrete mixers continued to churn throughout and the platform steadily started rising in height. Loud speakers blared devotional songs rendered to the tune of various popular Hindi film songs.'[12] In hindsight, when the temple's construction began after Bhoomi Pujan in August 2020, it was clear that all such past construction activity were mere smokescreens to provide a sense of progress to the cadre. Eventually, Rao was goaded to act and he requested the disputing parties to join the government on the negotiating table. The supporters of the Ram temple agreed to suspend kar seva as a break would provide opportunity to regroup.

The Rao government, however, did not utilize the breather. In fairness, though, neither the VHP nor the Muslim parties were serious on a mediated settlement. They remained rigid in their stance. But by its inaction the Centre left the door open for the VHP to later claim that the Centre made no effort in resolving the dispute through negotiation. Eventually, the VHP's three-month moratorium expired in late October and a fresh date was set for kar seva to resume. This day—6 December—would forever alter Indian polity. The RSS clan had consistently overplayed its hand and as a result the agitation was not completely in control of the early spearheads. The Shiv Sena, then an ally of the BJP, started pursuing an independent course for it sensed that an opportunity existed to stop being seen solely as a chauvinistic and anti-migrant regional party. Its ambition was to outdo the RSS clan in taking up 'Hindu causes'. As 6 December neared, the temple town resembled a sea of saffron bandanna-sporting and angry-looking Hindu youth, driven by the desire to seek 'revenge' by erasing 'the symbol of national shame'. It was amply evident that events were moving towards a denouement of sorts.

*

In December 1991, the Supreme Court transferred to itself all writ petitions pertaining to the acquisition of land in

Ayodhya. But it sat on the matter till November 1992, not stating if the restriction on construction could be lifted. Various constituents of the Sangh Parivar hoped the apex court would vacate the Allahabad High Court stay order on building any fresh structure or part of it on the 2.77 acres of acquired land. A select group of senior leaders from the saffron triumvirate—RSS, BJP and VHP—met on 2 November to weigh options in the event of the apex court not vacating the stay. But as the Liberhan Commission noted, they left no record of what transpired and what was agreed upon. However, on the basis of a newspaper report and the deposition of K.S. Sudarshan, the commission stated that the leaders decided that 'it would be preferable to give up the [Kalyan Singh] government rather than give up the construction of the temple'. Plans were also deliberated on how 'the Congress could be reduced to merely a reacting agent so that the Sangh could seize the political initiative'.[13] This was the first telltale sign of the saffron fraternity treating the Ram temple issue as part of a larger political project of establishing ideological dominance and seizing political power, whichever came first. That the Ram temple agitation was part of a wider political goal was already evident in a popular graffiti used in the course of the movement—*Ram drohi toh desh drohi*, if you are an opponent of the Ram (temple), you are a traitor. L.K. Advani rephrased this a few days later when he was accused of being opposed to the Indian Constitution: 'Those who were opposing "Vande Mataram" are opposing the Ayodhya movement,' he said. His declaration spawned a slogan—*Agar Hindustan mein rahna hoga, toh Vande Mataram kahna hoga.* Advani's assertion and the slogan were a response to long-felt discomfort among sections of Indian liberals and secularists who considered that Bankimchandra Chattopadhyay's song was steeped in religious symbolism and which is why it was not sung during official functions. In the years to come, 'Vande Mataram', like Jai Shri Ram, was used by the political leadership of the saffron brigade as a battle cry of a resurgent Hindu society.

When the Supreme Court was finally prodded into action, it showed itself as being blind to insincere statements being made by every party, including the Central and state governments. Inaction on part of the Centre and the judiciary benefited the Sangh Parivar for it could proceed with its plans to demolish the mosque. The apex court took the state government's assurance at face value and declined to appoint the Union government as the receiver for the mosque. Had this been done, the Centre would have been legally bound to protect the Babri Masjid and could not have been willingly complicit in its destruction.

Reports of the ground reality, from media as well as intelligence sources, suggested that Ayodhya was literarily bursting at its seams. Two Union cabinet committee meetings on 20 and 26 November, with Arjun Singh in the chair in the absence of Rao, took note of the worrisome assembly. Singh, Sharad Pawar and S.B. Chavan who comprised this group estimated that unless the inflow of kar sevaks was checked, their numbers would eventually swell to anything between four and five lakhs.[14] Yet, the state government argued before the Supreme Court that 'contemplation of immediate coercive action on part of Government might be counter-productive'.[15] The Centre fed the state government's intention to lie low amid continuing inflow of kar sevaks and damage to smaller Islamic structures like mazars and local mosques. It wrote a letter to the BJP ministry in Lucknow, reminding it of the 'violent reaction and damage to the disputed structure' in

1990. The court was thereby presented with an ingenuous argument: if a previous attack on the Babri Masjid by a smaller mob could not be prevented by security forces, how could the state government take stern action in November 1992 when large crowds had already gathered with the intention of razing the mosque to the ground.[16]

Eventually, on 25 November, the country's highest court observed that the 'situation is not without its emotive surcharges; at these trying times the capacity for statesmanship of those who bear the burden of government—of good government—is put to test. They should display statesmanship and deal with matters in such a way that would not result in the destruction of constitutional institutions and in the upsetting of social equilibrium.' Yet it provided no administrative direction and merely expressed hope that the state government would adhere to its commitment and not permit construction on the land whose acquisition by the state was still under scrutiny in the Allahabad High Court. The apex court merely warned that in the event of the state not being in position to prevent violation of its order, it shall 'have to consider prayers ... for appointment of a Receiver or direction to the Central government to ensure obedience of the court's order'.[17] The state counsel's response to this was a shade ominous for he declared that 'to assuage the religious feeling of Ram Bhakts, construction at some other place would take place'.[18] With this being the stated objective, there was little that the security personnel would be able to do on 6 December if the mob decided to focus energies on 'that place' (read disputed site) instead of the demarcated 'other place'. Oddly, the apex court did not see through this manoeuvre.

However, the apex court's observer, tasked to report immediately to it if any construction work was carried out, chose to be guided solely by the letter of the appointment and not its spirit. Consequently, he did not act as the court's 'eyes and ears on the ground and update it with any—and all—developments which might have had any bearing on the developing situation'. The Liberhan Commission noted that 'by construing the wide ambit of the SC's order in a very artificial and narrow perspective, the observer kept the Court in the dark and prevented the Court from having access to the material and happenings which might have enabled it to take more proactive stance and pass appropriate orders'. Figuratively speaking, the writing was scribbled all over the walls of the Babri Masjid. In hindsight, it appears that each of those who could protect it from the rampaging crowd wilfully chose not to read these lines.

As 'demolition day' loomed ahead, the BJP started bargaining with the Centre. The state government sought clearance from the Centre to allow the VHP and others to go ahead with the 6 December programme. Instead of offering to prevent any activity remotely resembling construction on the entire 2.77 acres of land, Kalyan Singh's regime promised to 'ensure the safety and security of the structure' if the Centre permitted kar seva. The Liberhan Commission later found this nothing but subterfuge, an act which 'itself speaks about the intention of the state [government]'.[19] Rao personally chose to rely on promises made by the VHP leaders and remain blind to what was unfolding on the ground. Vinay Katiyar, the Bajrang Dal chief, in his deposition stated that the prime minister asked him how kar seva could be conducted without violating the apex court's order. He had replied: 'It would be carried on undisputed land.'[20] While it was expected that leaders of the Sangh Parivar would speak in multiple voices to confuse the Centre, one thought that a leader of Rao's astuteness would comprehend the real intent and take preventive action. It is not that he was unaware of a public declaration by Champat Rai, the local VHP leader and manager for construction of the Ram temple, who was eventually appointed general secretary of the Shri Ram Janmabhoomi Teerth Kshetra Trust. At a conference in Ayodhya on 24 November, Rai asserted that 'it had been decided to adopt guerrilla strategy for 6 December'. His own words: '*Guerrilla shaily apnaenge kar seva mein.*'[21] Rao also had access to intelligence reports that Bajrang Dal and Shiv Sena were 'vying with each other for the "fame" of blowing up the disputed structure'.[22]

*

By early December, it was evident that assembled kar sevaks had no need to resort to guerrilla tactics as Rai threatened. Instead, they were free to do as they willed, and in broad daylight. Properties of Muslims in the temple town were targeted with forces looking away. The police registered a first information report regarding an incident on 2 December. It recorded damage to at least two mosques in Ayodhya, defilement of mazars and graves of ordinary people besides attacks on houses of a couple of Muslim residents of the town. Peculiarly, a local intelligence report that Justice Yadav cited in his judgement stated that these acts of desecration were committed by Muslims with the intention of provoking communal riots. On learning about these incendiary acts, the Union home secretary directed Central forces in Ayodhya to be on red alert. They merely remained 'alert', orders for 'action' never came. Justice Liberhan recorded that despite attack on Muslim properties, the administration 'did not become cautious' and took 'no steps to contain the crowd or their aggressiveness'.

Despite being instrumental in galvanizing the Ayodhya agitation with the Rath Yatra in 1990, Advani showed up late in Ayodhya—at midnight on 5 December. M.M. Joshi also reached at the same time and that left the duo with little to do but be bystanders. While they assured the local administration of peaceful kar seva, BJP lawmaker in the Lok Sabha, Swami Chinmayananda, who was arrested in September 2019 on rape charges (but eventually acquitted in March 2021), proclaimed that construction of the temple would be initiated. Ayodhya town did not sleep the night before the final assault. The streets reverberated with a variety of slogans: *mitti naheen khiskayenge, dhancha tor kar jayenge* (we shall not move the soil but will demolish the structure); *jo roke mandir nirman, bhejo usko Pakistan* (whoever opposes the Ram temple must be sent to Pakistan); *jis Hindu ka khoon na khaule, woh khoon naheen paani hai* (the Hindu whose blood does not boil is not blood but water); *Babur bole Jai Siya Ram, Akbar bole Jai Siya Ram* (both Babur and Akbar are now chanting 'hail' Lord Ram); and *badi khushi ki baat hai, police hamare saath hai* (it's a matter of joy that the police is with us). That night, VHP activists 'carried out the rehearsal of symbolic karseva in which only a couple of hundred people participated'. No outsider was allowed to witness it so no one has an idea of what the gathered kar sevaks were tutored about.[23] This was documented and photographed by the media[24] yet Justice Yadav angrily queried in his judgement: 'It is not for journalists to tell us whether the security measures were adequate or not.' The chief minister turned down the Union home secretary's advice to deploy more troops, and no further action was taken, possibly because the Centre realized that an estimated 2.5 lakhs kar sevaks had already trooped into the temple town.

As per the Hindu almanac, the kar seva was scheduled to commence at 12.15 p.m. on 6 December. A platform near the Babri Masjid was earmarked for the ritual. This decision, termed a 'sham paper decision' taken by the VHP's Kendriya Marg Darshan Mandal, was taken a day before the actual demolition.[25] The BJP disputed most conclusions of the Liberhan Commission. During a discussion in the Lok Sabha under Rule 193 on 7 December 2009, Rajnath Singh asserted that Justice Liberhan's conclusions were based solely on media reports. Ironically, Justice Yadav in his verdict too doubted the professional ability of journalists.[26]

Eventually on 6 December, select Hindu religious personalities associated with the VHP sat on the earmarked platform. They were assisted by almost one hundred RSS swayamsevaks, while baton-wielding constables of the PAC (accused of bias in favour of Hindus for decades) stood on watch. Other leaders associated with the movement were on a stage a short distance away. Many veterans sat on the terrace of an adjoining building. The BJP initially instructed its lawmakers and ministers not to participate in kar seva. Later, this order was inexplicably rescinded. Senior RSS–BJP–VHP leaders, including L.K. Advani, M.M. Joshi, Uma Bharti, Ashok Singhal and Sadhvi Rithambara met at Vinay Katiyar's residence in the morning before moving to the platform where symbolic kar seva was to begin shortly past noon. Their arrival enthused the kar sevaks gathered close by. Paying scant regard to the official mahurat, they broke through the security cordon and began performing rituals before being physically evicted by swayamsevaks. The ineffectiveness of the policepersons was proven. Yet, senior leaders took little action to prevent the gathered mob from becoming more belligerent. Instead, they retreated to the Ram Katha Park where many from their fraternity were already making fiery speeches. Possibly, they realized that it was much too late to dismount from the rampaging tiger.

Significantly, Advani deposed before the Liberhan Commission that he would not have joined the programme on 6 December had it not been for the organizers' acceptance of the apex court's order, agreeing to perform symbolic kar seva. Although this was at variance with his statement while mobilizing people to gather in Ayodhya, he added that he tried hard to convince the Centre to request the Allahabad High Court for an early judgement, before 6 December to be precise, on the matter of land acquisition. Two issues arise out of his statement: First, why did he not try to convince leaders in his own fraternity to postpone kar seva till after the verdict? Second, what would have been the outcome had the court nullified acquisition of the piece of land (as it eventually did)?

According to Justice Liberhan, the actual assault on Babri Masjid began around noon when a posse of young kar sevaks 'vaulted on the dome and thereby signalled the breaking of the outer cordon. Other karsevaks wielding pickaxes, hammers, iron rods, and shovels started scaling the Ram Deewar (or Ram Wall, well away from the disputed structure) and over the barriers of the outer, inner and isolation cordons, from the east, west and south directions. They stormed the disputed structure. The police deployed at the spot gave their canes and shields to karsevaks who brandished them openly.'[27]

The report continued that the actual assault which razed the mosque to the ground began within fifteen minutes of this, around the time of the scheduled start of kar seva. The extent of planning can be estimated from the fact that prior to the actual multipronged storming, a select team went inside the shrine and picked up the idol, the donation box and other objects connected with Hindu rituals from beneath the central dome to a preidentified safe place. It was only after this that the macabre dance of destruction began atop the domes. Justice Liberhan contended that this was a 'planned act in order to give the impression of spontaneous chaos'.[28] For the world to see, the mosque was being hammered by kar sevaks who had climbed atop the domes, but the real 'demolishers' were those who were trained. They smashed gaping holes in the wall. Thereafter, ropes tied to large iron hooks were inserted through these. These were then tied up and pulled by the crowd. The walls caved in, bringing the domes crashing down one by one—the first one at 1.55 p.m.

Leaders assembled there, including Advani, Joshi, Uma Bharti, Vijaya Raje Scindia and H.V. Seshadri, made 'feeble requests', 'either in earnest or for the media's benefit', to those atop the domes to come down—although no demolition was possible from top of the domes.[29] None of the leaders made appeals to the 1000-1500-strong crowd which had broken through the cordon and were milling around the Babri Masjid. No one asked them to refrain from going inside the structure and beneath the domes. The kar sevaks were neither worried for their own safety in the event of the domes collapsing over them nor did any leader warn them about this eventuality. Since September 1990, when Advani began his yatra, leaders of the Sangh Parivar had underlined the possibility of 'martyrdom' in this mission. In November 1990, those who had died in police firing in Ayodhya (official toll seventeen) were included in the list of martyrs for the cause. On 6 December, however, no one died.

A memorial for those who died in 1990 exists in Ayodhya. Furthermore, in April 2021, the deputy chief minister of UP, Keshav Prasad Maurya, promised to name a road in Ayodhya in memory of the two Kothari brothers. The siblings from Kolkata are listed among the leading 'martyrs' for hoisting a saffron flag atop the domes on 30 October 1990.

For Justice Liberhan, the feeble efforts of the leaders with a panoramic view of the proceedings to get kar sevaks to pull back, was indication of 'hidden intentions' to destroy the mosque. Although pictures of a jubilant Uma Bharti and other leaders including Joshi and Sadhvi Rithambara amid provocative slogan like *ek dhakka aur do, Babri Masjid tod do* (give another shove and smash the mosque)—that acted like a veritable war cry—were published in several publications, Bharti deposed before the commission that she tried to persuade them and when that failed, she even attempted to instil fear in their minds about possible police firing. But, she stated, the kar sevaks' stock reply was that they had not arrived in Ayodhya to 'eat *halwa* and *puri*'. The extent of planning can be estimated from the fact that the idol and the donation box containing unspecified amount of cash were put back at the same spot by 7 p.m. by which time preparatory work had started on constructing a makeshift temple. Indeed, kar seva eventually consisted of construction, only that it was not symbolic in nature but to raise a makeshift structure that existed till March 2020 when UP chief minister Yogi Adityanath shifted the idol and other accompanying religious paraphernalia in a public ceremony in violation of social distancing norms after imposition of a national lockdown due to the coronavirus pandemic.

*

From the time of the demolition, there was much speculation over the extent to which the action was pre-planned. The Liberhan Commission concluded that large amounts of money were raised to mobilize kar sevaks and conduct the programme on 6 December—'amounts transacted exceeded tens of crores of rupees,' he said. This, the retired judge concluded, was a 'categorical pointer to the planning and preplanning carried out for the entire process of the movement commencing with mobilisation onwards right till the very demolition'.[30] Without doubt, the mobilization of kar sevaks and their convergence at Ayodhya were neither spontaneous nor voluntary but organized, orchestrated as well as planned by astute managers well versed in ways of enlisting activists for political actions.

Liberhan firmly concluded that the Sangh Parivar was responsible for the demolition, both hardliners, as well as, what he termed, 'pseudo-moderates'. The closest he went to accusing BJP leaders was his formulation that it 'cannot be assumed even for the moment that L.K. Advani, A.B. Vajpayee or M.M. Joshi did not know of the designs of the Sangh Parivar'.[31] His words bore an eerie likeness to the ones used by the Justice J.K. Kapur Commission of Inquiry into the conspiracy to murder Mahatma Gandhi. Kapur had written: 'Facts (unearthed or established by the Commission) taken together were destructive of any theory other than the conspiracy to murder by Savarkar and his group.' Liberhan further wrote that the BJP 'was an essential element in the Parivar smorgasbord and essential to capture *de jure* power and authority, in furtherance of its goals of establishing Hindu Rashtra'.[32] For all the scant attention given to his report and its damnation by the current regime in India, the document remains a finely distilled work which examines claims and counter-claims of all parties and key individuals, at least those who agreed to appear before the commission.

While the role of the BJP and VHP leadership in the entire Ram temple agitation has been documented at length, little is known about how the RSS leadership managed the agitation. Did they directly intervene? Did they give directions from behind the curtains? Or is autonomy of affiliated organizations an article of faith within the saffron fraternity? Fact of the matter is that Madhukar Dattatreya (Balasaheb) Deoras was the sarsanghchalak from before the agitation's inception in 1984. He had personally overseen the revival of the VHP from the early 1980s and knew the political potential of the Ram temple demand.

The RSS has designated 'handlers' for affiliated organizations. These functionaries, in turn, nominated assistants at regional levels for regular monitoring. Moropant Pingle, a senior RSS person who had the potential to succeed Deoras, was the 'chief operational commander' during the crucial days prior to the demolition. He was ensconced in one of the bhawans or ashrams close to the Babri Masjid. Without stepping out once, he knew what was happening every minute courtesy loyalists acting as his eyes and ears.

I was told in conversations with people in the know of developments at the time of the Ayodhya agitation that the first group of activists leading the attack was personally selected by Pingle. The decision to raise this cohesive body of people was taken at Nagpur with Deoras's knowledge. These men literally came out from the dark and disappeared into it once the task was completed. In the years after the demolition, many people made claims regarding their role in the movement, but no one accepted involvement in the demolition. Even senior leaders against whom the criminal conspiracy case was being heard pleaded innocence in the special court which was winding up hearings as the Bhoomi Pujan drew close in August 2020. Despite publicly proclaimed bravado, accepting involvement in the demolition in court would have been an admission of guilt, making them liable to be convicted. Yet, there is no denying that the Babri Masjid demolition was a planned operation, and was known to a select group of people in the RSS, VHP and BJP, including of course the sarsanghchalak.

Several hours after the demolition, the Union cabinet finally met at 6 p.m. in Delhi and decided to impose President's Rule in UP. But Kalyan Singh put in his papers before the formal presidential proclamation. After the initial assault which brought down the domes, one group of kar sevaks continued the demolition, clearing the ground for the makeshift structure and collecting artefacts as personal trophies. Meanwhile, other groups started communal violence against Muslims and their properties. As many as eighteen Muslims died in the communal attacks in Ayodhya–Faizabad. An estimated 4000 of the displaced took refuge in an imposing white, typically Islamic, building—the yateemkhana or orphanage. This building was adjacent to the 'Bari Bua' or the big graveyard. The dead and the surviving coexisted cheek by jowl in the days after the demolition.

These attacks on Muslims of Ayodhya were executed with precision—much like the way Sikhs were targeted in the aftermath of Indira Gandhi's assassination. Unlike several towns and cities in north India, there were no Muslim ghettos in the temple town, and houses of Hindus and Muslims were often adjacent to one another in several colonies. Barring odd ones, the facades of the houses did not indicate the religion of the owner. People had lived in harmony for centuries in spite of the dispute. In December 1992, however, Muslims' houses were targeted one by one, without even one instance of an erroneous attack on a Hindu home. The mobs were in possession of lists of Muslim households, suggesting prior planning and some local involvement. Walls in several houses were vandalized with scribbles: 'You suffer because you are a descendant of Babur.' Possibly, the most ironical of attacks took place in Tehdi Bazar, a settlement that housed Muslim artisans who supplied 12,000 pair of wooden sandals—symbolizing the mythological sandals of Ram that his brother Bharat kept as a mark of authority during Ram's period of banishment—to the VHP when they launched yatras in October 1992. The local police stood by, inactive. Even as rioters and arsonists held Ayodhya to ransom, they remained mere bystanders.

When day ended and night cast its pall of darkness over the temple town, it was evident that not just its destiny, but that of the country had changed forever. The then vice-president, K.R. Narayanan, who became President in 1997, said that the demolition of the sixteenth-century mosque was the greatest political tragedy in India after Mahatma Gandhi's assassination. A large section in India disagrees with his formulation now. As subsequent events demonstrated, closure remains a myth as far as Ayodhya and Babri Masjid are concerned.

7

Through the Legal Maze

'Religion is never more tested than when our emotions are ablaze. At such a time, the timeless grandeur of the Law and its ethics stand at our mercy.'

—Abdal Hakim Murad

The legal dispute over the plot of land in Ayodhya, less than 1500 square yards in size, continued for 135 years, occasionally at a brisk pace, as during the weeks before the verdict on 9 November 2019 when the bench led by the Chief Justice of India, Ranjan Gogoi, raced against his impending retirement. Yet, and for most parts of these years, the case remained dormant as only the atypical judge was willing to sit in judgement on even peripheral matters related to the dispute. Most members of the judicature perfected the art of, as immortalized in a Bollywood film dialogue, of setting *tareeq pe tareeq* or date after date. Judges were reluctant to append their names permanently to the Babri Masjid–Ram Janmabhoomi case because they viewed it as a conflict that required political settlement. Significantly, Swapan Dasgupta, former journalist who was nominated to Rajya Sabha in 2017 before he joined the BJP to contest the West Bengal assembly elections in 2021 (and was renominated to the Upper House after he lost the poll), wrote in the aftermath of the Gujarat riots in 2002 that, it 'is the myth that a solution is up to the courts'.[1] He contended that the dispute had become a 'monumental exercise in passing the buck. Parliament is unwilling to take a stand for fear of antagonising the loser. So it takes refuge behind the courts.' Yet, it was eventually the highest court of the country that awarded the land to Hindu representatives enabling the government to claim that it merely abided by the judicial verdict.

By the time the case was settled and all review petitions rejected in the course of an in-chamber consideration by the newly appointed CJI, Justice S.A. Bobde, and his colleagues on 12 December 2019, no ambiguity remained that this had indeed been one of the rarest of rare civil disputes. It was a sad day when the curtains came down on the case after navigating domains of religion, mythology, history, archaeology, law, governance and politics. It was an ominous day because for the judges 'possession is indeed nine-tenths of the law' and that 'possessory title' was of greater consequence than 'property title'.[2] The judges were not guided by the consideration that 'possession' of the disputed property was acquired by force and backed by legal sleight of hand on two occasions—in 1949-50 and 1986. The judges went solely by legal books and not principles of justice. Indeed, the final verdict at the end of decades of contestation was a legal tour de force. But only that. For most luminaries, it was just a case. But was it just that?

At the centre of the clutch of civil suits, clubbed as one, was the legal entity that the Supreme Court of India, like other courts at lower levels of the legal pyramid, termed 'juristic person' or a 'jural deity', the idol of Hindu deity Ram.

For the apex court to rule in favour of parties representing the idol was more than a tad disheartening. Lead counsel of the Muslim parties, Rajeev Dhawan, remarked dolefully, 'We won on every point of law. They got the relief.'[3]

The pain in the senior counsel's words was understandable because the five judges of the apex court awarded the contested land to those individuals and organizations whose action on 6 December 1992 they found illegal and unlawful. They dubbed the Babri Masjid's demolition as nothing short of an 'egregious violation of the rule of law'. The judges added that the violence on the medieval structure was executed by activists mobilized explicitly for the act, 'in breach of the order of status quo and an assurance given to this Court'. The dichotomy between the deductions the judges marshalled from myriad evidence presented before them and the 'relief and directions' they pronounced was stark. A full stop on the last legal case surrounding the sixteenth-century structure that no longer exists was put on 30 September 2020 with another 'winner takes all' verdict. It was another sad, but not surprising day. The judge of the special Central Bureau of Investigations court, Justice S.K. Yadav, acquitted all accused of conspiring to demolish the Babri Masjid. The judgement contradicted the Supreme Court decree as well as the findings of the Justice Liberhan Commission. Despite this the special CBI court's judgement was not challenged in a higher court. In judicial hierarchy, Justice S.K. Yadav, who was appointed to the special CBI court, was much junior but he will remain the unchallenged arbitrator on criminal culpability for the demolition. He based his verdict, the last one of his career, on what was placed before him—evidence as well as questions. Less than seven months after exonerating a galaxy of Sangh Parivar leaders, Yadav was appointed the deputy Lokyukta of Uttar

Pradesh by the state government. A decade earlier, after the Allahabad High Court's judgement in September 2010 ordering division of the disputed property among three parties, it was evident that 'right questions' were not framed appropriately even once for any court that had heard the Ayodhya matter. As a result, 'right answers' were not given.[4]

The Supreme Court could not but be guided by what it was asked to adjudicate on—appeal(s) against the Allahabad High Court order. It was within its right to examine if the demolition had been a legal process or not. It could argue for providing 'restitution to the Muslim community for the unlawful destruction of their place of worship'. But it chose to pass a verdict on the limited question of who would leave the court that day with the land in their kitty and secure the right to build 'their' place of worship. Likewise, the CBI judge may have been personally aware of the viewpoint of the highest court as well as the Liberhan Commission report. But he refused to examine anything but what was provided by the country's highest investigate agency, albeit one that had a woeful success rate. Both courts worked within limited legal bandwidth because that is the way law is—providing justice is not the principal concern.

The apex court took ten years to decide on the appeals filed against the Allahabad High Court judgement. This was chiefly due to the unwillingness of Chief Justices to expedite the matter. The case moved to the fast track only after the elevation of Justice Dipak Misra as Chief Justice in August 2017 when he was put 'under a lot of pressure to decide the case'. He passed on the Ayodhya baton to his successor Justice Ranjan Gogoi whose hastening of the verdict will eternally be juxtaposed with the accusations of sexual harassment against him by a woman staffer of the court, the first time that a CJI faced a sexual harassment charge.[5]

This viewpoint appeared even more credible in March 2020 when Gogoi was nominated to the Rajya Sabha, the first time a government used its power to offer a post-retirement sinecure to a former Chief Justice of India. It was pointed out that Gogoi headed benches in several key cases in which the government had direct interest.[6]

Despite the time it took to arrive at its legal opinion, the apex court judgement provided no balm to those who had been at the receiving end of violence in December 1992. The five judges belied hopes of the finest legal luminaries that after the demolition no court would 'give any assistance to those who unilaterally by criminal acts destroyed the subject matter of the dispute and violated the Constitution and the law'.[7] Worryingly, legal precedents set in the course of the Ayodhya dispute, especially the criminal matter related to the demolition, are likely to raise its heads repeatedly in future. Even with the Covid-19 pandemic raging through 2020, there were considerable developments over two other shrines, for long on the list of Hindu temples requiring 'liberation'—the Kashi Vishwanath temple complex in Varanasi and the Krishna Janmabhoomi in Mathura. Civil cases were also filed by parties claiming to represent interests of Hindus over the Teele Waali Masjid in Lucknow and the Qutub Minar in Delhi that was asserted to have been built after destroying several Hindu and Jain temples.

Not just the civil suit to decide the title of the Ayodhya shrine, but the legal maze enveloped several other cases. These included the one heard by the Supreme Court after the Union government acquired a large tract of land surrounding the already demolished Babri Masjid in January 1993. At the same time, the Centre contentiously sought the opinion of the court on 'whether a Hindu temple or any Hindu religious structure existed prior to the construction of the

Ramjanmabhumi-Babri Masjid (including the premises of the inner and outer courtyards of such structure) in the areas on which the structure stood?' Other cases that required to be referred to determine how India's secular polity was 'wheedled within, rather than separated from, the religious' included the challenge arising out of the Supreme Court's decision upholding the aforementioned land acquisition and the appeal against it in the case popularly referred to as Ismail Faruqui.[8]

Yet other cases that had a bearing, at least obliquely, were the Hindutva cases penned by the otherwise remarkable Justice J.S. Verma, the September 2010 judgement of the Allahabad High Court which divided the disputed land among three parties, including representatives of Muslims, the January 2017 judgement on the Representation of the People Act regarding use of religion in election campaign and the 2018 verdict of the apex court rejecting a reference to a larger bench of the Ismail Faruqui case of 1994 regarding importance of mosque in Islam. Despite these significant cases, India is nowhere close to putting the past behind and moving on. If the special CBI court's verdict in the Babri demolition cases was not enough, ominous developments have continued through 2020 and 2021, suggesting that majoritarian forces are priming up to raise socio-political temperature over several other Islamic shrines and monuments. Besides the developments in the cases seeking 'restoration' of the Gyanvapi Mosque in Varanasi and Shahi Idgah in Mathura to Hindus,[9] a public interest litigation filed by a lawyer associated with the BJP, challenging the Places of Worship Act, 1991, has been admitted in the apex court. This has the potential to reopen the chapter of decades of Hindu–Muslim hostility. The PIL impinges on the status of the four shrines/monuments over which civil suits are pending. Furthermore, Hindu majoritarian groups had previously listed hundreds of mosques as being built on ancient temples and demanded their restoration. In the era of majoritarian triumphalism, there is no way of ascertaining if this list will be suddenly pulled out to serve political ends. The Supreme Court was clear in its November 2019 judgement that the PoW Act was much needed to ensure that majoritarian forces would not be able to constantly push the clock. It insisted that the day India became independent would serve as the appropriate day to mark a break from past conflicts. The demand for enactment of a law ensuring protection of all shrines as they were at the stroke of midnight 15 August 1947 had been made by secularists and some Muslim parties from the late 1980s. The only point on which the Rao government had made a concession was to leave out the disputed mosque/temple in Ayodhya from its ambit. The admission of the PIL now merely proves that the much-vaunted closure on points of conflict that emerged through the Ayodhya agitation remains a chimera.

*

The objective of the petitioners claiming to represent Hindu sentiments indeed came a long way from 1885, when Mahant Raghubar Das demanded that he be allowed to build a temple over the Ram Chabutra, to the fateful day in November 2019, when the five-judge bench of the Supreme Court ruled in favour of the Hindu parties and directed the Centre in one voice to facilitate establishment of a board of trustees to build a Ram temple that would sprawl beyond the 'inner and outer courtyards' of the contested site. It was forgotten that the original demand was not for such a gargantuan-sized piece of land. It was during the course of the political agitation launched in 1985, to secure the 'liberation' of Ram Janmabhoomi, that the goal of the movement was expanded—from unlocking the shut gates to handing over the disputed shrine to self-styled representatives of Hindus so that a Ram temple could be built. Additions or modifications to the charter of demands in the course of a political agitation are understandable, but when these get unquestioningly accepted by courts, they draw attention to what eighteenth-century Irish composer Kana O'Hara is attributed to have said: 'When the judgement's weak, the prejudice is strong.'

In the course of seemingly endless hearings at various levels of the judiciary, and in prodigiously written verdicts, considerable time and space were accorded to the issuc of 'barred by limitation', a statutory creation of law, based on the principle of diligence or a reasonable time to seek redressal of grievance—the claim has to be formally staked before a court within a stipulated time. Even the Supreme Court in its final verdict upheld the Allahabad High Court's conclusion that the Nirmohi Akhara's suit was time-barred because its suit was governed by Article 120 of the Limitation Act, 1908, that was in force when the case was filed in 1959. Providing reason for its rejection of the Nirmohi Akhara suit, the highest court argued that its ruling emerged from the Akhara's claim of being a shebait (a person or institution which serves a deity) as a result of which it was governed by the aforesaid article that specifies the limitation period to six years, and not twelve years as under Article 142 that permits claims to be made before expiry of twelve years. The Sunni Central Waqf Board's suit was filed days before the expiry in December 1961 and thereby maintainable.

It is well known that judges often disagree and are seldom unanimous in their conclusions. The Supreme Court judgement on the Ayodhya civil case raised eyebrows as the five judges were in almost complete agreement. In addition, the pronouncement 'broke three conventions' that the apex court had followed over seven decades.[10] Verdicts always carry a 'byline' and the 'author' reads it alone even though others may have the same opinion. But this epochal verdict did not carry a name and was read out by the Chief Justice of India, although legal eagles, adept at decoding writing styles of judges, fathomed that this was penned by Justice D.Y. Chandrachud. Additionally, the judgement carried an 'addenda', which too was anonymous. It was also not difficult to comprehend, by little more than 'comparison of the fonts used by judges in their judgements',[11] that the 116-page addenda was written by Justice Ashok Bhushan. Peculiarly, this had the characteristics of a comprehensive judgement and could well have been appended as a concurring judgement.

These decisions were possibly driven by political motivations or compulsions. Justice Gogoi spoke on behalf of his colleagues that they 'decided to speak to the nation in one voice on such an important and historic issue'. Justice Bhushan was thereby 'prevailed upon'[12] to add the new concept to an apex court verdict by terming his text, offering separate reasons for arriving at the same conclusion and relief granted, as 'addenda'. Yet, the question remained: By not identifying themselves, did the judges hide behind anonymity?

At the onset, the addenda addressed the question 'whether disputed structure is the holy birthplace of Lord Ram as per the faith, belief and trust of the Hindus'. It concluded that 'faith and belief of Hindus since prior to construction of Mosque and subsequent thereto has always been that Janmaasthan of Lord Ram is the place where Babri Mosque has been constructed'.[13] In their collective verdict, the judges spoke in one voice undoubtedly but in the process ended up addressing only one community and their aspirations. If what the Chief Justice stated actually implied that the judges had unanimously agreed to be mindful of the majoritarian 'societal' sense on the issue, it carries worrying portents not just for the independence of judiciary, but also for the future character of the republic.

*

The suit that became the main focus of attention during the hearing was the one filed in July 1989 by Deoki Nandan Agarwal, a retired high court judge and then vice-president of the VHP. It certainly cannot be sheer coincidence that the VHP successfully impleaded itself as a party in this case days before all suits were transferred to the Allahabad High Court whose chief justice thereafter constituted a three-judge bench on 21 July 1989 for the trial of the suits. Agarwal remained the plaintiff for thirteen years. On his death in 2002, a retired professor of history was appointed by the VHP as Ram Lalla's 'next best friend'. He eventually sought court permission to bow out in 2008 due to age and ill health. His application, however, ran into contestation and it was only in March 2010 that the Supreme Court permitted Triloki Nath Pande, an RSS pracharak and resident in Ayodhya since 1992, to be the plaintiff in the suit filed by Agarwal.

During hearings in the Supreme Court, the lawfulness of this suit on behalf of the deity being time-barred was raised. When Agarwal filed the suit in July 1989, almost forty years had elapsed since the idol was installed. The stipulated twelve years for claims to be made was long over. The last civil suit in the matter too had been filed in 1961, a clear gap of twenty-eight years. However, the apex court ruled that the suit was not time-barred because the deity 'not being a party to the earlier suits, its interests and concerns were not being adequately protected in the earlier suits including those instituted by the Hindu parties'.[14]

By the time the VHP became a party in the civil case in 1989, it was intent on dislodging other Hindu claimants. Agarwal's suit contended that 'some of the parties to the earlier suits who are worshippers are to some extent involved in seeking to gratify their personal interests to be served by obtaining control over the worship of the plaintiff deities'.[15] This claim by the VHP imputed motives to the previous petitioners in the case while professing moral uprightness despite the clear intention of using religion as a means of advancing the philosophy and politics of its ideological fountainhead, the RSS and other affiliates, including the BJP.

By the time the Sangh Parivar formally became a party to the dispute and a claimant to the contested land, the BJP had already passed the Palampur resolution officially embracing the demand for the Ram temple in its charter. The RSS too had passed several resolutions. If the other plaintiffs were open to accusations of 'gratifying personal interests', Agarwal and the VHP could not escape the charge of being driven by political interests. It is noteworthy that in mid-1989, Agarwal's suit categorically sought 'an injunction against interference in the construction of a new temple after the demolition of the existing building'.[16]

Eventually the apex court contended that the VHP, through Agarwal, was allowed to remain a de facto party because the 'interest of the deities was not being safeguarded by the persons or entities who were pursuing the earlier proceedings'. None of the courts—neither the district judge of Faizabad nor the Allahabad High Court or later the Supreme Court—examined the interconnection between the 'next best friend' and the VHP trust set up in 1985 and how this was part of the bigger agenda that later led to the events of December 1992.

Although the legal dispute over the shrine had started in 1885, there were long periods of dormancy which indicated that the issue was not a primary matter of contention between the two communities over the decades. Prior to January 1950, when Gopal Singh Visharad sought a simple declaration from the local court that he be allowed to offer prayers at 'the main Janmabhumi temple near the idols',[17] there were long periods when no claims were made over the shrine and no pleas were submitted seeking change in the arrangement worked out by the British administrators after events of the 1850s. In 1945, there was a litigation involving Shia and Sunni Muslims in the local court. The Shia grievance was that the Babri Masjid was listed as a Sunni mosque by the commissioner of Waqfs. This suit was settled in March 1946 in favour of the Sunnis and the site remained without legal dispute till December 1949 when the idols were forcibly installed.

Court cases involving the Babri Masjid–Ram Janmabhoomi can be bunched together period-wise as follows. First, those that emerged in the years prior to the conversion of the mosque into a de facto temple in December 1949. During this phase, Raghubar Das, the first Hindu plaintiff, pleaded with the sub-judge, Faizabad, that, by virtue of being the mahant of Ram Janmasthan, he be permitted to construct a 'temple on the Ramchabutra situated in the outer courtyard, measuring seventeen feet by twenty-one feet'.[18] His suit was filed two years after he started, on his own volition, constructing a temple over the chabutra, which was stopped by the district magistrate after Muslims objected. The judge dismissed the December 1885 suit because it apprehended conflict and riots between Hindus and Muslims. However, the court added a twist by asserting that there was no question or doubt regarding the possession and ownership of the Hindus over the chabutra. Significantly, even in the court's understanding, the Hindu claim was limited to the small platform and not beyond. The judge also accepted Hindu 'ownership' of the platform by virtue of possession. This reading of title rights in favour of Hindus was however struck down twice, by the district judge in the first instance in March 1886 and later by the judicial commissioner of Oudh in November 1886. The final word on this Hindu bid was that the mahant (as individual) had 'failed to present evidence of title to establish ownership of the Chabutra'.[19] The 1886 judgement even said that Muslims had title to the shrine.

Significantly, when the VHP demand began snowballing into a nationwide political conflict in the mid-1980s, Syed Shahabuddin suggested that Hindus be permitted to build a temple with garbha griha (sanctum sanctorum) on the Ram Chabutra and to enter from the eastern side from where Muslims entered till 22-23 December 1949. The Muslims, Shahabuddin proposed, could be provided access to the mosque from the northern gate which was made in 1877 by the colonial government after the spate of conflicts following the clashes of 1856 in the 'vicinity of the structure'.[20] He also suggested that the two shrines, if need be, could even share a common wall that could come up at the place where the iron grilled fence stood separating the inner and outer compounds. This suggestion was not without precedence; the 1968 agreement in Mathura between the Sri Krishna Janamasthan Seva Sangh and Shahi Idgah Trust had stood the test of time before this began to be challenged by the VHP and its affiliates.

The second phase involved cases and legal developments in the aftermath of the installation of the idol. The plea seeking the right to 'worship and visit without obstruction and disturbance', the idol inside the shrine was moved by the president of the Ayodhya unit of Hindu Mahasabha, Gopal Singh Visharad. He filed the first case in this matter, ironically ten days before India became a Republic, on 16 January 1950. This became the flag-bearer of the Hindu case in court. After the court passed an injunction against the removal of the idol and altering post-installation status quo, the field was open for other Hindu claimants. At an early stage of the case, the UP government counsel unambiguously stated in court that the disputed property was 'known as Babri Masjid (and) has been used as a mosque for the purpose of worship by Muslims for a long period and has not been used as a temple of Lord Ram ... On the night of 22 December 1949, the idols of Lord Ram were surreptitiously placed inside the mosque imperilling public peace and tranquillity.' Importantly, the state government used the term 'long period' and not a specific date as provided by the Muslims. It is evident that Hindu and Muslim parties in the dispute fed on one another's standpoint for different reasons. For Hindu nationalists, pinning the mosque's construction on the founder of the Mughal dynasty enabled demonization of Mughals, and by extension every Muslim. The Supreme Court in its judgement of November 2019 did not take any view on Babur ordering its construction. But the judges said that the 'belief and faith of the worshipper in offering namaz at a place which is for the worshipper a mosque cannot be challenged'.[21] That the Supreme Court honoured faith and belief of Hindus as well as Muslims is amply evident in its observation that the court 'as a secular institution, set up under a constitutional regime must steer clear from choosing one among many possible interpretations of theological doctrine and must defer to the safer course of accepting the faith and belief of the worshipper'.[22]

Paramhans Ramchandra Das, mahant of a local akhara, became the second litigant in December 1950. The judge responded by consolidating the two suits in February 1951, but without vacating his interim injunction. The Faizabad court's unwillingness to speedily hear the matter was adversely commented upon by the Allahabad High Court as early as 1955 when it heard an appeal against the aforementioned interim injunction. Although the court did not vacate the order, it nonetheless commented that it would be 'desirable that a suit of this kind be decided as soon as possible, and it is regretted that it remained undecided after four years'. Four years soon became another thirty-four years when in July 1989 the Faizabad judge transferred all cases to the Allahabad High Court. In between came two other cases, one by Mahant Raghunath Das of Nirmohi Akhara as shebait of the Ram Chabutra and the other by the Uttar Pradesh Sunni Central Board of Waqfs in December 1961.

In the course of discussions on the legal narrative of the Ayodhya civil cases, it was often asked why Muslims waited till 1961 before staking claim to what was a functioning mosque till December 1949. In the cases filed by Hindu parties in the local Faizabad courts, Muslims were defendants and they made no move to join the legal wrangling as plaintiff. This had primarily to do with the 'disarray among the Muslims of Ayodhya following the attacks on them after Partition'.[23] There was a history of attacks on Muslims and their properties in the aftermath of Partition and this evoked a sense of insecurity among them in the city. The suit on behalf of the Muslims certainly did not meet with approval of the dominantly Hindu legal community, and the Faizabad courts did not hear the plea till January 1964 when the civil judge consolidated all the four cases and made the one filed by the Sunni Central Waqf Board the leading case. The entire suit began being referred to hereafter as the title suit. From an instance of criminal trespass, the case had evolved into a civil dispute for ownership of property. Like most civil suits in India, this too was not prioritized. The political content of the dispute was obvious and would have weighed on the mind of the judges before whom the matter came up periodically. They did little but grant adjournments on one pretext or another.

A minor flutter was witnessed in 1970, but not on the core matter. The receiver of the shrine, Priyadatta Ram, died and a dispute arose over whether his successor could be appointed by the civil judge hearing the case or by a criminal court. The judiciary's lack of urgency to resolve the matter and get back to hearing the title suit can be assessed from the fact that it was as late as August 1987 when the Allahabad High Court settled this simple matter. But by then, the situation in Ayodhya and the disputed shrine's status had dramatically altered because a Faizabad court had thrown open the mosque-turned-temple to Hindu devotees in February 1986. This decision, detailed earlier, was however taken without any records of the title suit. After the receiver's death, all records pertaining to the case were 'summoned by the High Court and accordingly no proceedings took place in the suits at Faizabad'.[24] If the installation of the idols was the first step in dispossessing the Muslim of the Babri Masjid, the next step was taken in February 1986 when K.M. Pandey, a Brahmin district judge of Faizabad, ruled that the lock on the gate separating the mosque from the Ram Chabutra should be opened and the shrine be thrown open to Hindu devotees. As previously noted, the petitioner and the district collector on whose testimony the judge ordered the unlocking of the gate were Pandey Brahmins. Judicial impartiality was certainly not a prerequisite while deciding this matter.

Efforts to get the Supreme Court seized of the Ayodhya civil suit was made as early as January 1990 by Paramhans Ramchandra Das. He approached the apex court directly and contended that since 'only a *mutwalli* and not Waqf Board can enforce a legal right on a mosque', and since the *mutwalli* (manager or custodian of waqf) of the Babri Masjid was not the plaintiff, the Sunni Central Waqf Board's suit was not maintainable and hence pleaded for its dismissal. The Supreme Court heard the matter but directed the Allahabad High Court to listen to the arguments regarding it.

The top court was again drawn into the case next year when it was approached with pleas challenging the acquisition of 2.77 acres of land in Ayodhya by the BJP-controlled UP government in October 1991. Although the BJP's provocative act escalated tensions and gave a great fillip to the VHP to foment strife in the temple town, the apex court displayed little urgency and allowed the Allahabad High Court to delay its verdict till 11 December 1992, five days after the demolition. What made this delay crueller was that the acquisition was set aside. It remains a matter of speculation whether the events of 6 December

1992 could have been prevented if the apex court and the Allahabad High Court had acted with greater urgency on land acquisition and given specific directives to the Centre and the state to maintain status quo of the Babri Masjid.

As an institution, the Supreme Court partially atoned for its failure to safeguard a structure that had become the symbol of the basic feature of the Constitution, secularism. It did so only in part because the five-judge bench, which simultaneously heard the first important case after the demolition, agreed on only one matter—the presidential reference made by the government in January 1993 to answer whether a 'Hindu temple or any Hindu religious structure existed prior to the construction of the mosque'. Sadly, however, in its judgement dated 24 October 1994, on the separate matter of constitutional validity of the Acquisition of Certain Area at Ayodhya Act, 1993 (issued as an Ordinance initially and later replaced by an Act), the bench was divided. Two judges from India's minorities (a Muslim and a Parsi) struck the law down in its entirety, while three other justices ruled that only section 4(3) was unconstitutional. The minority ruling declared the Act unconstitutional because it 'offended the principles of secularism which was part of the basic structure of the Constitution, being slanted in favour of one religious community as against another'. However, the five judges were unanimous in rebuffing the presidential reference, although for different reasons. The majority judgement found the reference 'superfluous and unnecessary' and the minority opinion stated that the way the reference was drawn 'favours one religious community and disfavours the other'. The final judgement remarked that the government did not propose to settle the dispute in terms of the court's opinion and that its ruling was likely to be used as a 'springboard of negotiations'. The court also did not wish to adjudicate on the matter without hearing the views of the 'principal protagonists of the two stands', representatives of the Hindu and Muslim viewpoints. The court had little doubt that the 'dignity and honour of the Supreme Court cannot be compromised'.[25]

The court striking down Section 4(3) of the 1993 Acquisition Act was a double blow for the Rao government. The decision to acquire the land around the Babri Masjid had been a clever ploy for it stated that after passage of this legislation, 'any suit, appeal or other proceeding in respect of the right, title and interest' of the acquired land 'shall abate'. Effectively it meant that all cases would die down but with the nullification of the aforesaid section, suits pending before the Allahabad High Court were revived.

The Supreme Court exuded hope in 1994 that Ayodhya was 'a storm that would pass' and opined that the 'moderate Hindu has little taste for the tearing down of the place of worship of another to replace it with a temple'. The optimism turned out to be misplaced as the storm did not pass even after its Ayodhya verdict. Instead, foreboding clouds were already gathering over the horizon in Varanasi, Mathura, Lucknow and many other cities where many Islamic shrines/monuments remained on the to-be-restored list of the VHP.

Justice J.S. Verma made a worrying assertion in the October 1994 Ismail Faruqui judgement: 'A mosque is not an essential part of the practice of the religion of Islam and namaz (prayer) by Muslims can be offered anywhere even in open.' For the counsel for Muslims, who later argued that the assertion be scrutinized by a larger bench, implications of this viewpoint were immense, even devaluing 'a Muslim's constitutional rights of prayer'.[26] The observation underscores the enormous impact off-the-cuff remarks or observations have. The majority of judges in this case were also obviously mistaken in their assessment that few would like a temple for a revered god to be built over a site where a mosque was torn down in an act of vandalism. Instead, 'mandir waheen banayenge' had become the clarion call of those who wished to construct the temple not to deify Ram but to underline Hindu hegemony over Muslims. The judges reminded people of Mahatma Gandhi's words: 'India cannot cease to be one nation because people belonging to different religions live in it ... In no part of the world are one nationality and one religion synonymous terms, nor has it ever been so in India.' Yet they also waded into a matter that would later become another contentious issue before the apex court in another case even as the civil suit remained pending before it.

There was a dissenting opinion by Justice S.P. Bharucha who wrote on behalf of Justice A.M. Ahmadi and himself: 'No account is taken of the fact that the structure thereon had been destroyed in a most reprehensible act. The perpetrators of this deed struck not only against a place of worship but at the principles of secularism, democracy and the rule of law.' But the majority view prevailed as is the norm, although this contention was challenged and it was argued that the 1994 verdict must be examined by a larger bench of the Supreme Court before taking up the Ayodhya civil case. In September 2018, a three-judge bench of the Supreme Court turned down the plea seeking it to take a fresh look on whether mosques are essential to Islam and thereby protected by the Constitution. This however was again a split verdict. Chief Justice Dipak Misra and Justice Ashok Bhushan were against the matter being referred to a larger bench while Justice S. Abdul Nazeer said that whether a mosque is integral to Islam required detailed consideration. Arguments of the majority are widely reported and becomes the official narrative for the future. The minority judicial vote gets ignored, although Justice Nazeer's reasons for referring the matter to a larger bench required mention. He asked whether a detailed scrutiny on this issue was not required in the light of a legal precedent involving a Hindu place of worship, the Shirur Mutt. Can essential practice can be decided without a detailed examination of the beliefs, tenets and practice of the faith in question? Justice Nazeer also asked that a larger bench was required to examine if Article 25 protected 'belief and practices of particular significance of a faith or all practices regarded by the faith as essential?' Moreover, do 'Articles 15, 25 and 26 (read with Article 14) allow the comparative significance of faiths to be undertaken?'

The Ismail Faruqui case was the first verdict of Justice J.S. Verma, later CJI and a widely respected judge, which raised eyebrows for compromising the essence of secularism. The other controversial judgement delivered by Justice Verma on 11 December 1995 on behalf of himself and Justices N.P. Singh and K. Venkatasami has come to be known as the Hindutva judgement. It remains a widely debated verdict for the observation that Hindutva was a 'way of life of the Indian people'. According to him, Hindutva did not allude to 'hostility, enmity or intolerance towards other religious faiths'. In the 1990s, a clutch of pleas came up in the courts against electoral malpractices and use of religious appeals during campaign. Although there have been several verdicts that examined Hindutva and its relationship with Hinduism, Justice Verma's judgement remains a legal milestone.[27] The contentious aspect of his verdict, which ruled that seeking votes in the name of Hinduism was not a 'corrupt practise', was the fluid use of Hindu, Hinduism and Hindutva.

As has been amply established over the past quarter of a century since the first of the two cases were filed in 1995, the three words have different meanings and their synonymous use is wrong. Hindutva is clearly a political ideology which was codified by V.D. Savarkar in his well-known essay, *Hindutva: Who Is A Hindu?* Hindutva certainly cannot be termed a way of life—despite the objectives of the Indian right-wing, the Indian state is yet to become completely Hindu majoritarian in outlook and policy.

However, a welcome judgement came in *Abhiram Singh vs C.D. Commachen* in January 2017 which examined whether appealing to any social identity of candidate and voters constitutes a 'corrupt practice' under Section 123(3) of the Representation of the People Act, 1951. This verdict, again decided by a single judicial vote in the seven-member bench, broadened the scope and understanding of what constitutes 'corrupt practices' in elections under aforesaid section and act. Although debate prevails over interpretations of the verdict, the majority 4-3 judgement disallowed all references to religion, race, caste, language, etc., in electioneering.

Despite this, ambiguity remains over Justice Verma's Hindutva judgement over the question if it was merely an observation or not. Until the apex court examines the issue of Hindutva being a 'way of life', use of religion in electoral campaigns cannot be completely prevented. The 2017 judgement did not reinterpret this point that is certain to play a further role in Indian politics because it was not asked this question. As previously stated, courts have to be asked the right questions and only then correct answers can be expected.

In November 2019, the Supreme Court was of the view that the three Allahabad High Court judges 'adopted a path [of three-way bifurcation of the disputed property] which was not open to it in terms of the [legal] principles' and precedents it cited. While reversing the high court verdict of 2010, the apex court contended that none of the parties to the dispute asked for the relief the judges conceived and granted, that the 'High Court was not seized of a suit for partition'. Judgements are always subjective and rarely agreeable to parties involved in the dispute or to bystanders whose lives are affected by both the dispute and the judgement. The final Supreme Court verdict is no different. The high court judgement of 2010 however factored in the long-standing nature of the dispute and exhibited awareness that a halfway settlement would not lead to triumphalism within the 'victorious' community. Even though it did not provide a clear title to any party, and was as such criticized by each one of them, the high court judgement was clearly aimed at a political compromise. Although no party was satisfied with the judgement, it was the 'next best solution' in the given circumstances—after all, a compromise was the objective in every effort at negotiation, even in the Supreme Court–mandated process of mediation in 2019 where the Supreme Court backed a last-minute effort for an exclusive pact with the Waqf Board.

On 16 October 2019, the media reported that the Sunni Waqf Board had agreed to withdraw its appeal against the 2010 high court judgement and drop the claim for title to the 2.77 acres of land where the Babri Masjid existed prior to 6 December 1992. In return, the board wanted a guarantee that all other places of worship in India, over which Hindu parties were staking a claim, will be protected from similar campaigns seeking so-called restoration.[28]

Rajeev Dhavan asserted that this development was the result of the UP government and its chief minister's success in politically and administratively leveraging key leaders of the board. However, Athar Hussain, secretary of the trust formed to build the mosque in Ayodhya, said that the board and sections of the Muslim community which backed this deal, did not see the struggle as 'only a fight for Babur's land, but as a larger struggle to save the Constitution'.[29] However, no assurance on the PoW Act came either from the parties leading the campaign or from the state. The pitch was further queered by a sharp response from several Muslim parties who criticized the Waqf Board for taking a position on their behalf.[30] The board was seen as taking an accommodative stance. On the contrary, groups questioning the board for continuing parleys with the mediation committee were insistent that there would be no dilution in the original demand for reconstruction and handover of the mosque. Hardliners dead opposed to compromise of any sort existed among Hindu parties as well as those representing the Muslims viewpoint. For them, mediation was a sham exercise and a ploy to showcase themselves as being accommodative whereas the reality was different. There, however, is no doubt that while the Waqf Board was agreeable to yielding on Ayodhya in return for safeguards over other shrines on the majoritarian wish-list, each of the self-proclaimed representatives of Hindus was determined to grant no quarter.

Given that there had been little change on extreme postures since the agitation was kick-started in the late 1980s, the high court judges in 2010 took a gamble by forcing a settlement. The state of disarray of the Sangh Parivar in 2010 and the failure of the VHP to muster support for any programme with the potential to set up a head-on collision with the state or with Muslims were evident. Moreover, post-demolition, a makeshift Ram temple had been constructed and in almost two decades till 2010, most Hindu devotees had come to accept it as it stood. Among Muslims on the other hand, Narasimha Rao's promise to rebuild the mosque notwithstanding, the majority had come to accept that a 'token' award or at least a recognition was the best possible scenario. Leaders of the community were aware that after Rao's promise to the nation to rebuild the destroyed mosque, no mainstream political leader of significance reiterated that pledge. The high court verdict was the best possible closure to the dispute.

Albert Einstein told his assistant, Banesh Hoffman, in the late 1930s: 'When I am judging a theory, I ask myself whether, if I were God, I would have arranged the world in such a way.' The Allahabad High Court judges were possibly guided by this earthly concern in a conflict-ridden society but the apex judges chose to pronounce a judgement which could be legally justified while being politically suitable for dominant forces of the time. Consequently, when the judgement was delivered, it cast a pall of gloom among those who did not support majoritarian politics. Yet the judges provided hope by reiterating that 'the beliefs of one citizen do not interfere with or dominate the freedoms and beliefs of another'. Further ahead, the five of them appended their signatures to what one of them wrote—that the 'Constitution does not make a distinction between the faith and belief of one religion and another'.

While all these assertions can be cynically labelled as mandatory utterances required to maintain the facade of constitutional secularism, the same cannot be stated about its specific references to the Places of Worship Act passed by the same Rao government in September 1991 despite later being complicit in the demolition.

The apex court contended that the law was enacted with the intention of, first, prohibiting 'conversion of any place of worship. In doing so, it speaks to the future by mandating that the character of a place of public worship shall not be altered. Second, the law seeks to impose a positive obligation to maintain the religious character of every place of worship as it existed on 15 August 1947 when India achieved independence from colonial rule.' Although heartening, the judicial assurance may once again perhaps be stymied by governments of the future. The process for this has already been triggered with the Supreme Court admitting the PIL against the PoW Act. This has been done despite the then CJI S.A. Bobde being part of the larger bench that held the 1991 law as highly relevant to our times. Despite its overt emphasis on 'possessory title' and despite illogically stating that while the Babri Masjid may have been built as a mosque, Muslims were unable to prove its use as such, thc five judges armed inheritors of secular nationalism in the future for their struggles against majoritarian onslaught. But this safeguard could possible weaken too as another flank of assault has been opened.

8

The Silent March Ahead

'Faith: Belief without evidence in what is told by one who speaks without knowledge, of things without parallel.'

—Ambrose Bierce

Although the Ram temple agitation was flagged off in 1984, it required the two-headed programmes in 1989—Ram Shila Pujan and yatras—coupled with the shilanyas to secure acceptability for the idea of building a Ram temple in place of the Babri Masjid. Hereafter, large sections among Hindus nodded in the affirmative when RSS–VHP leaders asked where else but Ayodhya should a new Ram temple be built. Instead of being a demand for which a 'case' had to be established in the people's court, November 1989 onward, the temple became a matter beyond the pale of further debate.

Despite the BJP's phenomenal expansion in the 1989 elections, the temple–mosque discord, although not the dominant issue during the campaign, hung like a backdrop on the nation's political stage. From being a town chiefly of only religious significance to Hindus, Ayodhya became a political pilgrimage. The shilanyas ceremony forced

Rajiv Gandhi to launch his 1989 electoral campaign from Faizabad-Ayodhya just six days before the shilanyas, instead of from Nagaur in Rajasthan. In his speech, the prime minister did not articulate secular values of the Congress party, but promised to usher in Ram Rajya.

With passing years and elections, it became a norm for non-BJP political leaders to visit the temple town and remain mute on the blatant partisanship of the agitation for the Ram temple. In November 2016, when Rahul Gandhi hit the road in UP to campaign for the 2017 assembly elections, he visited Ayodhya and paid obeisance at Hanuman Garhi. Although staying away from the disputed site, the message was not lost on anyone—he was the first Gandhi to visit Ayodhya after the demolition. His mother had visited Varanasi a month earlier. Rahul Gandhi's visit was followed up with publicized temple visits in Gujarat during electioneering in the state in late 2017 and his assertion of being a Shiv Bhakt (devotee of Shiva). A party leader's assertion of Gandhi being a janeu dhari Brahmin (one who dons the sacred thread) was followed up with declaration of his gotra (religious clan or lineage).

It is an evidence of the Sangh Parivar's success in mainstreaming Ram and making religious identity one of the central issues in the political discourse that almost every party leader now swears in the name of Ram. A principal contemporary challenger to the BJP and former chief minister, Akhilesh Yadav, visited the temple town on numerous occasions and in December 2020 declared that Ram 'belongs to his party as much as anyone else'. Ram's acceptance as a political icon, to whom proximity must be displayed, is complete in UP and large parts of India. This is evident from contrasting responses of the Bahujan Samaj Party and its leader, Mayawati. In September-October 2010, as chief minister, she risked Hindu anger and disallowed boisterous celebrations in Ayodhya following the Allahabad High Court verdict. In contrast, in July 2021, the down-and-out leader deputed the BSP general secretary, Satish Chandra Mishra, as part of her renewed Brahmin outreach, to visit Ayodhya and holler from a public platform that the BJP had failed to make significant progress with temple construction. '*Kab banega mandir?*' (How long will the temple take), he asked.

In hindsight, it is evident that the Ayodhya issue acted as a political catalyst and was a harbinger of unabashed polarization. The shilanyas marked the point of transition from the old to the new. Yet, the emerging political centrality of the Ram temple was lost on V.P. Singh. His government paid scant attention to the matter. The new prime minister had myopic vision. He correctly assessed that the VHP-summoned Dharam Sansad in January 1990 would pass without precipitating a fresh crisis, and concluded that the movement was past its peak. Consequently, he declared a fifteen-point pro-minority programme—almost as a new year gift. But it was tough to satisfy the hard-nosed lot in any community. Shahabuddin was angered with this declaration because 'settlement of the Ayodhya dispute and enactment of a legislation to protect status quo of all places of worship as on August 15, 1947' was not mentioned.[1]

Building the Ram temple was not, per se, the objective of the VHP and other RSS affiliates. The medium-term and long-term objectives respectively were the BJP's electoral rise and securing support for religio-cultural nationalism. During the late nineteenth century, Indian nationalist consciousness swivelled on the religio-cultural axis. Large parts of India were welded into a single nation-state by creating a sense of community-based bonding among

Hindus. Starting from Bengal with Swami Vivekananda and Bankimchandra Chattopadhyay—the latter successfully seeding among the masses the idea of nation on the basis of dharma, elucidated 'in terms of *manushvata* and *samanjasya*, humanity and harmony'[2]—this sentiment gradually secured acceptance in several parts of British India. This early notion of nationalism was put on the backburner after 'inclusive' or 'multiple' sub-nationalisms (region and religion) were amalgamated into pan-Indian nationalism by the Congress, especially with the advent of Gandhi. The RSS, whose notion of nationalism was based on the aforesaid framework of the early years, used the Ram temple agitation to revive the unitarist view of national identity. It was put forth that although Ram was a Hindu god, the demand for a temple was not merely religious. The contention was that the notion of Ram as Maryada Purushottam symbolized the cultural or even national identity of all Indians irrespective of personal faith. Every Indian should consequently acquiesce to the need for a Ram temple at Ayodhya, and not doing so would undermine Indian nationalism and be indicative of the person's lack of patriotic commitment. It followed from this that any person not backing the demand was ranged against national interests. This sentiment found articulation in an early slogan of the agitation—*jo Ram ka nahee, woh hamare kaam ka nahee* (anyone who is not with Ram, is of no use).

The BJP formed majority state governments in the early months of 1990 in Madhya Pradesh, Rajasthan and Himachal Pradesh. It also became part of a coalition in Gujarat besides demonstrating creditable electoral presence in Maharashtra despite remaining on the opposition benches. These victories indicated the BJP's success in expanding its social base, spreading beyond the traditional Brahmin-trader groups that traditionally backed the party. It also made inroads in rural areas in the Hindi heartland and among women. After these successes, Advani spelt out the party's tasks in the course of an interview for a party publication to mark the BJP's first decade in existence. He said that expansion of 'the party's base geographically and socially must continue unabated'.[3] He additionally directed that 'conscious effort must be made to move eastwards and southwards'. Anniversary celebrations, evidence of the party's quest for geographical expansion, were held in Calcutta. In his presidential address, Advani skipped listing the Ram temple issue as a core concern and instead flagged the government's handling of internal security issues in Punjab, Kashmir and Assam as major thrust areas. Critics and adversaries alike erred by interpreting the omission as evidence of the party's realization that the 'Hindu card' bogey had been called. Advani's tactic became a recurring ploy for successive BJP leaders. Modi's campaign in 2014 was notable for the absence of acerbic Hindutva content, like in previous elections he led in Gujarat. This led middle India to believe that he had left the divisive narrative behind. Starting with Advani, the BJP repeatedly raised issues related to national security as part of its effort to underline, first, that it was not a 'single issue' party. Secondly, it wanted to reiterate that the BJP had a different perspective on homeland security and this reflected its stance on minority rights and privileges. Although the party had begun publicizing the thesis that the Congress presided over a soft state and 'appeased' minorities, in 1989-90 this was still on its way to becoming a pivotal point to prop up Hindu victimhood. There was no shift in the dominant opinion that minorities required special, if not preferential treatment. V.P. Singh's programme for the minorities was the result of an understanding that religious minorities required distinct 'packages' to emerge socio-economically at par with the majority community.

The prime minister, like his predecessor, wrongly concluded that a negotiated settlement on Ayodhya was achievable even though the standpoint of neither the VHP and its affiliates nor Muslim groups had undergone any significant alteration. Yet V.P. Singh chased the mirage. Acharya Sushil Muni, a politically ambitious Jain religious leader, was roped in to initiate dialogue. Bowing to the diktats of V.P. Singh, the priest kept out Shahabuddin as well as the VHP from meetings and peace committees. Playing along, the VHP did not press matters and announced a four-month-long moratorium on the agitation. Time showed this was a tactical ploy and not evidence of running out of steam.

*

The VHP was back in the headlines on 23-24 June 1990, announcing at the conclusion of its Kendriya Margdarshak Mandal session in Haridwar that it would begin 'constructing' the Ram temple from 30 October, once again to coincide with the Devotthan ekadashi festival. Simultaneously, the model of the proposed temple was unveiled. It was designed by Gujarat's established temple architect, Chandrakant Sompura, whose father had fashioned the Somnath temple. In 2020, after evaluating other options, the Shri Ram Janmabhoomi Teerth Kshetra Trust decided to build the new temple as per this design although the scale of the temple was made more 'grand' by increasing its size and number of domes. Engineering alterations were also required because of flow of underground water streams. This necessitated demolishing the separately owned Janmasthan temple built in the early years of the eighteenth century as it was almost adjacent to the Babri Masid. But there were worries too within the Hindu fold. Back in June 1990, many backers of the Ram temple felt that the VHP was hogging all the limelight and disallowing views of other groups from being articulated in these meetings. As a result, the resolution at the Haridwar meeting betrayed fears of a split and beseeched temple protagonists of all hues to 'forget all our internal differences and project the Hindu society as an impregnable fort'. Significantly, at this meeting, the VHP added another object of revulsion or hatred to the two already existing, Babri Masjid and Emperor Babur. Hereon, the chief minister of UP, Mulayam Singh Yadav, was ascribed a pejorative—Mulla Mulayam!

Every programme of the VHP from 1984 onwards included an element of spectacle—the consecration of bricks, for instance, in 1989 or the previous yatra from Sitamarhi, Sita's mythical birthplace in 1984. For Shila Pujan Yatras too, a web of programmes was conceptualized. As a first, Sankirtan Mandals or committees to organize daily sessions of bhajans in villages and towns to draw crowds were formed. VHP cadres were directed to use available infrastructure of local temples by infiltrating temple management committees. Plans were drawn to light a consecrated torch or *mashal* on 19 September at Ayodhya at the start of the Navratri period before Dussehra. The flame was symbolically named Ram Agni (fire of Ram). Several torches would be lit from the mother flame and carried to zonal centres where more torches would be lighted and taken to towns and villages. These torches would be called Ram jyotis. On the night of Diwali, people would be asked to assemble at village or town centres and light personal torches to take home and place them outside their doorstep. The VHP also asked Hindus to celebrate Independence Day that year by hoisting saffron flags and blowing conch shells in their houses, instead of joining government-organized functions. The Sangh Parivar was usurping every motif associated with Hinduism—saffron colour, conch shells and of course the ringing clarion call 'Jai Shri Ram', a battle cry that had replaced the softer greeting 'Jai Siya Ram' in which Siya was a colloquial rendering of Sita. The VHP was not just preparing its war machinery for the second year running, but was literally playing with fire.

The VHP's grand plan of sewing up pan-Hindu unity however hit a roadblock when V.P. Singh announced he was implementing the recommendations of the long-ignored Mandal Commission report. Reservation in government jobs and state-funded educational institutes for Other Backward Classes (OBCs) was violently opposed by upper-caste Hindus, leaving the BJP and its affiliates on the horns of a dilemma: which group to back—pro-reservationists or anti-reservationists? But while the BJP was bedevilled greatly over the posture to adopt, its affiliates had greater elbow room as they weren't engaged in competitive populism.

For the BJP, opposing a caste-based award entailed risking support of OBCs who had begun looking at the BJP as a potential electoral option from 1989 onward. On the other hand, if it backed the prime minister's decision, it faced desertions of upper castes from its fold. Others in the religio-cultural nationalist fold however were forthright. The *Organiser* in its issue dated 26 August 1990 accused V.P. Singh of undoing 'the great task of uniting Hindu society from the days of Vivekananda, Dayanand Saraswati, Mahatma Gandhi and Dr Hedgewar'. (It must be noted that Gandhi was included among spearheads of Hindu unification, indicating that advocates of political Hinduism had realized by then that it was essential to at least pay lip service to the Mahatma's memory. The past narrative of denigrating him for seeking equity for Muslims and other minorities was quietly dropped.) The *Organiser* effectively articulated the RSS unease with the reservation policy. In the same issue, the RSS mouthpiece claimed that reservation 'plays havoc' with the 'social fabric' and provides premium for 'mediocrity, encourages brain-drain and sharpens caste divide'. The discomfort of the RSS and its affiliates with India's reservation policy had persisted for decades although this was masked by calling for 'review' of the policy or often by advocating harmonious conversation between pro- and anti-reservationists.[4]

The stance of the RSS on affirmative action took a complete turnaround over the years and was spelt out on 10 August 2021. Dattareya Hosabale, the general secretary of the RSS declared at a public event that reservations were a 'historical necessity' and 'should continue' till the time certain social groups face inequality. This development, coupled with decisions like nominating a Dalit to the Ram temple trust, marked considerable progress in the RSS's objective of social inclusion post-Meenakshipuram conversions to forge Hindu unity.

But in 1990, following V.P. Singh's decision, the BJP leadership was of the view that upper castes had to be gradually prepared for accepting that reservations were 'here to stay'. Consequently, the BJP and its affiliates decided to tread the middle path and stated that it would rather that reservations were provided on economic criteria. The first task was to revive the Hindu unity witnessed in the run-up to the Shilanyas when Hindu masses, irrespective of caste, participated in Ram Shila Yatras and other associated rituals to counter Muslim response. Advani was of the view that after having put the Ayodhya issue on the backburner for some time, it was now necessary to lend full-throated backing for the VHP's kar seva programme. The question was how?

*

V.P. Singh's decision on the Mandal Commission recommendations coincided with the time when the television serial on the Mahabharata was heading for its finale on Doordarshan, on 8 July. Mirroring the mythological war between cousins, a massive conflict between former associates erupted within the ruling Janata Dal. By the end of July, a vertical split was inevitable. To overcome challenges within his party and simultaneously recasting his political constituency, V.P. Singh announced the implementation of recommendations made almost a decade ago to reserve jobs in government and seats in state-funded educational institutions for the OBCs. The proclamation met with expected, and now well-known reactions. Upper-caste protestors were first off the starting block, with an attempted self-immolation bid in Delhi becoming the symbol of anti-reservationists' anger against the prime minister.

This reaction was anticipated and Singh had thought through his move. He remained resolute because anti-reservationists were hopelessly outnumbered by pro-reservationists. If matters came to a head, backward classes could be mobilized to hit the streets. Resurgence of caste animus on a *rozi-roti* or bread-and-butter issue was of foremost worry for the Sangh Parivar, especially the BJP because its all-embracing Hindu vote bank was fragmented overnight. This was a conflict precipitated by two contradictory assessments of Hindu society—one which considered it primarily cohesive, the other seeing it as essentially fragmented and conflict-ridden. The single factor that determined whether unity would prevail or the collective would remain perennially locked in combat was caste. The challenge before the Sangh Parivar leadership was to keep them united on an issue with religious appeal and prevent them from locking horns on the issue of reaping benefits of the government's positive discrimination policy.

The RSS leadership was forced to begin internal deliberations after pro-reservationists hit the streets in full force in Bihar. The urgency within the Sangh Parivar underscored that with Mandal the prime minister had successfully checkmated the *kamandal*, the water pot used by Hindu ascetics or yogis to carry water, in this case typifying the Ram temple agitation. V.P. Singh's suo motu declaration demonstrated that his political alliance with the BJP was a relationship of convenience with no long-term future. Eventually, one of the two would survive, and as it was proved over time, it was the political force which kept its ear to the ground consistently, had the backing of a massive network of cadre and was in possession of a more seductive idea, that succeeded in its mission.

Close to political desperation in August-September 1990 to bring upper and backward castes to make common cause, the Sangh Parivar hatched an innovative plan that infused new life into the BJP. A novel image was created for L.K. Advani, at odds with how he was publicly seen until then: the quintessential gentle persuader. The BJP veteran wrote in his memoirs that in early September 1990, his wife, Kamala, and he, were 'spending a quiet evening in our Pandara Park home' when Pramod Mahajan, one of the four general secretaries of the party, dropped in unannounced. 'Although it was a casual visit, it was obvious that Ayodhya was uppermost on his mind too ... "I am thinking of undertaking a padyatra [journey on foot] from Somnath to reach Ayodhya on 30th October," I told Pramod and Kamala ... Pramod, a meticulous organiser of political campaign, quickly began a mental exercise ... After a pause, he remarked, "A padyatra is a good idea but not very useful for the purpose you have in mind. You'll at the most be able to cover a small part of Gujarat, Rajasthan, Madhya Pradesh, Delhi and half of UP." I asked him for an alternative.'[5]

The 'alternative' that Mahajan, the 'nuts and bolts' person in the BJP and with extensive connections in corporate India, conjured up was a 10,000-odd-kilometre journey starting at Somnath temple, a destination loaded with political symbolism for Hindu outfits. Eventually, Advani's religio-political voyage started on 25 September, birth anniversary of Deendayal Upadhyaya, and he was foisted atop a light commercial vehicle remodelled into a modern chariot. The route crisscrossed nine communally sensitive states before it was to enter its destination state of Uttar Pradesh and reach Ayodhya in time for the kar seva programme on 30 October. Mahajan drew up a gruelling schedule for his president—an average of 300 kilometres and at least six public meetings a day. By the time he had completed just one-fourth of his route, Advani realized he had a winner on his hands and termed his 'road show', as newspapers called it, the trigger for 'one of the biggest mass movements' in post-Independence India.[6] The Rath was perceived as divine by Hindus who gathered to see it drive past or hear him and imagined Advani as a person seeking to provide the rightful space for Ram. In speeches, he explained that the yatra was started from Somnath to 'contextualise Ayodhya in the historical lineage of Muslim aggression and to seek legitimacy for Mandir movement by drawing a parallel'.[7] A simplistic case built on half-truths, a standard tactic, was submitted to the public: If the 'secular' Nehru government 'agreed' to reconstruction of the temple at Somnath, how could the V.P. Singh government, supported by the BJP, not allow the VHP to begin construction with kar seva? This political argument, as distinct from the religio-cultural foundations of previous arguments, was indicative of the leadership of the Ayodhya movement passing from the hands of the VHP to the BJP, specifically Advani. Advani was the original *loh* purush or Iron Man, a spin on the moniker of Sardar Patel, long eulogized by the Hindu right for his nuanced divergences with Jawaharlal Nehru on issues of internal security and the reconstruction of the Somnath temple. Advani's tactics were simple—heighten fear and targeted anger, destroy or trivialize debate and move towards acquiring political power. Although a reluctant backer of the plan all along, Vajpayee did not say no to his colleagues' suggestion of walking up to the President and informing him, after Advani's arrest, of his party's decision to withdraw support from the government.

Much has been said about the existence of a 'moderate' section within the BJP-RSS in opposition to 'hardliners'. This was especially stated about leaders like Vajpayee and Jaswant Singh, the former armyman who metamorphosed into a 'gentleman-politician'. In later years, the same trope surfaced repeatedly in the context of new generations of leaders, the latest being in 2019 when it was presumed that Amit Shah was making a more decisive push for items on the Hindutva agenda in contrast to the 'sobering' Modi. But from the beginning there was little doubt that this was a deceptive manoeuvre to enable one set of leaders to mobilize a less strident section of society, while others engaged with the belligerent supporters, even as a smaller number of leaders reached out to the so-called 'fringe' sections. Despite ostensible divergences among leaders, they shared common views. Jaswant Singh, for instance, in an article in *Seminar* in February 1993 disagreed that the Babri Masjid's demolition was cataclysmic and instead argued that it marked a 'transition from the old order towards an emerging India'.[8] Before his death in September 2020, Jaswant Singh spent several years in political wilderness, like several others of his generation, but his articulation of the thought that the Ayodhya agitation was the turning point towards an emerging India, paved the way for Modi's concept of 'new India' to a generation that was unaware of this being an old maxim.

In the course of his first rath yatra, Advani was fashioned as mythical reincarnate, especially after 25 September when he picked up a bow at Somnath, outside the precincts of the Shiva temple, and drew the string with an arrow notionally pointed in the direction of Ayodhya. In speeches, he claimed that construction of the temple would enhance national pride and 'correct' a historical wrong. Advani's verbal ferocity was matched by actual bloodletting at several places as the yatra rolled towards Delhi, where it strategically halted for a few days to demonstrate the BJP's strength to the Union government. Applying tilak on the BJP president's forehead after drawing blood from the thumb became the norm, and he was often presented arms—bows, arrows, discs, maces, swords and trishuls or tridents in a symbolic call to arms against the 'other'. Mahajan asked Muslims in

Mandsaur, Madhya Pradesh, to either have faith in Ram or leave India, a slogan that was reiterated time and again, with modifications or without. BJP ally Shiv Sena's chief Bal Thackeray asked for the 'unholy green' to be wiped out. Advani's chariot left blood and gore in its wake. Between 1 September and 20 November there were 116 communal riots leaving 564 people dead. Most deaths occurred in Gujarat, Karnataka, Madhya Pradesh, Rajasthan and of course Bihar and UP. These states remained BJP strongholds for long periods of time thereafter.

Yet Advani's journey continued being showcased as a righteous mission, drawing increasingly large audiences. The Union government was warned that stopping the yatra would entail withdrawal of BJP's support. The Congress did not say it would step in to shore up Singh's regime. A failed effort was made to hammer out a compromise settlement while Advani was in the capital. V.P. Singh issued an ordinance broadly accepting the BJP's demand that kar seva be allowed on land outside the Babri Masjid save for a 30-ft perimeter. Singh withdrew the ordinance within forty-eight hours. This was indicative of both his choice and compulsion. While his heart guided him to intervene and recommended to the President to promulgate the law, his head reasoned that it would be a great political risk. Eventually, he could neither save his government, nor could he enlist support of large sections of Muslims over time.

The prime minister was testing the waters by issuing the ordinance which would have permitted kar seva, the way Rajiv Gandhi gave the green signal to the shilanyas in 1989, while simultaneously protecting the Babri Masjid structure. Muslim leaders as well as several stalwarts and satraps—most prominently the two Yadav leaders, Mulayam Singh and Lalu Prasad, within his party—protested after the ordinance was issued without prior consultation. Singh and Mulayam Singh were locked in a tussle for Muslim support in UP and the latter was vociferously cheered by the community for his provocative statement—*parinde ko par nahee marne doonga* (will not allow even a bird to flutter). History records V.P. Singh's conduct during those days as duplicitousness—allowing kar seva while maintaining status quo of the mosque structure. Eventually his Muslim supporters saw through the fact that his actions were very similar to Rajiv Gandhi's a year earlier.

Advani's yatra, the first instance of political pilgrimage in the Ram Janmabhoomi agitation, was eventually stopped in Bihar and he was placed under detention. The entire exercise was a meticulously choreographed drama aimed at scoring political points. Even the death of kar sevaks in the police firing on November 2 was milked and shobha yatras (memorial rallies) were taken out throughout India.

The BJP's decision to withdraw support remains the only instance in Indian political history when a government had to bow out of office because of the Ram temple issue. For spearheads of the movement, this was no mean achievement. From being a leader of the middle classes, Advani demonstrated his charisma among the masses. Being seen as Sardar Patel reincarnate had been the dream of many a leader since his passing in December 1950. Advani came to be enthroned as Loh Purush of the new era. The trouble, however, was that this title proved self-limiting and was snatched away in the not very distant future.

*

If eventually Advani failed to realize his ambition of becoming prime minister, the reasons lay in his later diffidence over the Ram temple issue. These self-doubts were not merely his, but shared by several in the Hindutva fraternity. These misgivings had nothing to do with Advani's capacity to lead an electoral campaign on the issue, but over the BJP being seen as a single-issue party. The contentious shrine's demolition had obliterated the structure whose existence served as a rallying call. Since a makeshift temple was immediately built at the site and rituals were being conducted, the matter of building a 'resplendent' temple became secondary. Most believed that it was a matter of time before the temple was constructed. Although vehemently opposed to the demand to rebuild the mosque, the majority of Hindus were unwilling to back the BJP solely on the basis of its advocacy of the Ram temple. This section in the electorate was willing to tilt to the right, but not with the aggression and vocalization associated with Advani.

In the years immediately after the demolition, the Indian economy had opened up, homegrown as well as cross-border terrorism became a recurring narrative, and fragmentation of the polity was appearing inevitable. The middle class emerged as a fast-growing political constituency and the BJP needed to induct this articulate and aspirational section into the Hindutva brigade. But this could be achieved only with a vocabulary different from the past, one that appealed chiefly to the middle, lower-middle and working class besides enrolling divergent rural Hindu social groups. The divisive ideology of religio-cultural nationalism had to be sugar-coated with the still-popular resonance of secularism. Nehruvianism was on its deathbed but lip service still had to be paid. These sentiments in the years immediately after the demolition had an effect on the eternal prime ministerial aspirant. Eventually, he became a victim of this dichotomy and made way for Vajpayee.

Almost a decade later, six years of which were spent as the second-most influential person in government, on his visit to Pakistan in June 2005, Advani—as part of a rebranding exercise—hailed Muhammad Ali Jinnah as 'secular' and as an 'ambassador of Hindu-Muslim unity'. Neither he nor the regime in Islamabad recalled that in a case dating back to 1948, Advani was named as a conspirator in a case to assassinate Jinnah. Two days prior to this public praise of the person who developed the two-nation theory, Advani distanced himself from the concept of 'akhand Bharat'. He also admitted to Partition being 'an unalterable reality of history'.[9] This tactic did not enable him to win over the middle ground in Indian politics and simultaneously lost his hold on the right.

Advani wrongly believed that entry to India's political centre stage could not be made from the right flank. In 2005, he failed to grasp that the UPA being in power notwithstanding, the appeal for the idea of Hindutva had grown and was slowly acquiring a critical mass. Despite stating explicitly in its election manifesto for the 1996 parliamentary election, the first after the demolition, that the BJP would 'facilitate the construction' of the Ram temple, the agitation's charioteer made way for a more amiable Vajpayee. There are conflicting reports regarding Advani's astonishing announcement in November 1995 that the party was reviving Vajpayee as its prime ministerial face. He claimed in his autobiography that he made the announcement without consulting anyone, a statement difficult to believe. Within the Hindu nationalistic fold, monumental decisions prior to 2014 were never taken without consultation with a larger collective. Certainly, the Sangh Parivar was of the view that with the Congress a declining force, the BJP under Vajpayee stood a better chance of winning more seats and convincing other parties to partner it in government. By their own admission, the Ram temple agitation may have resonated enough to muster thousands of volunteers to go to Ayodhya and tear down the mosque, but was still insufficient reason for more than a third of the people to vote for the party. Further canvassing was required to win over people and other parties to the BJP's viewpoint that India was 'one nation, one people, one culture' and that Indian nationalism was 'not merely bound by the geographical or political identity of India, but defined by our ancient cultural heritage'.[10]

The BJP's failure to attract new coalition partners in 1996 forced Vajpayee to step down as prime minister after just thirteen days. As a result, the Sangh Parivar had no option but to further tone down their bluster on the Ram temple. Consequently, the VHP began focussing on other issues, principally against religious conversions. Yet old habits die hard. In December 1997, amid campaigning for the 1998 parliamentary polls, Ashok Singhal made a blasphemous statement: 'It is time to catch the Muslims by their necks and tell them where their place lies.' He added, 'Kashi and Mathura (too) are ours.'[11] The BJP was aware that this would not just end all hopes of winning new friends but would make even the couple that were on board have second thoughts. Unsurprisingly, on the same day, Advani addressed a meeting in Tirupati, Andhra Pradesh, clarifying that the other two temples 'were not on the agenda of the BJP'.[12]

Further moderation was a compulsion once the party formed an omnibus coalition in March 1998. During negotiations, several parties made it clear that they would have no truck with the Hindu nationalistic party unless a consensual National Agenda of Governance was negotiated, spelling out priorities and listing these on the to-do list. When this was made public, it had no mention of the BJP's three contentious promises: Ram temple, abrogation of Article 370 of the Constitution and introduction of Uniform Civil Code. These promises were missing from the combined manifesto of the National Democratic Alliance (NDA) for the Lok Sabha polls in 1999 too. In these years, when the BJP was fighting shy of donning its Ayodhya colours and using vocabulary neither of religio-cultural mobilization nor of confrontation, the RSS chief, Rajendra Singh, justified the BJP's silence on the three divisive issues that defined its belief of cultural nationalism, 'the core of Hindutva ... the identity of our ancient nation'. In a speech, he explained the party's volte face: 'If you are ill, you don't take bath. But that does not mean that this will be an arrangement forever, in all circumstances.'[13]

It took the BJP two decades to secure support in the parliament to do away with Article 370 that gave Jammu and Kashmir its special status. In another three months, the party had the gratification of seeing a large section of society hailing the Supreme Court verdict on the disputed property in Ayodhya. In between, it had also sneaked in a promise which it delivered although it was not part of the 'contentious three': criminalizing triple talaq or instantaneous divorce among Muslims. Over the two decades after the demolition, the Ram temple campaign as a political instrument or tool of political mobilization was used just once—in 2002.

The BJP and its affiliates within the Sangh Parivar kept the Ayodhya issue in the national consciousness with a steady infusion of issues having the foundations of Hindutva in its core. The only time that the Ram temple caused massive political uproar, in March-April 2002, it led to the rise, in the national arena, of the man who from

2014 onward played a pivotal role in guiding the religio-cultural brotherhood to political power. Indeed, the rise of Narendra Modi is as much due to his consistent criticism by adversaries, as it is because of his steady articulation of the belief that Indianness, Bharatiyata and Hindutva are synonyms, the basis of India's national identity.[14] It is due to his persistence, not riven by self-doubt or circumspection like his one-time mentor, Advani, that enough Indians began believing in the notion that 'cultural nationalism is the most potent antidote to communalism, divisiveness, and separatism of every kind … a guarantor of national unity and national integration'.[15] The neo-converts drawn by Modi's appeal were instrumental in handing him two successive electoral majorities.

*

As early as October-November 1989, much before Gujarat began being referred to as Hindutva's laboratory, Modi had concluded that the Ayodhya agitation had opened the gates of electoral success for the BJP in Gujarat. Although secretary of the state unit, he was relatively junior at thirty-nine. His viewpoint, that the BJP should contest parliamentary elections independently, and not in alliance with the Janata Dal, was turned down by seniors, Advani included. During negotiations, Modi wanted parity—twenty-six parliamentary seats from the state apportioned equally. Others, unsure of the public appeal for the Ram temple agitation's timbre, agreed to twelve seats that the Janata Dal was willing to give it. Modi's confidence was not ill-founded—the BJP won each seat it contested, while the JD lost three of the fourteen it fought. Having scored a point within his party, Modi was elevated as principal negotiator for the assembly elections in February 1990.

Talks broke down because of his insistence on equal sharing of seats. Central leaders intervened and sewed a flawed alliance with the two allies contesting against one another in more than fifty seats. Yet, post-verdict, the two decided to collaborate because between them they had clear majority. The Janata Dal nominee, Chimanbhai Patel, became chief minister. In recognition of his political reading and organizational capacities, Modi was promoted as general secretary (organization) of the Gujarat unit. In due course, he was asked to anchor the Gujarat leg of Advani's Ram Rath Yatra. Nine months later, when fresh parliamentary polls were necessitated in 1991, the BJP improved its tally astonishingly—winning twenty out of the twenty-six seats in Gujarat with a vote share of 50.2 per cent. By then, the BJP had snapped ties with the Janata Dal and walked out of the state government.

The 'political Hindu', enthused by the idea of Ram temple, had unquestionably reared its head. Gujarat was labelled Hindutva's crucible and Modi was to become the chief 'chemist'. In UP too, the BJP won fifty-one of the eighty-five parliamentary seats. In the state polls held simultaneously, the party secured a majority and formed the government on its own. The BJP eventually secured a majority in the Gujarat Vidhan Sabha and formed the government in March 1995 on the wings of a campaign run on the promise of providing people a life devoid of '*bhay, bhookh aur bhrashtachar*' (fear, hunger and corruption). Fear, in the context of Gujarat, meant threat from growing radicalization among sections of Muslims. The slogan was evidence that gains from the Ram temple agitation were being extrapolated to other issues to promote the ideology of religio-cultural nationalism. This was a play on one of BJP's slogan for the 1991 Lok Sabha election that conjoined

Ram with economic bare necessities for people: Ram and roti.

Paradoxically, Modi's rise to national prominence was a consequence of a chain of events in which he had little role to play. The verbally gutsy leader with a marked preference for the provocative, he would have been preparing for a quiet end of the year, two months after Vajpayee took oath as prime minister for the third time in October 1999, when Indian Airline Flight number IC-814 was hijacked on the eve of the prime minister's birthday. Three months later, a change of guard was necessitated at the top of the RSS owing to sarsanghchalak Rajendra Singh 'Rajju Bhaiyya's' continuing illness. Days after taking over on 10 March 2000, the new chief, the acerbic K.S. Sudarshan, warned of the inevitability of another 'epic war' between Hindus and 'anti-Hindus' on whose conclusion 'every opposition to Hindutva will change'. He gloated that many who were previously ambivalent had already turned faithful.

Beginning with the Kargil conflict in 1999, the BJP and its affiliates became additionally vocal in claiming that a nexus existed between Pakistan, terrorists—homegrown as well as cross-border—and their supporters (read Muslims, opposition parties and civil society, especially human rights groups). Sudarshan's call for a holy war appeared appropriate to Hindu nationalists as days after his claim, thirty-six Sikhs were massacred by terrorists in Chittisinghpura, Jammu and Kashmir, during the visit of the president of the United States, Bill Clinton. Despite the American president affirming—during a visit in March 2000 that redefined Indo-US relations—that terrorist violence on Indian soil 'must end', cross-border terrorism continued in Kashmir. In early August, almost ninety Amarnath pilgrims were gunned down in a series of attacks. The year ended on a violent and symbolic note when terrorists sneaked into the Red Fort.

Despite rising terrorist violence, Vajpayee announced unilateral ceasefire in Jammu and Kashmir from December and invited General Pervez Musharraf of Pakistan for a summit at Agra in July 2001. Previously, in a tragedy wholly unrelated to internal security threats, but which eventually opened the door for Modi to emerge on the national arena, an earthquake on 26 January 2001 with its epicentre in Kutch district devastated Gujarat.

Insofar as the Ram temple was concerned, exasperation was mounting over the Vajpayee government's decision to merely await the Allahabad High Court verdict in the title suit. This angered the VHP and the RSS brass led by the mercurial Sudarshan, who were often at daggers drawn with Vajpayee. There was a perceptible difference in how the formation of a government with the BJP at its head was interpreted by the BJP and its affiliates within the Sangh Parivar, especially VHP. Christian missionaries and missionary activity came under attack in several violent incidents (including the lynching of Graham Staines, the Australian missionary, and his two minor sons) as a consequence of belligerence within its ranks causing political difficulties in navigating the coalition.

In this backdrop an assortment of saffron-clad saints owing allegiance to the VHP assembled for another session of the Dharam Sansad during the Kumbha Mela in Allahabad in January 2001. No immediate date was set for mass mobilization in Ayodhya. The announcement that construction of the temple would begin in Ayodhya fourteen months later, from 15 March 2002, lulled its adversaries and the BJP leadership into complacency. Advani and others had declared a decade ago that construction of the Ram temple was not the sole objective of the Ram Janmabhoomi agitation. But there were others within the ideological fold who were primarily committed to it. This was yet another instance of different affiliates within the Sangh Parivar having different priorities. After almost a decade of keeping the issue on the backburner, they would need fourteen months to stir up passions for the cause of the Ram temple once again.

*

At its annual meeting in March 2001, the Akhil Bharatiya Pratinidhi Sabha of the RSS 'endorsed' the VHP's plan to revive the Ayodhya movement. A resolution stated that the Vajpayee government had been given 'sufficient time for the Government to do away with the hurdles needlessly obstructing the temple construction over almost a decade' and that the 'ball is now in the Government's court'.[16] The plan was an encore of the 1989 and 1992 campaigns, involving a fusion of three elements. First, innovative Hindu worship rituals on the lines of shila pujan, shilanyas, etc., in which people were motivated to participate. The second feature was an ostensibly religious yatra but which was essentially a political march. The last element was providing the cadre and neo-converts the illusion of participating in the construction of the Ram temple, although this is a professional task requiring people with specific skills working under adequate technical supervision.

A three-month-long countrywide mass mobilization drive was scheduled between 18 October 2001 and 18 January 2002. It was to be resumed on 24 February in Ayodhya and slated to continue for the next hundred days. The first leg, named Shri Ram Naam Jap Yagna, was a drive to marshal people on the lines of the 1989 initiative of daily Ram bhajans in temples in villages, towns and cities. In 2001, a special *stotra* or hymn to pay obeisance to Lord Ram was written. Community as well as personal chanting of the mantra, especially composed for construction of a Ram temple, spawned a sense of civic participation among Hindus who turned out for these. Those who chanted the mantra without pause for sixty-five days qualified to participate in the next phase of the programme.

These qualifiers were provided tridents, saffron headbands and Ram Sevak identity cards, adornments of pride. Community chanting started in Gujarat days after Modi assumed charge as chief minister in October 2001. Nearly 2000 volunteers who qualified from the state left for Ayodhya on 22, 24 and 26 February 2002. They were to participate in the second phase of the specially conceived ritual, the Purnahuti Yagna, before returning to make way for the next group of qualifiers or Ram sevaks from another state. Starting 24 February, this second phase of ritual worship was to go on for a hundred days, by when the construction was supposed to start. The Purnahuti Yagna was certainly confrontational in character because kar seva was to begin from 15 March and unless the judicial directive on status quo in the entire government-controlled 67 acres of land was altered by the Supreme Court, the government would have to deploy forces to halt the programme and force VHP activists to vacate the site of the ritual.

The second element of the temple agitation revival package in 2001 was the yatra or political pilgrimage. Uncharacteristically, it was a low-key affair because the VHP was focused on mobilizing masses for the Ayodhya programme. Consequently, the Sant Chetawani Yatra or the march to serve a warning from holy men had Ashok Singhal at its head, with almost 3000 saffron-clad sadhus in tow. This Ayodhya to Delhi march flagged off on 21 January 2002 and reached the Indian capital symbolically on Republic Day, 26 January. They met Vajpayee the next day and he pleaded with the religious leaders to give the government more time to find a way out.

The third element of this confrontationist line-up in 2001-02 was kar seva or construction from 12 March. The principal demand was that the government must find means, prior to this date, to segregate disputed and undisputed portions of the 67 acres of land in government control. This phase, however, never got under way as we shall see. The VHP leadership was aware that starting to build the temple was no ordinary matter and they created several smokescreens to convey to the restive cadre that 'progress' was being made.

As noted previously, Modi was sworn in as Gujarat chief minister days prior to the launch of the three-pronged plan of the VHP. He was well aware of rising communal tension in the state as selected Ram Sevaks headed for Ayodhya on trains. The first batch reached the temple town on 24 February. After participating in the Purnahuti Yagna on 25 February, they boarded the Sabarmati Express to return to Gujarat. The train reached Godhra station on 27 February minutes before 8 a.m. What happened subsequently requires little reiteration.

The scale of violence and death that followed forced the UP government to flush out VHP volunteers from Ayodhya and led to the RSS agreeing to mediate between the VHP and the government. The RSS succeeded in getting the VHP to scale down its plans. On 4 March, the Shankaracharya of Kanchi Kamakoti Peetham also embarked on another attempt at finding a meeting point between the VHP and Muslim organizations, but it was destined to fail and left the

VHP with no option but to take a few steps backward even as communal violence in Gujarat continued abated.

When the matter reached the Supreme Court, the Centre showed its true colours and pleaded that the VHP be permitted to symbolically consecrate a sculpted pillar at a spot close to the makeshift temple but within the undisputed part of the 67 acres of land. The apex court judges of the time showed spine and turned down the Centre's plea. Its ruling disallowing any form of 'religious activity … either symbolic or actual' brought the curtains down on this round. However, this phase of agitation did not impair the political trajectory of the man under whose tenure the final steps towards the construction of a Ram temple at Ayodhya started to be taken. Without being present in Ayodhya in February-March 2002, Modi benefited the most from the gory fate that returning Ram Sevaks met with at Godhra.

*

Away from Ayodhya and Gujarat, three events in India and abroad in 2001-02 had a profound effect on the ideological orientation of social discourse in India. Since the mid-1980s people had increasingly questioned what had till then been articles of faith in the Indian republic but these three events provided an opportunity to decisively break from the past.

Globally, a spike in intercommunity dissonance was seen post 9/11 and almost overnight Samuel Huntington's *Clash of Civilizations*[17] merited reconsideration among those who argued that dialogue among civilizations would continue ceaselessly. After the attack on the World Trade Center and other American facilities, the launch of the global war on terror polarized the world. In India, the terrorist attack on Parliament in December 2001, preceded by the terrorist attack on the Jammu and Kashmir legislative assembly in Srinagar two-and-a-half months ago, aggravated the increasing dissonance. The fast-crystallizing prejudicial view of the majority towards minorities was accentuated by the third event of 2001-02: India and Pakistan getting embroiled in an eyeball-to-eyeball military confrontation and snapping diplomatic ties.

Despite these developments which laid the ground for Modi to firmly harness the BJP's pre-existing political constituency in Gujarat, the party's electoral slide remained unceasing. Because he was not a legislator when sworn in as chief minister, it was constitutionally obligatory for Modi to become a member of the state assembly within six months. In by-elections for three seats held in February 2002, the Congress wrested two. Modi managed to win his seat. But the post-Godhra violence turned political fortunes on its head. In assembly elections held in December 2002, Modi single-handedly swept the polls with a polarizing and divisive campaign.

Surprisingly, in an election campaign triggered by the tragedy that befell volunteers returning from Ayodhya, Modi did not significantly refer to the Ram temple issue except for occasionally invoking the slogan of Jai Shri Ram. The chief minister termed the post-Godhra riots an instance of '*kriya pratikriya ki chain*' (chain of action and reaction), indicating he did not think that any community was specifically targeted in the violence. His words echoed V.S. Naipaul's description of the Babri Masjid demolition as 'an act of historical balancing'.[18] Modi's campaign, however, went beyond the Ram temple and embraced the more divisive politics of 'othering'.

Modi's campaign narrative was initially aimed at harnessing the state's sub-nationalistic identity. His electoral plank of 2002 was founded on a web of issues articulated in the course of the Ayodhya campaign, overtly or covertly. By intermeshing issues, Modi played a pivotal role in steering the kernel of the idea which was introduced in the early 1980s into an expansive political plank or agenda. An instance of how he continued forging linkages between specific objectives and success of religio-cultural nationalists was evident in August 2020. The newly formed temple trust decided to invite Modi to perform the Bhoomi Pujan ceremony. He was given two dates to choose from, depending on convenience—3 August and 5 August. The latter date was chosen because it would mark the first anniversary of Article 370 of the Indian Constitution being abrogated. Modi's craftiness at intertwining completely unrelated events to propagate his vision of nationalism was evident in 2021 too. Speaking at an unrelated event on 5 August, he drew parallels between the Indian men's hockey team winning a medal after a gap of forty-one years earlier that day and his government's decision two years ago on Kashmir. Modi claimed that it furthered the idea of Ek Bharat, Shrestha Bharat. He also mentioned that exactly a year earlier, 'Indians took the first step towards the construction of a grand Ram temple after hundreds years.'

After the Godhra violence and Modi's successful campaign in 2002, the issue of Ram temple lost its capacity to mobilize or assemble people in Ayodhya to agitate. Yet he remained unswervingly on the Hindu nationalistic course, albeit disguising his ideological moorings during the 2014 campaign to woo new constituencies with a development spiel. For obvious reasons, no direct interconnection can be established or suggested between him and the nature of the Supreme Court's final verdict awarding the disputed site to Hindus. Yet the Centre's hand was felt throughout the process when the apex court finally fast-tracked the Ayodhya case. The Ram temple may cease to occupy much mind space among people. But the new mindset of Indians, framed in the course of the political movement for the temple, will be tough to alter in the years to come.

Acknowledgements

The thank you list for this book runs deep into time. It must begin with several editors, chiefs of bureau and other colleagues during the 1980s and 1990s for their initial patience and later guidance. There were several of them at different points of time but mention is essential of two editors: M.L. Kotru for reposing faith in my ability to report on the communal riots in Meerut in 1987, a first for a daily paper, *The Statesman*, despite not being on its rolls. Neena Vyas, for sharing bylines, M.K. Venu, for exchanging information and coming along on a two-wheeler and the late Jaswinder Singh (Jassi) for inputs on the Maliana massacre, all during the Meerut riots.

The late T.V.R. Shenoy, my editor in *Sunday Mail*, for allowing critical reports on the imbroglio despite his friends in the BJP, not that he did not have them in other parties. Seeing my steadiness in reporting on Ayodhya and related issues, he threatened to create a new byline for me—'Our Religious Correspondent'. Thankfully, it remained a threat. He also alerted me on the existence of the till then, shadowy K.N. Govindacharya, next among those who helped in comprehending the sangh parivar's dynamics. Consistently displaying democratic spirit, gradually waning in India, he continues doing so, despite awareness that I have a differing perspective. A similar openness was evident among several VHP leaders during the agitation's initial years. They included Surya Krishna, who I subsequently lost contact with and the now deceased Onkar Bhave. Many of BJP's early leaders in Delhi, were always willing to spend time individually and in small groups. K.L. Sharma, K.R. Malkani and J.P. Mathur are all no more but I owe a lot to them. The difference between conversations with them and other senior leaders in the Vajpayee–Advani league, was that these were informal conversations and frequently laced with raucous laughter. When he was deputed as BJP state prabhari or office bearer in Chandigarh and New Delhi, Prime Minister Narendra Modi graciously made himself available for detailed background conversations.

Thanks are also due to the éminence grisé on the 'other' side. Most prominent of these, the deceased Syed Shahabuddin made himself available without prior appointment. He too continued interacting till health permitted despite none too flattering comments on him in my writings.

Varsha consistently motivated me to revisit the Ayodhya issue and re-examine its centrality in Indian politics. She had an ally in Qurban Ali, although they did not act in tandem. In conversations, he impressed on the need for me to write again on the issue of the Ram temple agitation in its contemporary context for a new generation of readers.

When I eventually embarked on this book, decades-old historian friends, Gyanesh Kudaisya, Salil Misra and Rizwan Qaiser made valuable suggestions. The last of them, present at the release of each of my previous books, sadly shall not be witness to this one's publication, having passed away during the second wave of the Covid-19 pandemic. We rarely discussed this book specifically, but regular chats with Hilal Ahmed provided new perspective and were useful for this book.

A word of gratitude for several who are part of the RSS ecosystem and who continue interacting with me providing inputs and facilitating me to look at the picture from a perspective that I don't share or agree with. They include Dilip Deodhar and Virag Pachpore.

A heartfelt word of gratefulness to Karan Thapar, Mridula Mukherjee and S. Irfan Habib, redoubtable personalities, for taking time out of their pressing schedules to write words of praise that can be read on the book's cover after poring over the proofs in quick time. Their endorsement means a lot.

A word of special appreciation is due to Ravi Singh and Renuka Chatterjee (and Shantanu Ray Chaudhuri) of Speaking Tiger for first agreeing to publish this book and then persevering with it despite the rapidly changing times. They braved personal and professional challenges in these difficult times but remained firm on bringing out the book well in time.

Special thanks for Antoine Védeilhé, the journalist-photographer, part of the team making a documentary film that came to interview me, for taking my picture for the book. Thanks are also due to Sanjay Sharma, news cameraperson and friend for decades, and Praveen Jain, who dug into their archives for pictures that could be used in this book.

For well over a decade and half, Gyan Verma has been a daily sounding board, exchanging snatches of political developments and valuable perspective. Conversations with him often forced me, once again, to re-examine predilections honed in the environs of the Jawaharlal Nehru University through interactions with a vibrant academic community of faculty and alumni, reconnecting with whom is now possible, courtesy social media.

The larger family, like always, was available for

emotional unburdening, essential in the post-pandemic world. Heading the list are Saanvi, Tanisha and Ritisha, each gradually heading towards that stage of life when they will play roles in shaping India's future. Like for everyone, it was a trying period for their parents, Siddharth, Pragya, Abhishek and Vigya, but they never winced when I imposed upon them.

There are several others who aided me in understanding not just the Ayodhya conundrum, but the entire framework of emerging majoritarianism in India. My apologies to those who are inadvertently missed in this list. Lastly, despite the numerous who provide guidance and assistance, the responsibility for what is contained between the covers, is completely mine.

I hope readers will excuse the inadequacies they find.

Notes

1. Ram: From Mythical Hero to God to Political Icon

1. T.K. Arun, 'Hail the Verdict, Move On', *The Economic Times*, 11 November 2019, accessed-on 15 November 2019. https://economictimes.indiatimes.com/news/politics-and-nation/view-how-the-ayodhya-verdict-retains-the-secular-fabric-of-the-indian-state/articleshow/71998083.cms
2. Daniela Berti, 'Political Patronage and Ritual Competitions at Dussehra Festival in Northern India', PDF downloaded from https://hal.archives-ouvertes.fr/hal-00627913, 18 January 2021.
3. For further argument of this selective projection of various facets of the Ram story, read Pratap Bhanu Mehta, 'The reconfiguration of Hinduism is now complete', *Indian Express*, 11 November 2019, accessed on 16 November 2019, https://indianexpress.com/article/opinion/columns/ayodhya-verdict-supreme-court-ramjanam-bhoomi-babri-masjid-case-6112164/
4. Nilanjan Mukhopadhyay, *The Demolition: India at the Crossroads*, HarperCollins, New Delhi, 1994, p. 19.
5. Pratap Bhanu Mehta, 'The reconfiguration of Hinduism is now complete', *Indian Express*, 11 November 2019, accessed on 16 November 2019, https://indianexpress.com/article/opinion/columns/ayodhya-verdict-supreme-court-ramjanam-bhoomi-babri-masjid-case-6112164/

6. Accessed on 3 December 2019, https://www.outlookindia.com/newsscroll/i-stand-vindicated-advani-on-ayodhya-verdict/1659248
7. Ibid.
8. BJP's White Paper on Ayodhya, p. 1, accessed on 3 December 2019, http://library.bjp.org/jspui/handle/ 123456789/176
9. A few of these observations were also made in a Sahmat publication of the period. See Geeta Kapur, 'On the Hum Sab Ayodhya Exhibit', October 1993, accessed on 3 December 2019, https://www.tandfonline.com/doi/pdf/10.1080/14672715.1993.10416143. For further references, see 'Arjun Singh and BJP exploit the Sahmat show in Ayodhya', *India Today*, 15 September 1993, accessed on 3 December 2019, https://www.indiatoday.in/magazine/indiascope/story/19930915-both-arjun-singh-and-bjp-exploit-sahmat-show-in-ayodhya-811551-1993-09-15 and 'Ruckus over Ramayan Mela in Ayodhya', *India Today*, 15 January 1994, accessed on 3 December 2019, https://www.indiatoday.in/magazine/indiascope/story/19940115-ruckus-over-ramayan-mela-in-ayodhya-808676-1994-01-15
10. *Many Ramayanas: The Diversity of a Narrative Tradition in South Asia*, edited by Paula Richman, University of California Press, Berkeley, Los Angeles; Oxford, 1991.
11. For further reading, see 'Crying Wolf', *Frontline*, Vol. 25, No. 6, 15-28 March 2008 and 'The Rule of Unreason', *Frontline*, Vol. 28, No. 23, 5-18 November 2011, accessed on 3 December 2019, https://frontline.thehindu.com/static/html/fl2823/stories/20111118282312500.htm
12. 'Crying Wolf', *Frontline*, Vol. 25, No. 6, 15-28 March 2008.
13. 'The Rule of Unreason', *Frontline*, Vol. 28, No. 23, 5-18 November 2011, https://frontline.thehindu.com/static/html/fl2823/stories/20111118282312500.htm
14. Mukul Kesavan, *The Telegraph*, 27 October 2011.
15. I made this argument in my previous book, *The Demolition: India At the Crossroads*, on the basis of arguments of J.L.

Brockington, *The Righteous Rama: The Evolution of an Epic*, Oxford University Press, Delhi, 1984, who in turn also quoted Hermann Jacobi, *Das Ramayana: Geschichte und Inhalt nebst Concordanz der gedruckten Recensionen*, Bonn, 1893 (rep. Darmstadt, 1970), p. 65, as saying, 'Rama's deification and identification with Visnu are constantly present in the mind of the poet of the first and last books. But in the five genuine books, apart from a few interpolated passages, this concept is absent and by contrast Rama is thoroughly human. Such a transformation of Rama's character could only have taken place over a long span of time.'

16. Brockington cited R. Antoine, *Rama and the Bards: Epic Memory in the Ramayana*, Calcutta, 1975, p. 76. Calcutta: Writer's Workshop, 1975.
17. Romila Thapar, *Seminar*, January 1989, cited in *Frontline*, Vol. 26, No. 10, 9-22 May 2009.
18. Paula Richman, 'E.V. Ramasami's Reading of the Ramayana', in Paula Richman (ed.), *Many Ramayanas: The Diversity of a Narrative Tradition in South Asia*, University California Press, Berkeley, Los Angeles, Oxford, 1991. This citation taken from excerpts published in Scroll.in, 9 March 2018.
19. Ibid.
20. Mini Chandran, *The Writer, the Reader and the State: Literary Censorship in India*, New Delhi: Sage Publications, 2017. https://books google.co.in/books?id=wxtBDwAAQBAJ&pg=PT94&lpg=PT94&dq=Iramayanakkurippukal&source=bl&ots=xu54QR-bie&sig=ACfU3U2wazJhJSj3tB_83XYUbkrg57AM_w&hl=en&sa=X&ved=2ahUKEwjk7obivPblAhXg6nMBHa8xDyIQ6AEwC3oECAYQAQ#v=onepage&q=Iramayanakkurippukal&f=false, accessed on 12 December 2019.
21. A.S. Raman, 'Everybody in the school knew I was a born writer: Aubrey Menen', https://www.indiatoday.

in/magazine/interview/story/19780315-everybody-in-the-school-knew-i-was-a-born-writer-aubrey-menen-818633-2015-01-31, accessed on 12 December 2019.

22. Mini Chandran, *The Writer, the Reader and the State: Literary Censorship in India.*
23. 'Aubrey Menen's "Rama Retold" tells us to laugh at the Ramayana. No wonder it's still banned', Scroll.in, 1 October 2016.
24. Ibid.
25. *The Telegraph*, 21 June 2009, accessed 13 December 2019, https://www.telegraphindia.com/culture/sita-and-all-that-stuff/cid/615951
26. *Frontline*, Vol. 26, No. 10, 9-22 May 2009, accessed on 13 December 2019, https://frontline.thehindu.com/static/html/fl2610/stories/20090522261009200.htm
27. *The Hindu*, 16 December 2011, https://www.thehindu.com/features/metroplus/the-truth-is-in-diversity/article2720972.ece
28. This section is drawn from Nilanjan Mukhopadhyay, *The Demolition: India at the Crossroads*, HarperCollins, New Delhi, 1994, which referred to several academic articles and books including J.L. Brockington, *The Righteous Rama: The Evolution of an Epic*, Oxford University Press, Delhi, 1984, and Sukumar Sen, *The Origin and Development of the Rama Legend*, Rupa, 1977.
29. R.S. Sharma, 'The Ayodhya Issue', in *Destruction and Conservation of Cultural Property*, R. Layton, P. Stone, J. Thomas (eds), Routledge 2001, London, accessed on 13 December 2019, https://books.google.co.in/books?id=hEOFAgAAQBAJ&pg=PA128&dq=tulsidas+ayodhya&hl=en&sa=X&ved=0ahUKEwiw-uCL7PblAhXNfSsKHb3ZDggQ6AEIKDAA#v=onepage&q=tulsidas%20ayodhya&f=false

30. Ramachandra Guha, *India After Gandhi: The History of the World's Largest Democracy*, HarperCollins, New York, 2007, p. 576.
31. Arvind Rajagopal, *Politics After Television: Hindu Nationalism and the Reshaping of the Public in India*, Cambridge University Press, 2001, p. 31.
32. Ibid. From back cover of the book, https://books.google.co.in/books?id=PbgW2jTESKEC&pg=PA31&lpg=PA31&dq=was+a+great+gift+to+our+movement.+We+owed+out+recruits+to+the+serials+inspiration.&source=bl&ots=6z9P3PFxwJ&sig=ACfU3U0-ZD8nWqDQdGthu0dHquOpjfGCrA&hl=en&sa=X&ved=2ahUKEwjQ--zEx93mAhVGdCsKHTymCi8Q6AEwAHoECAgQAQ#v=onepage&q=religious%20partisanship&f=false
33. Namita Bhandare and Louise Fernandes, *Sunday*, 21-27 February 1993.
34. Ramachandra Guha, 'Ramayan: The Video', *Drama Review*, Vol. 34, No. 2, 1990, p. 128.
35. For further reading, Rakhshanda Jalil, *The Indian Express*, 24 September 2017; and Saquib Salim, *The Wire*, 11 October 2016, accessed on 13 December 2019, https://thewire.in/communalism/politicians-made-ram-hindu-indias-muslims-lost-maryada-purshotam

2. Ayodhya: From Antiquity to the Present

1. S.P. Udayakumar, 'Historicizing Myth and Mythologizing History: The "Rama Temple" Drama', *Social Scientist*, Vol. 25, Nos 7-8, July-August 1997.
2. Ritika Chopra, *Indian Express*, 27 November 2015, accessed on 15 December 2019, https://indianexpress.com/article/india/india-news-india/no-honorarium-ichr-chief-yellapragada-sudershan-rao-quits/

3. *Outlook* Interviews, 21 July 2014, accessed on 15 December 2019, https://www.outlookindia.com/magazine/story/ramayana-mahabharata-are-true-accounts-of-the-periodnot-myths/291363
4. https://indianexpress.com/article/india/india-others/pm-takes-leaf-from-batra-book-mahabharat-genetics-lord-ganesha-surgery/, accessed on 15 December 2019.
5. https://www.thehindu.com/news/national/need-to-rewrite-history-from-indias-point-of-view-amit-shah/article29724706.ece, accessed on 15 December 2019.
6. In the Supreme Court of India, Civil Appellate Jurisdiction, Civil Appeal Nos 10866-10867 of 2010, *M Siddiq (D) Thr Lrs Versus Mahant Suresh Das & Ors*, Part G, p. 92.
7. Gyanendra Pandey, 'Modes of History Writing: New Hindu History of Ayodhya', *Economic and Political Weekly*, Vol. 29, No. 25, 18 June 1994, pp. 1523-28.
8. *Indian Express*, 5 August 2020, https://indianexpress.com/article/india/ram-mandir-bhumi-pujan-full-text-of-pm-narendra-modis-speech-in-ayodhya/, accessed on 8 October 2020.
9. Ibid.
10. Romila Thapar, *Early India: From the Origins to AD 1300*, Penguin, 2003, New Delhi, p. 286.
11. Amit Shah at BHU, PIB Release, https://pib.gov.in/newsite/PrintRelease.aspx?relid=193845, accessed on 15 December 2019.
12. Nistula Hebbar, *The Hindu*, 23 October 2019.
13. Amit Shah at BHU, PIB Release, https://pib.gov.in/newsite/PrintRelease.aspx?relid=193845, accessed on 15 December 2019.
14. http://www.ebooksread.com/authors-eng/great-britain-india-office/imperial-gazetteer-of-india-volume-12-aer/page-14-imperial-gazetteer-of-india-volume-12-aer.shtml, accessed on 15 December 2019.

15. Sushil Srivastava, *The Disputed Mosque: A Historical Inquiry*, Sage, New Delhi, 1991, p. 51.
16. B.B. Lal, *Puratattva: Bulletin of Indian Archaeological Society*, No. 16; 1985-86, https://www.amazon.in/Puratattva-Vol-16-Bulletin-Archaeological/dp/B0075MCOUU
17. Ibid.
18. B.B. Lal, *Indian Archaeology: A Review of Explorations and Excavations*, 1976-77, ASI annual publication, 1980, p. 53, http://nmma.nic.in/nmma/nmma_doc/Indian%20Archaeology%20Review/Indian%20Archaeology%201976-77%20A%20Review.pdf
19. https://www.hindustantimes.com/lucknow/ram-temple-site-in-ayodhya-a-buddhist-sthal/story-aDrCNpNa4sRnkI72niQ2hP.html#:~:text=Claiming%20that%20the%20ancient%20artefacts,Survey%20of%20India%20(ASI), accessed on 8 October 2020.
20. Srivastava, *The Disputed Mosque: A Historical Inquiry*, Sage, New Delhi, 1991, p. 66. He cited Abdur Rahman Chisti's 1682 text, *Mirat-i-Masudi*.
21. Wolseley Haig, *Cambridge History of India*, III, p. 29, The University Press Cambridge, 1928, cited in The Heritage of Ghazni and Bukhara, http://www.columbia.edu/itc/mealac/pritchett/00islamlinks/ikram/part1_02.html#n06), accessed on 16 December 2019.
22. Srivastava, *The Disputed Mosque: A Historical Inquiry*, Sage, New Delhi, 1991, p. 63.
23. Neeladri Bhattacharya, 'Myth, History and the Politics of Ramjanmabhumi: Anatomy of a Confrontation', in *Anatomy of a Confrontation: The Babri Masjid-Ram Janmabhumi Issue* (edited by Sarvepalli Gopal), Penguin Books, 1991, p. 122.
24. Allahabad High Court Judgement, Other Original Suit (O.O.S.) No. 1 of 1989 (Regular Suit No. 2 of 1950), *Gopal Singh Visharad since deceased and survived by Rajendra Singh Vs. Zahoor Ahmad and others*, AND Other Original

Suit No. 3 of 1989 (Regular Suit No. 26 of 1959), *Nirmohi Akhara and others Vs. Baboo Priya Datt Ram and others*, AND Other Original Suit No. 4 of 1989 (Regular Suit No. 12 of 1961), *The Sunni Central Board of Waqfs, U.P. and others Vs. Gopal Singh Visharad (since deceased) and others*, AND Other Original Suit No. 5 of 1989 (Regular Suit No. 236 of 1989), *Bhagwan Sri Ram Lala Virajman and others Vs. Rajendra Singh and others*, Findings, p. 238. This point was also raised previously, including in K.M. Panikkar, 'A Historical Overview', in *Anatomy of a Confrontation: The Babri Masjid-Ram Janmabhumi Issue* (edited by Sarvepalli Gopal), Penguin Books, 1991, pp. 28–29 and *The Demolition: India at the Crossroads*, HarperCollins, New Delhi, 1994, p. 77.

25. K.M. Panikkar, 'A Historical Overview, in *Anatomy of a Confrontation: The Babri Masjid-Ram Janmabhumi Issue* (edited by Sarvepalli Gopal), Penguin Books, 1991, p. 28.
26. Ibid.
27. Sushil Srivastava, *The Disputed Mosque: A Historical Inquiry*, Sage, New Delhi, 1991, pp. 64–65.
28. Ibid., p. 20.
29. Ibid.
30. Ibid., p. 35.
31. In the Supreme Court of India, Civil Appellate Jurisdiction, Civil Appeal Nos 10866-10867 of 2010, *M Siddiq (D) Thr Lrs Versus Mahant Suresh Das & Ors*, pp. 562, 669.
32. Hans Bakker, 'Ayodhya: A Hindu Jerusalem, An Investigation of "Holy War" as a Religious Idea in the Light of Communal Unrest in India', *International Review for the History of Religions*, Vol. 38, No. 1, June 1991, pp. 80-109.
33. Amritlal Nagar, *Gathering the Ashes*, Translated by Mrinal Pande, Harper Perennial, New Delhi, 2014, citation from excerpt published in *National Herald*, 10 November 2019, https://www.nationalheraldindia.com/book-extract/book-

extract-drawing-a-blank-in-ayodhya-of-1957, accessed on 8 December 2019.

34. Saiyid Zaheer Husain Jafri, 'Mid-19th Century Communal Tussle in Ayodhya Has a Lesson for Today's Awadh', *The Wire*, 6 September 2018, https://thewire.in/history/mid-19th-century-communal-tussle-in-ayodhya-has-a-lesson-for-todays-awadh, accessed on 8 December 2019; also see Dhirendra Jha and Krishna Jha, *Ayodhya: The Dark Night, The Secret History of Rama's Appearance In Babri Masjid*, HarperCollins, New Delhi, 2012, pp. 7–15.
35. Saiyid Zaheer Husain Jafri, 'Mid-19th Century Communal Tussle in Ayodhya Has a Lesson for Today's Awadh', *The Wire*, 6 September 2018, https://thewire.in/history/mid-19th-century-communal-tussle-in-ayodhya-has-a-lesson-for-todays-awadh, accessed on 8 December 2019.
36. In the Supreme Court of India, Civil Appellate Jurisdiction, Civil Appeal Nos 10866-10867 of 2010, *M Siddiq (D) Thr Lrs Versus Mahant Suresh Das & Ors*, Part D, p. 63.
37. Cited by Krishna and Dhirendra Jha, *Ayodhya, The Dark Night: The Secret History of Rama's Appearance in Babri Masjid*, New Delhi: HarperCollins, 2012, p. 26.

3. The Desecration

1. Cited by Krishna and Dhirendra Jha, *Ayodhya, The Dark Night: The Secret History of Rama's Appearance in Babri Masjid*, New Delhi: HarperCollins, 2012, p. 26.
2. Report of the Commission of Inquiry Into Conspiracy to Murder Mahatma Gandhi, Ministry of Home Affairs, 1969, Vol. 1. Chapter XII, Para 12B.10.
3. Christophe Jaffrelot, *The Hindu Nationalist Movement and Indian Politics: 1925-1994*, C. Hurst & Co., London, 1996, p. 91.
4. Durga Dass (ed.), *Sardar Patel's Correspondence, 1945-50*, Vol. 6, Navajivan Publishing House, Ahmedabad,

1973, pp. 63-64, https://archive.org/stream/in.ernet.dli.2015.110524/2015.110524.Sardar-Patels-Correspondence-Vol-6_djvu.txt, accessed on 20 December 2019.

5. Ibid.
6. Cited by Gyanesh Kudaisya, Quoting Leader 21 June 1948, *Region, Nation, 'Heartland': Uttar Pradesh in India's Body Politic*, SAGE Series in Modern Indian History, Sage, p. 371.
7. Ibid.
8. Krishna and Dhirendra Jha, *Ayodhya, The Dark Night: The Secret History of Rama's Appearance in Babri Masjid*, New Delhi: HarperCollins, 2012, p. 38.
9. Krishna and Dhirendra Jha, *Ayodhya, The Dark Night: The Secret History of Rama's Appearance in Babri Masjid*, New Delhi: HarperCollins, 2012, citing Harold A. Gould, *Grassroot Politics in India*, Oxford and IBH, 1994, pp.164-66.
10. Ibid, citing a *National Herald* report dated 18 June 1948.
11. Cited in Nilanjan Mukhopadhyay, *The Demolition: India at the Crossroads*, HarperCollins, New Delhi, 1994, pp. 85-86.
12. Land situated beyond two miles of the municipal limits, which has reverted to the state government and has not already been appropriated by it for any purpose.
13. Krishna and Dhirendra Jha, *Ayodhya, The Dark Night: The Secret History of Rama's Appearance in Babri Masjid*, New Delhi: HarperCollins, 2012, p. 47. They cite Hindu Mahasabha papers.
14. The nine-day recitation was an annual feature as it coincided with the period when Hanuman was believed to be born, the difference in 1949 being that the scale was bigger and there was a sense of imminence in Ayodhya.
15. *The Demolition: India at the Crossroads*, HarperCollins, 1994, pp. 86–87.

16. Ibid.
17. Abhiram Das pleaded not guilty and was acquitted on 30 July 1953. The Nirvani Akhara priest's discharge in the case was reported by the pro-Mahasabha newspaper, *Virakta*, under a headline which glorified the incident: *Janmabhoomi Ki Shaandaar Vijay* (Glorious victory of the Janmabhoomi). Legal subterfuge played a role in Abhiram Das's easy acquittal.
18. Cited by Krishna and Dhirendra Jha, *Ayodhya, The Dark Night: The Secret History of Rama's Appearance in Babri Masjid*, New Delhi: HarperCollins, 2012, p. 112.
19. Harold A. Gould, 'Religion and Politics in a U.P. Constituency', Essay in *South Asian Politics and Religion*, Ed, Donald Eugene Smith, Princeton University Press, 1966, pp. 62-64.
20. Ibid.
21. Krishna and Dhirendra Jha, *Ayodhya, The Dark Night: The Secret History of Rama's Appearance in Babri Masjid*, New Delhi: HarperCollins, 2012, p. 19, citing *The Pioneer*, 23 December 1949.
22. Krishna and Dhirendra Jha, *Ayodhya, The Dark Night: The Secret History of Rama's Appearance In Babri Masjid*, New Delhi: HarperCollins, 2012, pp. 99-100, citing Hindu Mahasabha Papers, N.B. Khare, Oral History Transcripts, Acc. No 310, NMML, p 117.
23. Ibid., p. 20, citing Hindu Mahasabha papers, C-170, NMML, p. 12.
24. Krishna and Dhirendra Jha, *Ayodhya, The Dark Night: The Secret History of Rama's Appearance in Babri Masjid*, New Delhi: HarperCollins, 2012, p. 81.
25. Ibid.
26. All citations from P.V. Narasimha Rao, *Ayodhya: 6 December 1992*, New Delhi: Penguin, 2006, p. 8.
27. Ibid., p. 16.

28. Ibid., p. 20.
29. Ibid., p. 21.
30. Ibid., p. 22.
31. Krishna and Dhirendra Jha, *Ayodhya The Dark Night: The Secret History of Rama's Appearance in Babri Masjid*, New Delhi: HarperCollins, 2012, pp. 115-16.
32. Nilanjan Mukhopadhyay, *The Demolition: India at the Crossroads*, New Delhi: HarperCollins, 1994, p. 193.
33. Krishna and Dhirendra Jha, *Ayodhya, The Dark Night: The Secret History of Rama's Appearance in Babri Masjid*, New Delhi: HarperCollins, 2012, pp. 112–13.
34. Recap by Khan of what had happened in 1950. Allahabad High Court Judgement, Other Original Suit (O.O.S.) No. 1 of 1989 (Regular Suit No. 2 of 1950), *Gopal Singh Visharad since deceased and survived by Rajendra Singh vs. Zahoor Ahmad and others*, AND Other Original Suit No. 3 of 1989 (Regular Suit No. 26 of 1959), *Nirmohi Akhara and others vs. Baboo Priya Datt Ram and others*, AND Other Original Suit No. 4 of 1989 (Regular Suit No. 12 of 1961*), The Sunni Central Board of Waqfs, U.P. and others vs. Gopal Singh Visharad (since deceased) and others*, AND Other Original Suit No. 5 of 1989 (Regular Suit No. 236 of 1989), *Bhagwan Sri Ram Lala Virajman and others vs. Rajendra Singh and others*, Pleadings, Suit No 5 (69), p. 71.
35. Jawaharlal Nehru, *Selected Works*, Series 2, Vol. 14, Part II, General Editor, S. Gopal, Jawaharlal Nehru Memorial Fund, New Delhi, 1993, https://archive.org/stream/HindSwaraj-Nehru-SW2-14II/nehru.sw2.vol.s14.II_djvu.txt
36. Ibid., Part 1, 1972, https://nehruselectedworks.com/pdfviewer.php?style=UI_Zine_Material.xml&subfolder=&doc=s2v14.pdf|10|594#page=459, accessed on 22 December 2019.
37. For further reading on why Nehru did not act more decisively, see Gyanesh Kudaisya in https://www.

outlookindia.com/magazine/story/ayodhya-in-the-time-of-jawaharlal/300943

38. For further reading, see Nilanjan Mukhopadhyay, *The Demolition: India at the Crossroads*, HarperCollins, New Delhi, 1994, pp.117–25.

4. Getting Started

1. https://www.newsbharati.com/Encyc/2015/7/6/Dalai-Lama-and-RSS-Strengthening-spiritual-relationship.html, accessed on 27 December 1949.
2. Importantly, this was not the first occasion that the sarsanghchalak made this assertion. He had made it previously in 1978, but not from a big platform. *Hindu Vishva*, Vol. 13, 1978, p. 92. Deoras's speech cited above from *Hindu Vishva*, Special Number, Second World Hindu Conference, March-April 1979, p. 13.
3. Christophe Jaffrelot, *The Hindu Nationalist Movement and Indian Politics: 1925-1994*, C. Hurst & Co., London, 1996, p. 347.
4. See Nilanjan Mukhopadhyay, *The RSS: Icons of the Indian Right*, Tranquebar, New Delhi, 2019, p. 121.
5. https://vhp.org/conferences/world-hindu-conference/world-hindu-conference-2-whc-ii/, accessed on 27 December 2019.
6. Nilanjan Mukhopadhyay, *The RSS: Icons of the Indian Right*, Tranquebar, New Delhi, 2019, p. 285.
7. Ibid., pp. 286–87.
8. Prabhu Chawla, *India Today*, 15 September 1981, https://www.indiatoday.in/magazine/indiascope/story/19810915-sudden-spurt-in-conversions-of-harijans-to-islam-forces-govt-to-study-the-issue-773219-2013-11-11, accessed on 29 December 2019.
9. Ibid.

10. Ibid.
11. All quotes from *RSS Resolves: Resolution of Akhil Bharatiya Karyakarini Mandal*, 1981, Suruchi Prakashan, New Delhi, 2007, p. 101.
12. Satish Sabharwal and Mushirul Hasan, 'Moradabad Riots, 1980: Causes and Meanings' in Asghar Ali Engineer, ed., *Communal Riots in Post-Independence India*, Sangam Books, 1984 , p. 209.
13. Christophe Jaffrelot, *The Hindu Nationalist Movement and Indian Politics: 1925-1994*, C. Hurst & Co., London, 1996, p. 364.
14. A.G. Noorani, 'Karan Singh's Career', Review in *Frontline*, 10 February 2012, of Jawaid Alam, ed., *Kashmir & Beyond 1966-84: Select Correspondence between Indira Gandhi and Karan Singh*, Penguin Books India, 2011.
15. D.R. Goyal, *Rashtriya Swayamsevak Sangh*, Radhakrishna Publishers, revised edition, 2000, p. 156.
16. Ashok Singhal, *Organiser*, 1 April 2007.
17. Sumit Mitra, *India Today*, 30 November 1983.
18. Nilanjan Mukhopadhyay, *The Demolition: India at the Crossroads*, HarperCollins, New Delhi, 1994, p. 130.
19. Nilanjan Mukhopadhyay, *The RSS: Icons of the Indian Right*, Tranquebar, New Delhi, 2019, p. 315, also in Christiane Brosius, *Empowering Visions: The Politics of Representation in Hindu Nationalism*, Anthem Press, 2005, p. 145.
20. *India Today*, 30 November 1983.
21. Neeladri Bhattacharya, 'Myth, History and the Politics of Ramjanmabhumi', in Sarvepalli Gopal, ed, *Anatomy of a Confrontation: Myth, History and the Politics of Ramjanmabhoomi*, Penguin, New Delhi, 1990, pp. 130–31.
22. Donald Eugene Smith, *South Asian Politics and Religion*, Princeton University Press, 1966, p. 67.
23. Deendayal Upadhyaya, 'Jana Sangh', *Seminar*, January 1962.
24. Nilanjan Mukhopadhyay, *Narendra Modi: The Man, The*

Times, Tranquebar, New Delhi 2013, p. 192, citing A.G. Noorani who quoted Richard H Davis, *The RSS and the BJP: A Division of Labour*, Leftward Books, 2000, p. 71.

25. L.K. Advani, *My Country My Life*, Rupa & Company, New Delhi, 2008, p. 362.
26. VHP Pamphlet, 'Dharam Sansad', April 1982, cited in Nilanjan Mukhopadhyay, *The Demolition: India at the Crossroads*, HarperCollins, New Delhi, 1994, p. 128.
27. Ashok Singhal in his deposition to the Liberhan Commission. Report of the Liberhan Ayodhya Commission of Inquiry, https://www.mha.gov.in/about-us/commissions-committees/liberhan-ayodhya-commission, p. 338, accessed on 29 December 2019.
28. P.V. Narasimha Rao, *Ayodhya: 6 December 1992*, Penguin, 2006, p. 23.
29. Ibid., p. 31.
30. Nilanjan Mukhopadhyay, *The RSS: Icons of the Indian Right*, Tranquebar, New Delhi, 2019, pp. 336-50.
31. *RSS Resolves*, Suruchi Prakashan, New Delhi 2007, pp. 123-26.
32. Salman Khurshid, *At Home in India: The Muslim Saga*, Hay House, New Delhi, accessed on 30 December 2019 from https://bit.ly/3dBhSPi
33. Shekhar Gupta, Inderjit Badhwar and Farzand Ahmed, *India Today*, 31 January 1986.
34. *The Telegraph*, 5 March 2017, https://www.telegraphindia.com/india/leftist-who-became-minority-voice/cid/1518990, accessed on 30 December 2019.
35. Ibid.
36. Ramachandra Guha, *India After Gandhi: The History of the World's Largest Democracy*, HarperCollins, New York, 2007, p. 581.
37. Justice Deoki Nandan Agarwal, *Ram Janma Bhoomi: A Historical and Legal Perspective*, publication of the Sri Ram Janma Bhumi Mukti Yajna Samiti, Lucknow 1989.

38. L.K. Advani, *My Country My Life*, Rupa & Company, New Delhi, 2008, pp. 332-33.
39. P.V. Narasimha Rao, *Ayodhya: 6 December 1992*, Penguin, 2006, p. 31.
40. Justice Deoki Nandan Agarwal, *Ram Janma Bhoomi: A Historical and Legal Perspective*, publication of the Sri Ram Janma Bhumi Mukti Yajna Samiti, Lucknow, 1989.
41. Ibid.
42. Text of resolution, cited previously in Nilanjan Mukhopadhyay, *The Demolition: India at the Crossroads*, HarperCollins, New Delhi, 1994, p. 144.
43. Hilal Ahmed, 'Mosque as Monument: The Afterlives of Jama Masjid and the Political Memories of a Royal Muslim Past', *South Asian Studies*, Vol. 29, Issue 1, 2013, also available and accessed on 30 December 2019, https://www.csds.in/uploads/custom_files/1526551516_Mosque%20as%20Monument.pdf
44. Ibid.
45. S. Premi, Ghulam Nabi Khayal and Aiay Kumar, *India Today*, 15 March 1986, https://www.indiatoday.in/magazine/indiascope/story/19860315-muslim-leaders-split-over-muslim-women-protection-of-rights-on-divorce-bill-800651-1986-03-15, accessed on 30 December 2019.
46. *RSS Resolves*, Suruchi Prakashan, New Delhi, 2007, pp. 135-36.
47. Abdul Gafoor Abdul Majeed Noorani, *The RSS: A Menace to India*, Leftword Books, New Delhi, 2019, pp. 226-27.
48. http://www.girilaljainarchive.net/1986/02/editorial-scrap-the-bill/, accessed on 30 December 2019.
49. All quotes from BJP E-Library, http://library.bjp.org/jspui/bitstream/123456789/251/2/Policy%20Document.pdf, accessed on 30 December 2019.
50. 'Two Years of Misrule: A Chargesheet', BJP Publication, October 1986.

51. Hilal Ahmed, 'Mosque as Monument: The Afterlives of Jama Masjid and the Political Memories of a Royal Muslim Past', *South Asian Studies*, Vol. 29, Issue 1, 2013, also available and accessed on 30 December 2019, https://www.csds.in/uploads/custom_files/1526551516_Mosque%20as%20Monument.pdf
52. Conversation with Syed Shahabuddin, December 1986, cited in Nilanjan Mukhopadhyay, *The Demolition: India at the Crossroads*, HarperCollins, New Delhi, 1994.
53. Nilanjan Mukhopadhyay, *The Demolition: India at the Crossroads*, HarperCollins, New Delhi, 1994, p. 215.
54. Press statement by L.K. Advani, March 1987.

5. The Giant Leap

1. Nilanjan Mukhopadhyay, *Narendra Modi: The Man, The Times*, Tranquebar, New Delhi, 2013, p. 258.
2. Prabhu Chawla, *India Today*, 15 February 1987, https://www.indiatoday.in/magazine/cover-story/story/19870215-finance-to-defence-pm-rajiv-gandhi-removes-v.p.-singh-from-the-limelight-798500-1987- 02-15, accessed on 4 January 2020.
3. Inderjit Bhadwar and Tania Midha, *India Today*, 15 June 1987.
4. Hilal Ahmed, 'Mosque as Monument: The Afterlives of Jama Masjid and the Political Memories of a Royal Muslim Past', *South Asian Studies*, Vol. 29, Issue 1, 2013, also available and accessed on 4 January 2010, https://www.csds.in/uploads/custom_files/1526551516_Mosque%20as%20Monument.pdf
5. Asghar Ali Engineer, 'Meerut: The Shame of The Nation', in *Delhi-Meerut Riots: Compilation, Documentation and Analysis*, Ajanta Books, Delhi, 1988, cited in Nilanjan Mukhopadhyay, *The Demolition: India at the Crossroads*, HarperCollins, New Delhi, 1994, p. 217.

6. Inderjit Bhadwar, *India Today*, 15 June 1987, https://www.indiatoday.in/magazine/cover-story/story/19870615-devastating-communal-riots-sweep-through-meerut-and-its-adjoining-areas-in-uttar-pradesh-798979-1987-06-15, accessed on 4 January 2020.
7. Ibid., https://www.indiatoday.in/magazine/cover-story/story/19870615-devastating-communal-riots-sweep-through-meerut-and-its-adjoining-areas-in-uttar-pradesh-798979-1987-06-15
8. Fatalities were estimated at about 400. See Violette Graff and Juliette Galonnier, 'Hindu-Muslim Communal Riots in India II (1986-2011)', *SciencesPo*, Mass Violence and Resistance, Research Network, https://www.sciencespo.fr/mass-violence-war-massacre-resistance/en/document/hindu-muslim-communal-riots-india-ii-1986-2011.html, accessed on 10 January 2020.
9. Asghar Ali Engineer (ed.), *Delhi Meerut Riots: Analysis, Compilation and Documentation*, Delhi, Ajanta, 1988, pp. 80–85. Cited by Hilal Ahmed, 'Mosque as Monument: The Afterlives of Jama Masjid and the Political Memories of a Royal Muslim Past', *South Asian Studies*, Vol. 29, Issue 1, 2013, also available and accessed on 30 December 2019, https://www.csds.in/uploads/custom_files/1526551516_Mosque%20as%20Monument.pdf
10. Cited in Nilanjan Mukhopadhyay, *The Demolition: India at the Crossroads*, HarperCollins, New Delhi, 1994, p. 219.
11. Signatories to the statement included I.K. Gujral, who later became prime minister of India, and P.N. Haksar, who had been Indira Gandhi's principal secretary. Cited in Nilanjan Mukhopadhyay, *The Demolition: India at the Crossroads*, HarperCollins, New Delhi, 1994, p. 219.
12. Statement of a VHP leader, B.L. Sharma 'Prem', cited in Nilanjan Mukhopadhyay, *The Demolition: India at the Crossroads*, HarperCollins, New Delhi, 1994, p. 220.

13. L.K. Advani, Presidential Speech, October 1988, Ahmedabad.
14. 'Two Years of Congress Misrule: A Chargesheet', BJP publication.
15. Nilanjan Mukhopadhyay, *The Demolition: India at the Crossroads*, HarperCollins, New Delhi, 1994, p. 222.
16. L.K. Advani, presidential remarks, BJP National Executive meeting, July 1987.
17. Sanjeev Kelkar, *Lost Years of the RSS*, Sage, New Delhi, 2011, conversation with D.B. Ghumare, a journalist, p. 190.
18. Available on multiple websites. This one from https://www.outlookindia.com/website/story/the-first-claim-on-resources/233334
19. Sanjeev Kelkar, *Lost Years of the RSS*, Sage, New Delhi, 2011, p. 191.
20. Ibid.
21. Ramesh Patange, 'Manu, Sangh and I', *Vivek Weekly*, Hindusthan Prakashan Sanstha, Pune, 2012, translated from the Marathi original by Suresh Desai, translation available at http://www.hvk.org/specialreports/mms/ch3.html, accessed on 10 January 2020.
22. Ibid.
23. Pankaj Pachauri, *India Today*, 30 June 1989, https://www.indiatoday.in/magazine/special-report/story/19890630-rss-works-with-renewed-zeal-to-emerge-as-militant-political-force-816240-1989-06-30, accessed on 10 January 2020.
24. Ibid.
25. https://www.outlookindia.com/newsscroll/rss-is-a-movement-that-can-change-the-country-world-rajasthan-bjp- chief/1619299, accessed on 10 January 2020.
26. Note of Union home minister Buta Singh to Rajiv Gandhi, cited by Nilanjan Mukhopadhyay, *The Demolition: India at the Crossroads*, HarperCollins, New Delhi, 1994, p. 234.

27. Shahabuddin's letter to Buta Singh dated 6 October 1988.
28. Buta Singh's note, cited by Nilanjan Mukhopadhyay, *The Demolition: India at the Crossroads*, HarperCollins, New Delhi, 1994, p. 239.
29. Not to be confused with the All-India Muslim League that existed in pre-independence India and spearheaded the formation of Pakistan. IUML is a political party with presence primarily limited to Kerala and Tamil Nadu.
30. Conversation with Sultan Salahuddin Owaisi, October 1988, cited in Nilanjan Mukhopadhyay, *The Demolition: India at the Crossroads*, HarperCollins, New Delhi, 1994, p. 240.
31. Speech of Ahmed Bukhari, 26 November 1988.
32. Buta Singh's note to Rajiv Gandhi, 4 January 1989.
33. Press Statement, AIBMAC, 31 January 1989.
34. VHP Pamphlet, 'Shila Pujan: Ram Mandir Ki Ore', March 1989.
35. VHP Pamphlet, 'Indraprastha Vishwa Hindu Parishad Dharmayatra', September 1989.
36. Aarefa Johari, 'Ram temple fundraisers leave behind stickers on doors—sparking fear and concern', Scroll.in, 13 February 2021, https://scroll.in/article/986670/ram-temple-fundraisers-leave-behind-stickers-on-doors-sparking-fear-and-concern, accessed on 11 March 2021.
37. Nilanjan Mukhopadhyay, 'Why the Manner of Ram Temple Donation Drive is Worrisome', newsclick.in, 17 February 2021, https://www.newsclick.in/Why-Manner-Ram-Temple-Donation-Drive-Worrisome, accessed on 11 March 2021.
38. Deeptiman Tiwary, 'Ram temple to be ready by 2025, but devotees will be let in earlier', *Indian Express*, 5 August 2021, https://indianexpress.com/article/india/ayodhya-ram-temple-to-be-ready-by-2025-but-devotees-will-be-let-in-earlier-7438863/

39. Christophe Jaffrelot, *The Hindu Nationalist Movement and Indian Politics: 1925-1994*, C. Hurst & Co., London, 1996, p. 388.
40. Bilingual VHP Newsletter, 'Ram Shila Pujan Samachar', September 1989.
41. Ibid.
42. Ibid.
43. Ibid.
44. Ibid.
45. Ibid.
46. Ibid.
47. C. Rajeshwar Rao and Shameem Faizee, 'Babri Masjid Ram Janmabhoomi Controversy: Dangerous Communal Situation', CPI Publication, April 1989.
48. Jaffrelot, *Hindu Nationalism*, p. 389.
49. Manini Chatterjee, 'Saffron Scourge: The VHP's Communal Fascism', *Frontline*, 10 September 1993.
50. Team PGurus, 'Donations to Ram Mandir Crosses Rs 2500 cr, Mandir to be Built in Three Years', https://www.pgurus.com/donations-to-ram-mandir-crosses-rs-2500-crore-mandir-to-be-built-in-three-years/, accessed on 12 March 2021.
51. https://www.sciencespo.fr/mass-violence-war-massacre-resistance/en/document/hindu-muslim-communal-riots-india-ii-1986-2011.html#title0, accessed on 10 January 2020.
52. Pankaj Pachauri, Inderjit Bhadwar, 'With Ramshila movement, militant Hindus launches offensive to counter Muslim fundamentalists', *India Today*, 31 October 1989.
53. Interview with Kamaljeet Rattan, *The Economic Times*, December 1992.
54. http://library.bjp.org/jspui/bitstream/123456789/264/1/Untitled-2.pdf
55. The BJP White Paper of 1993.

56. *Sunday Mail*, 3 December 1989, cited in Nilanjan Mukhopadhyay, *The Demolition: India at the Crossroads*, HarperCollins, New Delhi, 1994, p. 256.
57. M.V. Kamath, *Expanding Horizons: BJP's First Decade*. BJP Publication, New Delhi, April 1990. Cited in Nilanjan Mukhopadhyay, *The Demolition: India at the Crossroads*, HarperCollins, New Delhi, 1994.
58. N.J. Nanporia, *The Independent*, Bombay, 1 December 1989. Cited in Nilanjan Mukhopadhyay, *The Demolition: India at the Crossroads*, HarperCollins, New Delhi, 1994, p. 256.
59. Ibid.
60. M.V. Kamath, *Expanding Horizons: BJP's First Decade*, BJP Publication, April 1990.
61. Jay Dubashi, 'From Shilanyas to Berlin Wall', *Organiser*, 26 November 1989.
62. Swapan Dasgupta, 'A truth nobody will ever admit', *The Times of India*, 5 July 2009.
63. Buta Singh interview with Kamaljeet Rattan, *The Economic Times*, December 1992.
64. Conversation with the author in January 1990.

6. Demolition Day

1. Led by Justice M.S. Liberhan, it was appointed by the Government of India on 16 December 1992 and mandated to submit its report within three months. It became one of the longest-running commissions of inquiry. Its term was extended forty-eight times and eventually the report was submitted to Prime Minister Manmohan Singh in June 2009.
2. Justice M.S. Liberhan in an interview to *The Indian Express*, 2 October 2020, https://indianexpress.com/article/india/justice-liberhanbabri-masjid-demolition-6657370/, accessed on 22 October 2020.

3. Judgement of Justice S.K. Yadav, pp. 1115-16.
4. Liberhan Commission Report, Section 43.42, p. 249.
5. File No. 16/200/52/D/92, cited in the Liberhan Commission report, p. 212.
6. Ibid.
7. Report of the Liberhan Commission of Inquiry, Section 41.41, p. 211.
8. Nilanjan Mukhopadhyay, *The Demolition: India at the Crossroads*, HarperCollins, New Delhi, 1994, p. 346.
9. Ibid, p. 345.
10. S. Srinivasan, *The Federal*, https://thefederal.com/the-legend-of-ramjanmabhoomi/jai-shree-ram-ho-gaya-kaam-mosque-falls-in-ayodhya-bjp-rises-in-delhi/, accessed on 15 March 2021.
11. Nilanjan Mukhopadhyay, *The Demolition: India at the Crossroads*, HarperCollins, New Delhi, 1994, conversation with the author, p. 337.
12. Ibid., p. 340.
13. Liberhan Commission report, Sections 41.9-10, p. 203.
14. Ibid., Section 41.41, p. 211.
15. Ibid., Section 41.42, p. 212.
16. An Intelligence Bureau report of 22 November mentioned this and was cited by Justice Liberhan. Ibid., Section 41.46.
17. Ibid., Section 41.50, p. 214.
18. Ibid., Section 41.51, p. 215.
19. Ibid., Section 41.56, p. 217.
20. Ibid., Section 41.59, p. 217.
21. Ibid., Section 41.67, p. 220.
22. Ibid., Section 41.68, p. 221.
23. Ibid., Section 43.30, p. 246.
24. https://theprint.in/in-pictures/unseen-photos-of-how-babri-masjid-demolition-was-planned-and-executed-in-1992/474297/#:~:text=Nearly%2028%20years%20ago%2C%20on,how%20incidents%20were%20going%20to, accessed on 20 October 2020.

25. Liberhan Commission report, Section 44.2, p. 250.
26. See https://eparlib.nic.in/bitstream/123456789/758406/1/0712_III.pdffor debate, p. 103, accessed on 20 October 2020.
27. Liberhan Commission report, Section 44.18, p. 254.
28. Ibid., Section 22.19, p. 254.
29. Ibid., Section 44.24, p. 256.
30. Ibid., Sections 158.8 and 158.9, p. 917.
31. Ibid., Section 166.6, p. 942.
32. Ibid., Section 166.9, p. 943.

7. Through the Legal Maze

1. Swapan Dasgupta, 'Ayodhya dispute: Judicial solution becomes an escape route from lack of political resolve', *India Today*, 25 March 2002.
2. Prabir Purakayastha, newsclick.in, 10 November 2019, https://www.newsclick.in/supreme-court-babri-masjid-possession-nine-tenths-law, accessed on 19 September 2020.
3. Conversation with the author, 22 February 2020.
4. Warisha Farasat, 'Ayodhya Verdict: Does It Provide Closure?' Kafila (a team blog focussed on political and media critiques), 11 September 2010, https://kafila.online/2010/11/09/ayodhya-verdict-does-it-provide-closure/, accessed on 25 September 2020.
5. Author conversation with Rajeev Dhawan. The conversation took place before Justice Gogoi's nomination to Rajya Sabha.
6. 'In Unprecedented Move, Modi Government Sends Former CJI Ranjan Gogoi to Rajya Sabha', *The Wire*, 16 March 2020, https://thewire.in/law/cji-ranjan-gogoi-rajya-sabha-nomination
7. H.M. Seervai, 'Babri: Constitution Disregarded', *The Economic Times*, 1 October 2010, these were online excerpts

from a two-part series of articles written in the newspaper in April 1993, https://economictimes.indiatimes.com/babri-constitution-disregarded/articleshow/6662068.cms?from=mdr, accessed on 25 September 2020.

8. Deepak Mehta, 'The Ayodhya dispute: The absent mosque, state of emergency and the jural deity', *Journal of Material Culture*, Volume 20, Issue 4, December 2015, pp. 397–414.
9. Nilanjan Mukhopadhyay, 'With the Ayodhya Dispute "Settled", Sangh Parivar Inches Towards Kashi and Mathura', newsclick.in, 16 September 2020, https://www.newsclick.in/Ayodhya-Dispute-Settled-Sangh-Parivar-Inches-Kashi-Mathura, accessed on 25 September 2020.
10. Dhananjay Mahapatra, 'Author of Ayodhya verdict not named, but it bears Chandrachud's imprint', *The Times of India*, 10 November 2019, https://timesofindia.indiatimes.com/india/author-of-ayodhya-verdict-not-named-but-it-bears-chandrachuds-imprint/articleshow/71989381.cms, accessed 28 September 2020.
11. Ibid.
12. Ibid.
13. In the Supreme Court of India, Civil Appellate Jurisdiction, Civil Appeal Nos 10866-10867 of 2010, *M Siddiq (D) Thr Lrs vs Mahant Suresh Das & Ors,* Addenda, p. 116.
14. Ibad Mushtaq, 'Read the suit-wise summary of the Ayodhya judgement', *The Leaflet*, 11 November 2019, https://www.theleaflet.in/read-the-suit-wise-summary-of-the-ayodhya-judgement/#, accessed on 25 September 2020.
15. In the Supreme Court of India, Civil Appellate Jurisdiction, Civil Appeal Nos 10866-10867 of 2010, *M Siddiq (D) Thr Lrs Versus Mahant Suresh Das & Ors*, Part N, p. 477.
16. Ibid., Part K, p. 224.
17. Ibid., Part A, p. 7.
18. Ibid., Part A, p. 8.
19. Ibid.

20. Ibid., Part A, p. 9.
21. Ibid., Part H, pp. 114-15.
22. Ibid., Part H, p. 115.
23. Nilanjan Mukhopadhyay, *The Demolition: India at the Crossroads*, HarperCollins, New Delhi, 1994, p. 196.
24. Ibid., p. 197.
25. Citations of the 24 October 1994 Supreme Court judgement have been taken from multiple sources, namely, Fali S. Nariman, *The State of the Nation*, Hay House, 2013, https://www.google.co.in/books/edition/The_State_of_the_Nation/MQ89BAAAQBAJ?hl=en&gbpv=1, accessed online on 25 March 2021; Arvind Lavakare, 'A question of squaring up', 2 April 2002, Rediff.com, https://www.rediff.com/news/2002/apr/02arvind.htm, accessed on 25 March 2020; A. Surya Prakash, 'Ayodhya case: the Answers are out there', *New Indian Express*, 9 May 2017, accessed online 25 March 2021; and *Dr M. Ismail Faruqui Etc, Mohd. ... vs Union of India and Others* in Supreme Court, available online and accessed on 25 March 2021, https://bit.ly/3cXQEAc
26. Rajeev Dhawan, 'Why the Supreme Court's Judgement on Mosques is Fatally Flawed', *The Wire*, 1 October 2018, https://thewire.in/law/why-the-supreme-courts-judgement-on-mosques-is-fatally-flawed, accessed on 26 March 2021.
27. Prabhash K Dutta, 'Supreme Court revisits 21-year-old verdict on Hindutva ahead of crucial elections', *India Today*, 17 October 2016, https://www.indiatoday.in/india/story/supreme-court-verdict-hindutva-interpretation-elections-346972-2016-10-17, accessed online on 25 March 2021.
28. 'Sunni Waqf Board Will Drop Babri Land Claim if Other Mosques Are Guaranteed Protection', *The Wire*, 16 October 2019, https://thewire.in/law/breaking-sunni-waqf-board-files-for-settlement-drops-claim-to-babri-masjid-land, accessed on 26 March 2021.

29. Conversation with Athar Hussain, 27 January 2021.
30. Press Trust of India report, 'Don't accept Ayodhya panel "settlement", shocked at Waqf Board "withdrawing claim": Muslim parties', 18 October 2019, *The Economic Times*, https://bit.ly/3cpRirg, accessed on 26 March 2021.

8. The Silent March Ahead

1. Press statement, Insaf Party, 5 January 1990.
2. Inder Nath Choudhuri, *Indian Renaissance and Rabindranath Tagore*, Vani Book Company, 2019, p. 229.
3. M.V. Kamath, *Expanding Horizons: BJP's First Decade*, BJP publication.
4. Nilanjan Mukhopadhyay, 'Modi, BJP & RSS: Why Reservation Issue Inspires Different Tunes', https://www.thequint.com/voices/opinion/rss-chief-mohan-bhagwat-and-reservation-what-is-being-put-on-national-agenda, accessed on 20 September 2020
5. L.K. Advani, *My Country My Life*, Rupa & Company, New Delhi, 2008, p. 373.
6. Advani's speech in Delhi, cited in Nilanjan Mukhopadhyay, *The Demolition: India at the Crossroads*, HarperCollins, New Delhi, 1994, p. 287.
7. K.M. Panikkar, 'Religious Symbols and Political Mobilization: The Agitation for a Mandir at Ayodhya', https://www.jstor.org/stable/3520346?read-now=1&refreqid=excelsior%3Aad1fb91ad89a3a1ed5ea51353368b8c6&seq=7#page_scan_tab_contents, accessed on 16 November 2019.
8. Jaswant Singh, An emerging India, *Seminar*, 402, February 1993, https://www.india-seminar.com/2001/500/500%20jaswant%20singh.htm, accessed on 18 November 2019.
9. Radhika Ramaseshan, 'Advani salutes "secular" Jinnah', 4 June 2005, *The Telegraph*, https://www.telegraphindia.com/

india/advani-salutes-secular-jinnah/cid/873488, accessed 26 March 2021.

10. BJP Election Manifesto, 1996, p. 10.
11. Cited by Abdul Gafoor Abdul Majeed Noorani, *The RSS: A Menace to India*, Leftword Books, New Delhi, 2019, p. 240.
12. Ibid.
13. Ibid.
14. BJP Election Manifesto, 2004.
15. Ibid.
16. *RSS Resolves*, Suruchi Prakashan, New Delhi 2007, p. 291.
17. Samuel P. Huntington's *The Clash of Civilizations and the Remaking of World Order* is a 1996 book and an elaboration of the scholar's essay in *Foreign Affairs* in 1993. The book theorized on the nature of post-Cold War world order. His primary thesis was that after the collapse of the Soviet Union, the 'most important distinctions among peoples are (no longer) ideological, political, or economic. They are cultural.'
18. Nilanjan Mukhopadhyay, *The Demolition: India at the Crossroads*, HarperCollins, New Delhi, 1994, p. 267.

Index